*Unity and Disintegration in
International Alliances:
Comparative Studies*

Comparative Studies in Behavioral Science:

A WILEY SERIES

Robert T. Holt and John E. Turner, *Editors*
Department of Political Science
University of Minnesota

The Logic of Comparative Social Inquiry
    by Adam Przeworski and Henry Teune

The Analysis of Subjective Culture
    by Harry C. Triandis

*Comparative Legislative Behavior: Frontiers
of Research*
        edited by Samuel C. Patterson and John C. Wahlke

*Mass Political Violence: A Cross-National
Causal Analysis*
        by Douglas A. Hibbs, Jr.

*Unity and Disintegration in International
Alliances: Comparative Studies*
        by Ole R. Holsti, P. Terrence Hopmann,
        and John D. Sullivan

Unity and Disintegration in International Alliances: Comparative Studies

OLE R. HOLSTI
University of British Columbia

P. TERRENCE HOPMANN
University of Minnesota

JOHN D. SULLIVAN
Claremont Graduate School

A WILEY-INTERSCIENCE PUBLICATION

John Wiley & Sons

NEW YORK   LONDON   SYDNEY   TORONTO

Library of Congress Cataloging in Publication Data

Holsti, Ole R.
  Unity and disintegration in international alliances.

  Includes bibliographical references.
  1. Alliances. I. Hopmann, P. Terrence, joint author. II. Sullivan, John D., joint author.
III. Title.

JX4005.H65   327'.1   72-10150
ISBN 0-471-40835-2

Printed in the United States of America

10 9 8 7 6 5 4 3 2 1

To Ann, Marita, and Rosemarie

The last decade has witnessed the burgeoning of comparative studies in the behavioral sciences. Scholars in specific disciplines have come to realize that they share much with experts in other fields who face similar theoretical and methodological problems and whose research findings are often related. Moreover, specialists in a given geographic area have felt the need to look beyond the limited confines of their region and to seek new meaning in their research results by comparing them with studies that have been made elsewhere.

This series is designed to meet the needs of the growing cadre of scholars in comparative research. The emphasis is on cross-disciplinary studies, although works within the perspective of a single discipline are included. In its scope, the series includes books of theoretical and methodological interest, as well as studies that are based on empirical research. The books in the series are addressed to scholars in the various behavioral science disciplines, to graduate students, and to undergraduates in advanced standing.

University of Minnesota   *Robert T. Holt*
Minneapolis, Minnesota   *John E. Turner*

Preface

When the ideas for this book began to take shape some five years ago, we had hoped to achieve several goals: to test some of the classical explanations of international alliances through rigorous and replicable studies; to demonstrate the rich diversity of data and methods that may be applied to the study of alliances; and to use the findings as a springboard for some reasonably clear-cut assessments about the relative merits of alternative candidates for *a* theory of alliances. The extent to which we have succeeded in the first two tasks must be judged by the reader. But it is now clear to us that the third goal was either misconceived or premature. Thus, the reader will find us less ready to pronounce that Theory A or Proposition X is universally superior to the alternative formulations of Theory B or Proposition Y, and more inclined to search for the circumstances under which each explanation is valid. The latter task is, of course, the more complex and demanding, and we cannot claim to have completed it. Perhaps this is another way of saying that the research process has made us more modest, realistic, and cautious about our goals. We view our efforts, then, as a preface to the study of alliances; we hope it will assist others to write a more definitive conclusion.

A few words about the plan of the book may be in order. Chapter One is a critical survey of some literature on alliances, with special emphasis on theories and propositions that purport to explain their formation, performance, disintegration, and effects. The chapter is based on an extended search by the three authors through the literature for propositions in which alliances serve as either the independent or dependent variable. That is, we extracted all statements that link alliances to their causes and effects. An extensive but not exhaustive linking of the propositions appears in Appendix C. The initial search was not restricted except by language— we attempted to survey monographs, texts, and articles in English, irrespective of discipline or definition of alliance or coalition. But Appendix C includes only a sample of the vast literature on coalition-formation in experimental settings, supra-national community-building, and electoral or legislative coalitions. Our focus, in short, is on international alliances. Also excluded from Appendix C are purely definitional propositions; for example, "An alliance is distinguished from a coalition by the number of member nations." To facilitate the use of the appendix we have placed the propositions into twenty-two categories, twenty of which are concerned with the causes of alliances and their performance. The other two categories focus on the national and international effects of alliances.

The empirical studies in the next five chapters are marked by wide diversity in scope. Chapter Two considers several alternative explanations of alliance formation and performance. These are then tested with data on all alliances formed between the end of the Napoleonic Wars and the outbreak of World War II. Among the variables included in the analysis are both national attributes (e.g. regime stability) and such characteristics of alliances as ideological similarity, the number of member nations, geographical dispersion, and the number and ambiguity of goals. Probably the most widely cited hypothesis in the literature is that alliance cohesion is directly related to the degree of external threat. The third and fourth chapters are a detailed test of this proposition, using data from NATO and the Communist system. Chapters Five and Six also examine the cold war alliances, but with a focus on the two leading dissident members of these coalitions—France and the People's Republic of China. Hypotheses about differences in the ability of pluralistic and authoritarian alliances to cope with intra-bloc conflict are tested. In light of findings that emerge from the preceding studies, the concluding chapter is a brief reassessment of alliance theories.

The research and writing of this book has been marked both by close collaboration among the authors and by a division of labor. Holsti is responsible for Chapter One, Sullivan for Chapter Two, and Hopmann for Chapters Three and Four. Holsti prepared Chapters Five and Six, revising and expanding an earlier version co-authored with Sullivan. Holsti and Hopmann collaborated on the conclusion. Appendixes A, B, and C were prepared by Sullivan, Hopmann, and Holsti, respectively.

In preparing this book we have benefited from assistance, constructive criticism, and encouragement of several persons and organizations. Robert Holt and John Turner contributed valuable suggestions on the entire manuscript. A Canada Council Leave Fellowship permitted Holsti to enjoy a year free of responsibilities other than research and writing. Additional support was provided by the Faculty of Graduate Studies Committee on Research at the University of British Columbia. The Center for Advanced Study in the Behavioral Sciences provided an idyllic setting for final revisions and editing of the manuscript. He is also indebted to

K. J. Holsti for a detailed critique of Chapter One, to James N. Rosenau for constructive comments on several earlier drafts of Chapters Five and Six, to Fern Miller, William Moul, and John Terry for assistance in collecting data, and to Ann Holsti, Joan Ippen, and Jean Wrinch for typing. Hopmann received valuable assistance and advice from Davis B. Bobrow, Andrew L. Haines, Barry B. Hughes, and Kuan Lee. Data processing was made possible by grants from the Stanford University Computation Center, as well as the Computer Center and the Data Processing Center at the University of Minnesota. The Graduate School and Office of International Programs at the University of Minnesota provided financial support. Sullivan received financial support from the World Data Analysis Program of Yale University, under grant GS614 from the National Science Foundation, and contract N-0014-67-A-0097-0007 from ARPA, Behavioral Sciences, monitored by the Office of Naval Research. For helpful advice he is indebted to Nazli Choucri, John Ferejohn, Jeffrey Milstein, Norman Nie, Robert C. North, Bruce Russett, Randolph Siverson, Michael Sullivan, and Sidney Verba. Data analysis for Chapter Two was performed with the Statistical Package for the Social Sciences, written by Norman Nie. During the initial stages of our research all three of us received support from the Stanford Studies in International Conflict and Integration, directed by Robert C. North. Eric Holsti devoted many hours to helping prepare the index. Mary Dick and others on the Wiley staff were helpful at all stages of transforming a manuscript into a book. Our individual and collective thanks to all of the above does not imply that they share responsibility for any errors of commission or omission in this book.

OLE R. HOLSTI
P. TERRENCE HOPMANN
JOHN D. SULLIVAN

Contents

CHAPTER ONE

International Alliances: A Survey of Theories and Propositions

Introduction

Kautilya, the Indian statesman-philosopher, wrote some twenty-three centuries ago that a state may maintain six patterns of relations with others, one of the six being alliances. In the *Arthasastra* he went on to advise under what circumstances alliances should be undertaken or avoided, and he described in some detail the attributes that a state should seek in its alliance partners, as well as those that characterize undesirable allies. Kautilya may thus have written the first systematic treatise on alliance as an instrument of statecraft, antedating the more renowned advice in Machiavelli's *Discourses* by almost two millennia.

Kautilya's guidelines were inspired by the inter-state politics of ancient India. Machiavelli, unaware of Kautilya's writings, drew much of his material from the history of Rome but, as with Kautilya, his prescriptions were to be applied to the political situation of his day. Yet despite the evident differences between India of the third century B.C., republican Rome, and fifteenth century Italy, contemporary readers of *Arthasastra* and *The Discourses* are immediately struck by the similarities in the advice they offered to statesmen. There is also a very modern flavor in much of these writings. Consider Kautilya's precept that "A state located between two powerful states should seek collaboration and protection from the stronger of the two." Whether or not one agrees with this particular strategy, it is necessary to be conversant with neither the politics of ancient Indian principalities nor Indian institutions and culture to understand it. Or consider Machiavelli's dictum that "Alliances are broken from considerations of interest; and in this respect republics are much more careful in the observance of treaties than princes." Were a more modern term such as "autoc-

1

racies" substituted for "princes," we would scarcely be surprised to find the statement in a contemporary work on international politics or comparative politics—or in the memoirs of a recently retired foreign minister.

As these examples suggest, alliances are apparently a universal component of relations between political units, irrespective of time or place. Alliance policies are, moreover, at the core of a nation's foreign policy orientation, often taking on symbolic as well as practical importance. The most enduring phrase of George Washington's "Farewell Address" was his admonition against "permanent alliances," a maxim which, along with Thomas Jefferson's warning against "entangling alliances," remained for over a century a virtually unquestioned shibboleth. Consider also some of the terms associated with cold war alliances—the Truman Doctrine, NATO, the Warsaw Pact, the Brezhnev Doctrine, SEATO, the Japanese-American Security Treaty, the Sino-Soviet Pact, neutralism and nonalignment. Aside from their importance as instruments of statecraft, these terms have also been among the most potent symbols of post-1945 international politics.

There is thus good reason to agree with Modelski's assertion that alliance is among the "dozen or so key terms of International Relations." [1] Were we to assume a correspondence between the evident importance of alliances in world affairs and our understanding of their causes and consequences, we would expect the existing literature to be marked by well-developed theories resting on firm foundations of empirical data. Determining whether such expectations have been fulfilled is one major purpose of this chapter. The present survey is undertaken with a view to identifying areas of consensus and disagreement among students of alliances, and, in a number of instances, suggesting some tentative hypotheses that may resolve the contradictions. We have two other goals: to provide a setting for the empirical studies in the chapters that follow, and through this review, along with the more comprehensive list of propositions in Appendix C, to assist others to pursue further research on alliances.

This survey is divided into several major topics. Initially we shall examine theories of *alliance formation*. What motives lead statesmen to join or avoid alliances? Are some states more likely to form alliances than others? Can we deduce patterns of alignment from the international distribution of power, or does the premise that like states will attract each other better inform our predictions? The next section considers various explanations of *alliance performance*. How is influence distributed within an alliance? What makes for cohesion among the member states? What factors distinguish effective alliances from ineffective ones? The third section surveys some of the more prominent explanations of *alliance termination*. Why do some alliances endure while others disintegrate rapidly? What are the likely consequences of nuclear weapons and their proliferation for alliances? The final part of the chapter turns to the *effects of alliances*. Do alliances serve to maintain stability by maintaining an equilibrium and by increasing the predictability of international affairs? Are they a prime cause of war, or are they the seeds of more lasting forms of integration? What are the domestic effects of alliance participation?

The limitations of this review should be made explicit. Because the literature on alliances is so vast as to rule out a comprehensive discussion, the focus is on the most prominent—that is, most frequently cited—theories and hypotheses. Many others may be found in the propositions that appear in Appendix C, but even that survey is at best representative rather than exhaustive. A number of issues could have been discussed under several headings. The spread of nuclear weapons, for instance, may have implications for alliance formation, performance, and termination. To avoid repetition, and because most theorists have considered nuclear proliferation as a possible agent of alliance dissolution, our discussion appears under the latter heading only. Similarly, the "size principle" of coalition theories is relevant to several aspects of alliances, but our discussion is located under the heading of alliance formation.

Definitions of Alliance. The lack of an accepted definition of alliance is perhaps the first indication that the literature is characterized by a marked absence of agreement on many issues. Some authors use the terms *alliance, coalition, pact* and *bloc* interchangeably, whereas others distinguish among them on various criteria.[2] Nor is there agreement on classifying types of alliances. Most authors seem to agree that the adjectives "offensive" and "defensive" are too value-laden to be of much utility. It is, moreover, distinctly unfashionable for signatories to a treaty of alliance to proclaim aggressive purposes; not even Ribbentrop and Molotov did so as they signed the Nazi-Soviet Pact of 1939. Categories such as "preservation" and "redistribution" are among the suggested alternatives.[3] "Defensive pact," "neutrality and nonaggression pact," and "entente" are also used widely, but not necessarily uniformly. But the differences are not merely semantic, as authors diverge in their fundamental conception of alliances. They are variously considered as *techniques of statecraft, international organizations,* or *regulating mechanisms in the balance of power.*[4]

For present purposes it is sufficient to take note of the disagreements without taking sides. There is little to be gained by a restrictive definition, and a broad one offers the distinct advantage of enlarging the scope of our review. We will thus not limit ourselves to any one of these usages. We require only that the agreement to collaborate be made by formal treaty—open or secret—and that it be concerned directly with national security issues. The first stipulation rules out the accidental or temporary coordination of foreign policy acts such as occurred in 1956 when the United States and the Soviet Union found themselves on the same side with respect to the Suez crisis. The second requirement excludes a broad range of formal agreements on trade, cultural affairs, and the like. For our purposes, then, *an alliance is a formal agreement between two or more nations to collaborate on national security issues.*

Alliance Formation

With rare exceptions, the decision to participate in alliances is made by sovereign and independent nations.[5] In this initial section we shall consider two closely related questions about the motives that give rise to alliance policies. First, *why do nations choose to undertake or shun external commitments?* There is little agreement among alliance theorists. Many place considerable emphasis on the external environment, stressing such factors as the structure of the international system or the level of conflict and threat among its member nations. Others are more inclined to look also at the attributes of the nation; some types of nations are regarded as "alliance prone," whereas others are seen as more likely to remain free from external military ties. Second, *why do nations elect to join a particular coalition in preference to others?* One position is that nations with important characteristics in common are more likely to align than dissimilar nations. A different view is held by a substantial group of theorists who regard alliances as the pragmatic expression of transient, albeit urgent, interests, rather than as the international manifestation of sentimental ties arising from common ethnic, cultural, ideological or other attributes.

Balance of Power Theories. Among the oldest and most popular theories of alliances are those derived from balance of power or equilibrium theories,[6] in which the emphasis is almost exclusively on the international system. The motives for alignment and for the particular coalition of states derive largely from the structure, distribution of power, and the state of relations among nations in the international system. Alliances, therefore, are formed as a matter of expediency. Nations join forces in order to aggregate sufficient capabilities to achieve certain foreign policy goals. One of the most important motives for coalition formation is to prevent any nation or combination of countries from achieving a dominant position. The following propositions are a representative sample.

Perceived imbalances in the distribution of international power will give rise to alliance formation (A-11; see also A-15, A-17, A-18).[7]

External threat, rather than national strength or weakness, is the primary source of alliances (P-2).

The classic examples used to illustrate these principles are the Quadruple Alliance—Great Britain, Austria, Prussia and Russia—which defeated Napoleon in 1814–1815, ending French hegemony over Europe, and the World War II alliance led by the United States, the Soviet Union, and Great Britain which defeated German and Japanese attempts to establish domination over Europe and Asia, respectively.

Balance of power approaches thus locate the motivations for alliance formation primarily in the attributes of the international system and the situation—the distribution of power, threats to the balance of power, and the like. Conversely, they tend to deny that alliance policies are significantly affected by national characteristics; democratic and autocratic nations use alliances as instruments of statecraft, as do large and small ones, rich and poor ones. Indeed, few alliances are homogeneous with respect to the attributes of member nations.

Alliance partners, moreover, are said to be chosen on the basis of common need, not for reasons of shared values, institutions, or a sense of community.

Alliance policy is a matter of expediency, not principle (P-8).

Alliances are formed primarily for security rather than out of a sense of community (P-3).

These contentions are supported by a wide variety of historical examples; aside from those provided by the coalitions of the Napoleonic Wars and World War II, the Nazi-Soviet Pact of 1939 is often cited to illustrate the point that the wellspring of any given alliance is the calculus of interest rather than sentiments of community.

Although balance of power approaches are usually associated with political scientists and historians, they often rely on a set of assumptions which are analogous to classical free market economics. Central to both is the notion of the "invisible hand"—that is, if men (or institutions) pursue their own interests rationally, an equilibrium is established which serves the general good. Just as the intelligent pursuit of profit in a competitive free market is intended to serve the welfare of the community by ensuring low prices and high quality, so the intelligent and disciplined pursuit of the national interest maintains international stability while permitting sufficient change to prevent the system from becoming overly rigid.

The analogy can be developed further to take into account alliance policies. If any member of the system threatens to become dominant, the interests of the community require some form of collective action. In the economic realm this may take the form of antitrust action; in international politics the alliance is the traditional means of preventing a hegemony. But *permanent* alliances are themselves as detrimental to the system as oligopolies or monopolies, and must therefore be avoided. Permanent alliances give rise to more intense international tensions and they tend to inhibit peaceful change by reducing flexibility: "He who plays the balance of power can have no permanent friends. His devotion can be to no specific state but only to balanced power. The ally of today is the enemy of tomorrow. One of the charms of power politics is that it offers no opportunity to grow weary of one's friends." [8]

Balance of power approaches to alliance have a normative as well as a descriptive element. That is, international stability requires that statesmen adhere to certain rules,[9] one of the most important of which is that they *must* form alliances to prevent any nation or combination of nations from achieving a position of hegemony. Failure to do so when the situation demands it is not merely irrational, it is also a serious dereliction of duty.

Balance of power theories are no doubt a useful point of departure for understanding some of the motivations underlying alliance policies, at least for some periods or regions.[10] But the number of alliances that don't "fit" the theory is sufficiently large to raise serious doubts that we can derive from these formulations a general theory of alliances, much less a universal law of history.[11] Balance of power advocates do not deny the existence of deviant cases, arguing instead that these merely represent lapses from rational policy. This is not an altogether satisfactory manner of coping with the issue, however, as it tends to render the theory incapable of disproof. At the very least it suggests that the cases of "irrational" alliance should be examined to determine whether they reveal any regularities. Such findings might then be used to clarify the many ambiguities [12] in alliance theories based on the concept of balance of power.

Coalition Theories. In contrast to balance of power explanations of alliance formation, aspects of which can be found in some of the earliest known writings on politics,[13] coalition theories are of very recent origin.[14] The proposition of central interest is the "size principle."

Coalitions will increase in size only to the minimum point of subjective certainty of winning (K-1).[15]

The basic elements of coalition theory are drawn deductively from the logic of N-person "game theory"—usually of the zero-sum variety—rather than inductively from historical evidence, yet they share a number of characteristics with balance of power or equilibrium models. Both theories place heavy emphasis on calculation of advantage, adequate information, and rationality in alliance formation. Both also tend to assume that national attributes other than power are at best of secondary importance for purposes of explaining alliances. But on one point they appear to differ. Whereas an important goal of "ideal" balance of power systems is to *prevent* the rise of a dominant nation or group of nations, the primary motivation in game theory approaches is to form just such a coalition.[16] Stated somewhat differently, the statesman in a balance of power system must simultaneously be motivated to pursue policies of self-extension and self-restraint; [17] in coalition theories the actors are assumed to be motivated by the single goal of winning, and doing so under conditions that maximize their share of the gain—that is, with as few partners as are necessary to achieve victory.

Without question coalition theories are elegant and intuitively appealing. They are also among the best examples of how mathematical reasoning (as opposed to mathematical or statistical methods of data analysis) can provide insights into important substantive questions. There are, moreover, a large number of experimental studies [18] as well as investigations of political coalitions in elections, conventions, multiparty legislatures and the like, which have often provided empirical substantiation for predictions drawn from coalition theories. But a number of difficulties arise when this approach is applied to international politics; to date efforts to do so have invariably been impressionistic analyses, often based on the collapse of victorious coalitions following global wars.[19]

The first problem is the premise that whatever an alliance wins must be divided competitively among its members; that is, alliance partners are assumed to be in a "zero-sum" situation in which the gain of any one nation must involve a similar loss to the others. In some circumstances this assumption may be valid. If war offers the prospect of winning territory, indemnities, or other kinds of tangible booty there are evident advantages to forming an alliance no larger than is necessary to gain victory. If a coalition of two nations is sufficient to vanquish and devour a third—for instance, the partition of Poland in 1939—there is little motivation to invite others into the alliance. In any case, the process of dividing the spoils may itself become a source of friction and, as predicted by the theory, lead to dissolution of the alliance.

But the zero-sum premise is not applicable to all coalitions. Even in offensive alliances the interests of the partners may be complementary, permitting a noncompetitive (or non-zero-sum) division of rewards. More importantly, alliances are often formed for purposes of defense or deterrence. In that case the success of the alliance is measured by its ability to *prevent* conflict, not by the territorial or other gains derived from a successful prosecution of war. In alliances of this kind the rewards are not divided competitively. To the contrary, each member gains from their collective ability to deter an aggressor, and any increase in the security of one nation accrues to the benefit of all. Alliances of deterrence have been important in virtually all periods of history. Indeed, the "ideal" balance of power system is one in which *ad hoc* coalitions are continually being formed to avert any major threat to the fundamental structure of the international system. For purposes of deterrence, the motives of allied nations are to form large alliances rather than the smallest successful coalition (F-3); large ones may actually serve the common interest better by reducing the probability of miscalculation on the part of a potential aggressor.

The zero-sum premises of coalition theories are particularly questionable in the light of contemporary international politics. The competing military blocs which emerged after World War II have generally functioned as alliances of deterrence rather than offense. In areas of central concern to NATO and the Warsaw Pact, there is little prospect that either side can gain territory or any other tangible benefits without incurring catastrophic costs. At least in the more developed areas of the world it thus appears that the central motives for keeping alliances at the minimum necessary size are of limited relevance.

A second difficulty, one that is shared with balance of power theories, is the demanding requirement that statesmen be able to measure capabilities with sufficient precision to define a minimum winning coalition.[20] In an election, convention, or legislature this rarely poses a severe problem. An American presidential candidate knows that 270 electoral votes will win under any conditions, even if the opponent gains a majority of the popular votes. Similarly, it is certain that fifty-one or sixty-seven votes (depending on the kind of issue) in the United States Senate or 133 votes in the multi-party Canadian House of Commons will ensure a winning margin. Moreover, although pre-voting influence may be unequally distributed among convention delegates or legislators, at the voting stage each person wields equal power. There is thus little difficulty in defining a "minimum winning coalition." In these circumstances coalition theories appear especially relevant. But rarely do these conditions prevail at the international level. Important elements of strength such as morale and popular support for the regime, whether of allies or adversaries, can rarely be assessed with complete accuracy; even the tangible components of power may elude precise measurement. To simplify the problems we can consider the capabilities of allies and adversaries as tangible and intangible. This yields a four-fold table. There is reason to suspect that in at least three of the four cases it may be difficult to measure capabilities with sufficient accuracy to satisfy the premises of the minimum winning coalition theories (Figure 1).[21]

One answer to this criticism is that the size principle is based solely on *subjective* estimates of capabilities. But if it is thus limited, the size principle appears to lose most of its explanatory power. If each exception to the

COMPONENTS OF POWER

	TANGIBLE (military power, technology, etc.)	INTANGIBLE (morale, popular support, etc.)
POWER OF ALLIES	Information readily available and easily verified	Information often difficult to obtain and to verify
		Tendency to believe that ally is a "good regime"; therefore it possesses this aspect of legitimacy
	Probable Assessment: Accurate Estimate	Probable Assessment: Tend to Overestimate
POWER OF ADVERSARIES	Information usually available but it may be difficult to verify it	Information difficult to obtain and to verify
	Better to "play it safe" by overestimating	Tendency to believe that enemy is a "bad regime"; therefore it lacks this aspect of legitimacy
	Overestimates may be useful in bureaucratic bargaining for scarce resources	
	Probable Assessment: Tendency to Overestimate	Probable Assessment: Tendency to Underestimate

Figure 1. An hypothesis on assessment of capabilities.

theory can be attributed to the subjective nature of capability estimates, then the theory cannot be disconfirmed. And by explaining everything it in fact explains nothing.)

Several other considerations may reduce the significance of coalition theories for the contemporary international system. As the number of independent nations increases, so does the difficulty of defining a winning coalition, with the consequence that we may expect larger alliances to be formed (A-5). Moreover, the predominant form of warfare today is that in which conventional measures of power, even rather sophisticated ones, may be inadequate. It is easy to point to errors of calculation made by Lyndon Johnson or Robert McNamara in the Vietnam War; it is much more difficult to develop an index that would have permitted them to define with accuracy what aggregation of power would have been necessary for victory. Indeed, in conflicts of this type it is difficult even to define what is meant by "winning."

Finally, when international politics are characterized by intense ideological conflict for which domestic energies and mass emotions are mobilized, the process of alliance formation is unlikely to be dominated solely by calculations of capabilities. Consider, for example, the period since the end of World War II. Both the United States and the Soviet Union have been engaged in a competition to line up as many allies as possible, often with a less than comprehensive assessment of the assets and liabilities which might accrue to the alliance. Because the conflict between the two blocs has usually been defined in ideological and zero-sum terms, it has been difficult to write off any area of the world as a peripheral concern (F-6).[22] By any detached assessment of the balance sheet, it is reasonably clear that to date Cuba and South Vietnam have been net liabilities to the Soviet Union and United States respectively, and no doubt other examples, contemporary and historical, could be cited.

These limitations are sufficiently important to suggest that coalition theories, and their central "size principle," are probably an inadequate base from which to construct a theory of alliance formation.[23] Nevertheless, one important normative element does emerge from the notion of minimum winning coalitions. It provides a counterbalance to an evangelical approach to alliance formation, in which allies are feverishly collected with only secondary considerations for the net advantages to be derived from such commitments. In this respect the prescriptions of coalition theorists converge with those of the "realist" school of international politics.

National Attributes and Alliance Participation.   A clear contrast to the balance of power and minimum winning coalition theories is provided by those who emphasize one or more national attributes—other than power or capabilities—as important considerations in alliance policies. These approaches do not deny that calculations of national interest or power will have an impact on alliance formation, nor do they rule out the effects of systemic or situational considerations. Virtually all of them agree, for example, that irrespective of national attributes, nations faced with an external threat are more likely to seek allies than those in a benign situation. But in addition they emphasize that we cannot treat nations as undifferentiated entities if we wish to understand their propensity to see alliances as useful instruments of foreign policy (as opposed to such alternatives as neutralism), and their choice of alliance partners when there are available options. The common denominator is a suspicion that fundamental foreign policy orientations reflect motives that draw upon many sources,[24] some of which may be explained by national attributes.

The first group of propositions links one or more national attributes to the propensity of states to join or avoid external military commitments. The most general of these suggest that alliance policies reflect leadership needs (P-17), general domestic needs (P-32), including the requirements of internal stability, status (P-33, P-36), and economic interests (P-57).

Beyond these very general observations the literature includes a large number of propositions which link one or more attributes to a greater or lesser propensity to seek alliances. Several theorists have emphasized the importance of historical experience.

The more successful a nation's past experience with self-reliant policies, the less the tendency to join alliances (P-25; see also P-26, P-53).

New states tend to pursue a policy of avoiding alliances (P-45; see also P-42 and P-44).

A study of Swedish and Norwegian policies following World War II provides some support for the first proposition. Both nations successfully avoided being drawn into World War I and both tried to remain neutral during World War II, but only the former was successful. The threat of Soviet imperialism during the late 1940s led each of the Scandinavian nations to choose a policy that was consistent with its success or failure against Hitlerian aggression: Norway joined NATO and Sweden chose neutrality rather than joining any alliance.[25]

The second proposition receives considerable support from the contemporary international system, as virtually all states which have achieved independence since 1945 have chosen policies of "neutralism," although not necessarily neutrality, with respect to cold war conflicts. American history also appears to provide support; for a century and a half after gaining independence from Great Britain the warnings of Washington and Jefferson against "entangling alliances" represented the core of conventional wisdom on matters of foreign policy. Persuasive as these examples may be, however, history is not devoid of counter-examples. Nations which gained independence in 1918 as the German, Austro-Hungarian, Russian, and Ottoman Empires collapsed did not, as a rule, shun alliances; witness the creation in 1920–21 of the Little Entente between Czechoslovakia, Yugoslavia, and Rumania, and formation of the looser Balkan Entente by Yugoslavia, Greece, Turkey and Rumania in 1934. Moreover, in several instances involving European nations it has been necessary to obtain formal agreement of the major powers to guarantee the new state's neutrality. Article VII of the settlement by which Belgian independence from Holland was recognized in 1839 declared Belgium to be a "perpetually neutral" state under the collective guarantee of the European powers. A similar stipulation was attached to the treaty by which Austria was freed from four-power occupation in 1955. This suggests the modified hypothesis that newly independent states are likely to avoid alliances only when they are geographically removed from the centers of great power conflict.

Other writers have suggested a relationship between a nation's political structure and its alliance policy (P-16). Few have put it as poetically as Queen Margaret in Shakespeare's *Henry VI:*

> For how can Tyrants safely governe home,
> Unlesse abroad they purchase great allyance?

More frequently, political stability has been associated with a propensity to join alliances (P-18) and instability has been seen as an impetus to go beyond nonalignment and to pursue a policy of "militant neutralism" (P-50). A leadership group faced with domestic instability may actively court allies in the hopes of gaining external support for a tottering regime. According to purely utilitarian criteria, small, poor, and unstable nations are relatively unattractive alliance partners (P-51). Nevertheless, such nations have often been sought as allies and they have even become the focal point of acute crises or bloody wars involving great power alliances; twentieth century examples include Bosnia (1908–1909), Serbia (1914), Cuba (1961 and 1962), and Indo-China (1953–54, and since 1965).

In the foregoing discussion we have been concerned solely with the attributes of a *single nation,* identifying some of the characteristics that are thought to predispose nations to pursue certain alliance policies. At this point we turn our attention to a somewhat different question: Given a propensity to seek allies, does the choice of partners reflect any discernible pattern of preferences? "Affiliation theories" approach alliance formation from a sociometric perspective, addressing themselves to the similarities and differences of two or more nations as an element in their propensity to align. The initial premise is that nations are likely to be selective in their choice of allies, exhibiting a preference for partners with whom they share common institutions, cultural and ideological values, or economic interests (P-31, P-59).

Ideology is by far the most controversial aspect of affiliation theories. There are many advocates of the view that a common ideology is both an impetus and a unifying bond in alliances.

Alliances generally presuppose national or ideological affinities that go beyond expediency (P-24).

There are at least equal numbers who maintain that alliance commitments are not (and should not be) made on the basis of ideology, whether the reference is to the religious wars of the sixteenth and seventeenth centuries or the hot and cold wars of the twentieth.

Religious or ideological homogeneity has not been a traditional prerequisite of alignment among states (P-14; see also P-56).

Ideology provides the rationalization for alliances (P-27).

As the issue of ideology also has relevance for the problems of alliance duration and termination, we will return to a more detailed consideration of it later.

Relative capabilities have, not surprisingly, been considered an important factor in alliance formation, but there is little consensus on its effects. Consider the following propositions:

Faced with a perceived threat, weak nations will seek strong alliance partners (P-20).

The attraction of strong states for the weak is based primarily on economic need (P-21).

A weaker power will be commonly anxious to seek alignment with geographically remoter powers (P-29).

As a nation's economic position relative to other nations declines, it will be motivated to seek alliances (P-40).

Underdeveloped nations will seek to pursue a policy of nonalignment with existing blocs (P-43, P-39).

If a nation is economically developed relative to other nations, it will not be motivated to seek alliances (P-41).

Although all of these propositions have been valid explanations for one alliance or another, the contradictions among them clearly suggest that none of them is adequate for all alliances. This is but one of the many areas of alliance theory in which it becomes important to specify the range of circumstances under which each of two or more competing propositions is likely to be valid. The task, then, is to identify the intervening variables that will permit us to state the limiting conditions for each proposition. This is what we shall attempt to do in Chapter Two, as we shall return to some of the issues introduced in this section.

Alliance Performance

The examination of alliance formation centered on the nations which choose to undertake or avoid external commitments, and the sources of their motivations for doing so. Varied as these motives may be, presumably all nations prefer to join alliances that offer them an effective role in determining goals, strategy, and tactics; that provide a "fair" share of the rewards without undue costs; and that offer the maximum probability of success in achieving their goals. There is little disagreement, however, that alliances differ markedly in these qualities. In this section we shall consider three related characteristics of alliances and the factors that are alleged to contribute to the differences between alliances in these respects. First, how and why do alliances differ in the *distribution of internal influence?* Who gets what, how and why? Second, how and why do alliances differ in the level of *cohesion* and coordination? Finally, what factors are associated with alliance *effectiveness?*

Distribution of Influence Within Alliances. Alliances are concluded between nations that possess the legal attributes of sovereignty and independence. In this respect they are equals, but many alliances include nations of rather wide disparity in the many characteristics which may contribute to power.[26] This is especially true of multipartite coalitions. The Warsaw Pact may be drawn up in the language of a contract between equal sovereign units but, as the Hungarians and Czechs have discovered, some are considerably more equal than others. The Warsaw Pact may be atypical in this respect, but we cannot assume that the norm of equality among sovereign entities accurately describes the realities of intra-alliance politics.

The conventional position is that alliance influence and allocation of benefits reflect the distribution of capabilities among its members (L-31, L-32, M-4, Q-5, Q-30). This view appears to fit common sense, historical examples can be adduced in support, and some supporting evidence may be found in both small group (L-31) and experimental studies (Q-30).

Despite the intuitive appeal of the proposition that influence is proportional to strength, it is rejected by a number of theorists who maintain that weakness may actually be a source of advantage in intra-alliance bargaining. This is but one of the many paradoxes that appears in the literature on alliances.

The stronger alliance partner is in a weaker bargaining position within the alliance, because it is usually the keener of the two to maintain the alliance (Q-35).

Small nations usually have disproportionate power in intra-alliance bargaining because (1) it is hard for a large nation to threaten credibly to reduce its contribution and (2) a large nation has less to gain by bargaining hard than does a small nation (Q-32; see also Q-37).

A small power has disproportionate influence in an alliance because it has the ability to commit its larger ally, who cannot accept the losses attendant upon the weaker partner's defeat (Q-33).

As is often the case, however, advocates of two quite contradictory propositions are able to draw supporting examples from one historical instance or another. In the absence of rigorous evidence that either theory is capable of explaining all cases, it may be useful to suggest some additional propositions with a view to stating the conditions under which each of the opposing views is likely to be valid.

The "tighter" the international system, the greater the likelihood that small allies will enjoy disproportionate influence.

The reasoning behind this hypothesis is that in a "loose" international system—one with a large number of unaligned states and more than two alliance systems—it may be easier and cheaper for a powerful ally to shop for new partners than to give in to an overly demanding ally. If leaders of both nations recognize this fact, their bargaining influence will probably come close to reflecting their capabilities. Conversely, in an international system that is polarized or approaching polarization, the number of potential alternative allies is limited. Moreover, when competition between the blocs takes on the attributes of a zero-sum game the loss of even a minor ally may be perceived as too costly. Weaker allies such as Serbia and Austria-Hungary in 1914, Poland in 1939, South Vietnam during the 1960s and many others have used this situation to good advantage in their relations with alliance leaders.[27]

The more pluralistic the alliance, the greater the likelihood that small allies will enjoy disproportionate influence.

The second hypothesis assumes that the nature of the alliance is closely related to the typical means of resolving intra-alliance differences. In a pluralistic alliance [28] the *de jure* norm that each member is a sovereign nation is more likely to be taken seriously. It is at least likely to rule out overt threats of force, or the promulgation of alliance doctrines, for example the "Brezhnev Doctrine," which even permit one nation to overturn the government of a recalcitrant ally.[29] In an authoritarian alliance, on the other hand, a small nation can bargain only within the limits established by the alliance leader, rendering it less likely that the former can wield disproportionate influence over the latter. The final proposition follows much the same line of reasoning:

Small nations are more likely to achieve disproportionate influence in an alliance composed of democratic states than in one of authoritarian nations.

Nations with a tradition of conflict resolution by bargaining instead of violence are more likely to employ similar means in resolving intra-alliance differences. A bargaining situation in which certain means of persuasion are proscribed should reduce the advantage of the more powerful party.

Alliance Cohesion and Efficacy.   Few aspects of alliances have received as much consideration as bloc cohesion. The term cohesion has been used in various ways. Some writers refer to the ability of alliance partners to agree upon goals, strategy, and tactics, and to coordinate activities directed toward those ends. Others use the term in a way that overlaps with alliance efficacy. Finally, some refer to cohesion as the antonym of disintegration, that is, as the ability of the coalition to survive.[30] At this point we shall consider cohesion in the first usage as well as alliance efficacy, the ability of the alliance to achieve its goals. We do so to avoid repetition because many theorists treat cohesion as a necessary condition for effectiveness. But when a distinction between the two appears, it shall be noted. One leading student of alliances argues, for example, that the requirements for cohesion may actually be incompatible with those for efficacy (N-10), a point illustrated by the proposition that extensive intra-alliance consultation tends to increase solidarity (L-14), but it may be detrimental to the effective conduct of military operations (N-14). Efficacy is especially likely to suffer when cohesion is based on coercion (N-12).

Although there are some doubts that alliance cohesion increases efficacy, most theorists agree that effective and successful alliances enjoy greater unity (L-27, O-9, O-14). Among the reasons is that the more successful the group, the more likely it is to restructure its hierarchies to reduce status inconsistencies (L-29), an attribute often cited as a major obstacle to cohesion, whether of groups or alliances (L-11, L-17, L-29, L-35). And an interesting set of propositions drawn from the economic theory of "collective action" suggests that alliances which supplement public benefits with private or noncollective ones are more cohesive than alliances that provide only collective benefits. Support has been found in both experimental research (L-6) and in studies of NATO.[31]

THREAT. Probably the most widely stated proposition about alliances is that cohesion depends upon external danger and declines as the threat is reduced (G-1, G-2, G-5, G-6, G-7, G-10, G-11, G-13, G-17, G-18, G-20, G-22, I-13). The proposition is, of course, an extension of several major themes in the literature: that alliances are formed primarily *against* something, and only secondarily *for* something (M-1); and, that they tend to reflect shared interests in a specific situation rather than a sense of community arising from common values, culture, and the like. From these premises it tends to follow that, as the threat which gave rise to alliance recedes, so will cohesion within the alliance. Typical propositions of this type link increasing external threat to greater cohesion, a greater propensity to rally around the alliance leader (G-22), and a willingness to subordinate conflicting purposes to a single goal (H-5). Conversely, inter-alliance negotiations (G-26), peace (G-30), and generally declining international tensions (E-11) are associated with eroding cohesion.

Although few writers have denied that external pressure tends to create internal cohesion, a number of important qualifications have been suggested. One group of propositions places emphasis on the degree to which the threat is felt equally by all bloc members. If only part of the alliance membership is threatened (G-3, G-23), or if the threat strikes at the basis of group consensus, severe divisions may arise (G-25). Similarly, unless the external danger creates an equitable division of labor among alliance members, cohesion is likely to suffer (G-24). For this reason, although wartime alliances obviously face considerable external pressure, they may be characterized by internal tensions because military operations rarely result in burdens of an equal magnitude upon the partner nations (G-9). As long as the threat seems to call for a cooperative solution—"Unless we hang together we shall hang separately"—cohesion will probably be enhanced (G-15). But should a solution appear which favors one ally at the expense of others, the alliance may not only lose unity, but disintegrate. France's willingness in 1938 to cope with the threat of war with Germany by sacrificing the integrity of its Czech ally is a case in point. Finally, an alliance confronting an external threat for which there is no solution may also experience reduced cohesion (G-16).

A related line of reasoning suggests that external conflict may enhance cohesion for the short run, while establishing the conditions for longer-range problems of internal unity. According to these propositions, threat from without tends to create organizational rigidities in alliances and reduced tolerance for diversity (G-29), whereas declining international tensions give rise to more flexible and less hierarchical arrangements (G-19, G-21). At least some students of alliances consider rigid alliances less likely to remain cohesive in the long run.

Despite the popularity of propositions linking external threat and cohesion, rigorous supporting evidence has usually been derived from studies of groups other than alliances or from experimental research. Chapters Three and Four describe a study which tests these and related hypotheses in the two cold war alliances, NATO and the Communist system.

DECISION MAKING STRUCTURE. Of the many alliance attributes that have been associated with cohesion, decision making structure, size, and duration are perhaps the most important.[32]

Alliances differ widely in the kinds of political and administrative arrangements which govern their activities. Two nations may undertake wide-ranging commitments to assist each other under given circumstances and yet fail to establish institutions and procedures for communication and co-ordination of activities. This tended to characterize the alliance between Germany and Austria-Hungary during the years leading up to World War I.[33] The Warsaw Pact may perhaps be used to illustrate the other extreme. There is little question that basic alliance decisions are made in Moscow and all key positions in the alliance have been filled by Russians.[34] In contrast to the Dual Alliance between Vienna and Berlin, the Warsaw Pact thus represents a highly *centralized* and *hierarchical* alliance.

There is a notable lack of agreement among alliance theorists regarding the consequences of alternative decision making structures. One line of reasoning suggests that hierarchical and centralized alliances are more likely to be both more cohesive and more effective in coping with the external environment.

Other things being equal, a coalition will be more stable to the extent that decision making is centralized, i.e., the coalition is hierarchically organized (O-13).

Centralization of alliance decision making leads to greater alliance cohesion (L-24).

A hegemonic alliance would repress strains underneath the supremacy of the leading ally (L-4).

The more structurally centralized ("system dominant") as well as the more autocratic ("directive") the organizational structure of a bloc, the greater the potential energy with which the bloc could act (N-4).

A very autocratic bloc, "because of its control over resources, can readily respond to external threats or opportunities" (N-5; see also N-6).

This position is analogous to the theory—articulated by Alexis de Tocqueville, Walter Lippmann, Raymond Aron, and George Kennan, among others—that democratic nations are poorly equipped to cope with external problems.

The diametrically opposite position, that pluralistic and decentralized alliances are likely to enjoy greater solidarity and effectiveness, also has wide currency in the literature.

A loose system of states in alliance may be more cohesive than a tight one (L-20).

The more highly structured the alliance, the greater the likelihood of conflict among members (L-21; see also L-3, S-24).

Alliance cohesion based on the oppressive rule of a single power, or a single principle, will give rise to reduced efficacy (N-12; see also N-17).

Pluralistic alliances have greater vitality (N-20).

Small group and experimental studies tend to support the case for pluralistic organizations (L-26). Although such findings can be a suggestive source of insights, we cannot dismiss the possibility that significant properties of small groups and alliances are not sufficiently isomorphic to support the assumption that what is true of the former will necessarily be valid for the latter. Thus the issue can only be settled by investigations of international alliances. A study of French and Chinese alliance policies in Chapters Five and Six will test the alternative proposition that autocratic alliances may be more cohesive and effective than pluralistic ones as long as there are no issues which might seriously challenge the established order within the coalition, but once such issues develop they are likely to poison all facets of relations between the contending partners. Conversely, although pluralistic alliances will not be free of disagreements, even differences on central concerns are likely to remain confined to the single issue at stake, rather than "spilling over" into other issue-areas. Put somewhat differently, the price that authoritarian alliances pay for faster reaction time and related advantages may be a quality of brittleness which does not facilitate coping with serious internal problems.

There is greater agreement that a division of functions enhances alliance unity. Calvocoressi suggests that in the absence of a division of labor there will be dissension arising from lack of distinct and useful functions for the minor members (L-22), a view for which some experimental support exists (L-10). But the substantive nature of the division is no doubt also an important consideration, as some distributions of roles are unlikely to find general favor. For example, proposals to divide NATO functions in a way that would have the United States take primary responsibility for nuclear deterrence and would leave the task of conventional defense in the hands of the Europeans have gained something less than enthusiastic support in Paris, Bonn, Brussels, and other European capitals.

In discussing alliance structures and procedures, a number of theorists place special emphasis on the bloc "leader." Not all coalitions have a nation in an acknowledged position of primacy, but the formation after World War II of the alliances led by the United States and Soviet Union has given the topic special importance.

A general observation is that alliances led by superpowers are particularly prone to erosion (O-4). This is especially likely if the leading nation plays an oppressive role within the bloc (N-12), or if the interests of minor members are neglected (G-12). A related proposition is that when the legitimacy of the core nation's leadership is open to question because of the absence of established rules of succession, an oppressive degree of conformity may be imposed on other allies (Q-23); the long run effects are likely to be reduced unity. Moreover, in an international system dominated by superpowers, the disparity between their power and that of allies gives rise to interests common to the superpowers and not shared by their allies (C-2). Some events during the 1950s and 1960s, notably the Suez crisis, the Sino-Indian border war, and the Nuclear Test Ban Treaty, did indicate a willingness of the alliance leaders to subordinate bloc unity to the more general interests of the superpowers. Whether this proposition is applicable only to the era of nuclear weapons could only be determined by examining earlier international systems that were dominated by two extraordinarily powerful protagonists.

Another set of propositions stresses the capabilities and competence of the bloc leader (Q-11, Q-26). A decline in the strength of the leader makes the alliance especially vulnerable to erosion (R-4, T-2). Conversely, a wealthy bloc leader is capable of offering economic aid and other types of side payments to smaller partners which may, in turn, render the alliance more effective (O-12). A rich nation can do so without disrupting domestic programs, whereas a relatively poor bloc leader may be tempted instead to drain the resources of its allies.

Although there seems to be general agreement on these propositions and they seem intuitively reasonable, they appear to be tailored to a very limited number of cases—the experiences of the United States and the Soviet Union during the past two decades. Whether they have more general application remains to be demonstrated. For example the proposition linking the wealth of the bloc leader to cohesion and efficacy fits the two cold war alliances—compare the Marshall Plan program of aid to Western Europe with the niggardly aid from the Soviet Union to its allies, the unfavorable trade terms imposed on nations such as Poland, or the effort to maintain Rumania as an agricultural supplier within the Communist system. It remains to be tested in other alliances, however, or even against alternative explanations of cohesion in NATO and the Warsaw Pact.

DURATION. Another of the many contradictions in the literature concerns the effects of time. Against the thesis that strains will develop within alliances of long duration (L-8) stands the counter-argument that the longer an alliance endures, the greater its solidarity and legitimacy (L-16). The issue appears to be closely related to two of the conflicting theories on alliance formation that we encountered earlier. The former positions seem to be more consistent with the general view that alliances are established purely as a matter of expediency. Thus, as the problems that gave rise to the alliance are resolved or fade into relative insignificance, or as new issues arise on which the erstwhile partners may not share a common interest, we could expect a loosening of cohesion. The thesis that alliance solidarity will grow with time, on the other hand, appears to arise from the premise that whatever the original impetus for coalition formation, alliances will resemble other institutions that take on a life and rationale of their own, which may eventually have little or no direct relationship to their initial purposes. At the same time they may create feelings of community which permit an alliance to survive even severe crises, as the Anglo-American alliance survived the Suez and Skybolt crises of 1956 and 1962.[35] An even stronger version of this theory holds that cooperative activity in one sphere may "spill over" into others, ultimately paving the way for some form of international integration. We shall examine this thesis in greater detail when we turn our attention to the effects of alliances.

SIZE. Large alliances are usually considered less cohesive and effective than small ones (N-15, N-18), a proposition that has received support from small-group research (L-25), but less attention from students of international alliances. There are several reasons why this seems intuitively, but not necessarily empirically, true. First, the larger the alliance, the smaller the share of attention that nations can give to each other ally. Secondly, as the size of the alliance increases, the number of dyads within the alliance rises even faster. In a partnership of two nations, there is but a single pair of nations between which activities must be coordinated. With five nations in a coalition the number of dyads increases to ten, and a bloc of fifteen nations includes 105 bilateral relationships. Not only do the problems of coordination increase, but so do the opportunities for dissension. Finally, the larger the alliance, the less important the contributions of any single member (especially minor partners), and the easier it is for any partner to rationalize the argument that failure to meet all alliance obligations will not really make any difference.

CAPABILITIES AND CREDIBILITY. Alliance cohesion has been linked to both steadily rising capabilities (L-5) and the credibility of deterrence (L-23). It is generally recognized that each state brings both assets and liabilities to the partnership (S-8). The typical manner of assessing the capabilities of a coalition is to total the assets of member nations. We are often presented with statistical data, for example, comparing the populations, number of divisions, aircraft, or ships for two or more alliances. The assumption is that the strength of an alliance may be determined by summing the contributions of each nation.

The alternative view is that the power of an alliance is not equal to the sum of its parts (S-3, S-13, S-14). Under some circumstances the whole may be greater than that possessed by its members individually. Given close coordination and similar equipment, economies of scale may be achieved. Probably the more usual case is that for various reasons alliance capabilities are less—perhaps substantially less—than that of the individual nations combined, resulting from poor staff coordination, mistrust, incompatible goals, logistical difficulties, dissimilar military equipment and organization, and other problems. This is what Napoleon had in mind when he stated, "If I must make war, I prefer it to be against a coalition." [36] A century later Marshal Foch remarked, "My admiration for Napoleon has shrunk since I found out what a coalition was." [37] Perhaps there are some parallels between corporate mergers and alliances in this respect. Some mergers clearly result in a firm that is far more effective than its parts— witness the case of General Motors. Others seem to prove only that the combination is equal to the sum of its liabilities. Two companies with vast assets but mediocre management, the New York Central and Pennsylvania railroads, produced the most spectacular bankruptcy in American corporate history soon after their merger.

A problem faced by virtually every alliance is that of ensuring the credibility of its commitments. If adversaries possess serious doubts on this score, the alliance may serve as an invitation to attack. Equally important, if allies themselves have doubts about the assurances of their partners, the alliance is unlikely to survive for long. According to some, nuclear weapons have introduced and nurtured precisely this type of question about the viability of contemporary commitments, a point to which we shall return later.

It is sometimes suggested that "irrational" alliance commitments may be undertaken as part of an overall strategy of increasing the credibility of deterrence (P-37). For example, a nation may undertake a vast commitment of resources in a peripheral region to support a minor ally of far less value than the costs of the commitment. This strategy is intended to convey to the adversary—and to other allies—that if one will expend vast resources to protect areas of little value, then it should be clear that an even greater effort will be made in support of other areas.

But like other strategies of buttressing credibility by "irrational" commitments, this one may backfire badly. In 1939, after agreeing to dismemberment of Czechoslovakia, Great Britain undertook a virtually unlimited pledge of support for Poland. However commendable the motives of the Chamberlain government may have been, a number of European leaders were astounded that Britain had, in effect, left it to Warsaw and Berlin to decide whether England would be drawn into war, an action without precedent in British history. If this pledge was viewed as incredible and unprecedented by others, it is scarcely surprising that Hitler and Ribbentrop were convinced that the commitment would not be honored (N-23, N-24).

NATIONAL ATTRIBUTES. Finally, many theorists begin with the assumption that nations with substantially different attributes are less likely to be compatible alliance partners. With the possible exception of ideology, to be discussed later, the relative capabilities of nations in alliance has received the most attention. Earlier we encountered the thesis that alliances led by superpowers are especially vulnerable to internal dissension, the implication being that relative equality in strength enhances unity. Aside from the very special case of the two superpowers, there appears to be widespread agreement that great inequalities in size and strength among alliance members is a likely source of dissension (Q-2, Q-14, Q-17, R-7). A dynamic version of the thesis is the proposition that unequal *changes* in strength favor disunity (Q-4, S-22).

The relative merits of democracies and autocracies as partners has been debated in many treatises on alliances, including those of Kautylia and Machiavelli. The result is a distinct lack of consensus. To some the former are inferior on two counts. By definition they experience relatively frequent changes in ruling elites, with the consequence that commitments to allies may also change; and the demands of domestic politics may take precedence over the requirements of alliances. The American election campaign of 1952 and its aftermath is a good case of the latter point. One of the two leading candidates for the Republican nomination, Senator Robert A. Taft, was a long-standing opponent of permanent American commitments to European defense. During the campaign and its immediate aftermath, statements by John Foster Dulles about a "rollback of communism" and an "agonizing reappraisal" of American defense commitments were scarcely reassuring to Western European allies. Not until later in 1953, after the East German riots and the French defeat of the European Defense Community brought forth no significant response from Washington, was it clear that these slogans were intended for domestic consumption. Ironically, Dulles failed to appreciate that the often moralistic rhetoric of neutralist statesmen which he found offensive was also important for reasons of domestic politics in India and elsewhere, as a symbolic expression of national independence by ex-colonial nations.

Other observers take a kinder view of democracies, finding that, when under attack, they are more likely to expand alliance functions (R-3), they tend to turn alliances into communities of friendship (M-2), and they are less likely to renege on commitments by seeking a separate peace (S-19; but cf. S-20). But history is filled with enough examples of ineffective alliance performance to lend some weight to the arguments of those who maintain that neither democracies nor dictatorships are markedly superior in this respect (T-6, S-7). In Chapter Two we shall attempt to shed further light on this question with data on all alliances between the end of the Napoleonic Wars and the outbreak of World War II.

A third set of propositions suggests that differences in national bureaucratic structures and processes may be an increasingly important barrier to coordination of alliance strategies. They emphasize that national security policy is the product of constant intramural conflict within highly complex and varied bureaucratic structures.[38] As a result, even the closest allies may fail to perceive accurately the nuances in the "rules" of the bureaucratic politics "game" as it is played abroad, and how the demands of various constituents may shape and constrain alliance policies (Q-3, Q-18, Q-22).

Bureaucratic conflict models of foreign policy appear to provide a useful alternative or supplement to approaches that place great emphasis on rationality and calculation, to the virtual exclusion of organizational considerations. To date they have been used almost exclusively to explain post-1945 alliance politics among developed western democracies. They have, moreover, focused largely on the tensions between the imperatives of internal bureaucratic bargaining and the demands of allies. Future research should establish more clearly the scope and limitations of this approach to alliance politics.[39]

Alliance Duration and Disintegration

Palmerston once noted that nations have neither permanent enemies nor allies, only permanent interests. More recently Fedder has asserted that they are not "particularly viable" components of the international system (N-1; see also T-9). It is true that the endurance of alliances can better be measured in years than decades or centuries, but this scarcely explains why they disintegrate. Is it because the conditions which gave rise to the alliance have passed, rendering it superfluous? Or is the alliance either too successful (eliminating external threats) or too unsuccessful (it is defeated in a general war)? Or do allies discover, like newlyweds, that two cannot necessarily live as cheaply as one or, indeed, as cheaply as they did before

the alliance (V-5)? Was the alliance unable to bridge the chasm of fundamental differences in values? Do few nations possess the resources, internal cohesion, and coherence of interests to be effective allies (S-11)?
Moreover, such general observations do not help to explain why some coalitions endure for relatively long periods, whereas others are stillborn virtually from the moment of conception.

Balance of power theorists and their critics tend to agree on one point:
Alliances that endure without change over significant periods of time
merely introduce rigidities into the international system, with the result
that they are a source of instability in the long run. Under what conditions,
then, are we likely to find such rigid coalitions? Among the conditions that
are thought to discourage alliance shifting are vast disparities in power between bloc leaders and their partners (E-8), cleavages of an ideological nature between alliances (E-7, F-5), and commitment to the status quo by alliance leaders (E-13), which precludes the possibility of offering territorial
compensation to nations that shift their allegiance from one alliance to
another (E-5). Conversely, an increase in the number of major powers enhances fluidity in alliance commitments (E-10).

Nuclear Weapons. Expanding membership in the "nuclear club" has
generated an extensive debate on the likely consequences of nuclear weapons for alliances. Given the limited period that such weapons have been in
existence, it is almost inevitable that theorizing on this question has, for
the most part, drawn more heavily on abstract logic than on empirical evidence. This is not to say that discussion of the problem has remained confined to theoreticians, however, for few alliance-related questions have
taken on such importance in the councils of state as the myriad problems
posed by the revolution in weapons technology.

A majority of those who have considered the political impact of nuclear
weapons have stressed their negative consequences for alliances, with varying degrees of emphasis.

Nuclear weapons have made alliances obsolete (I-11; see also E-1, E-3).

*Nuclear weapons introduce inconsistencies into traditional alliances, be-
cause no country will die for another (I-9).*

*Development of nuclear weapons may have a divisive effect on alliances
(G-8; see also G-28).*

There are several related themes in the argument of those who foresee
that nuclear weapons will play a divisive or disintegrative function. One is
that contemporary military technology permits nations to gain preponderant power without external assistance (F-1, P-48), but at the same time it

has restricted the utility of military power, further reducing the value of alliances (I-8). Another strand of the argument is that nuclear deterrence may not be reliable, and therefore it will be less than credible if it takes the form of one alliance member providing a "nuclear umbrella" for the others. Put in its starkest form the question is: What nation will risk its own annihilation by using its nuclear capabilities as a means of last resort to punish aggression against its allies? Any doubts on that score will reduce the credibility of deterrence and the utility of the alliance (L-23, I-4, I-6). If an alliance is a doubtful deterrent, then clearly an alternative form of security policy must be sought; for some the answer is neutralism, for others it is disengagement from alliances, combined with self-reliance.

The other side of the argument is that one may unwittingly become a nuclear target as a result of an ally's quarrels. Here is another of the many paradoxes of international politics in the nuclear age. Doubts about the credibility of the ally's pledges of assistance seem to encourage disengagement from alliance commitments; but fear that the alliance commitments will actually be honored, resulting in a nuclear war, lead many to the same conclusion—that it is safer to withdraw from external military ties.

Finally, it has not escaped notice that one may perhaps avoid both of these dilemmas by abstaining from alliances, and yet gain all of the real advantages of the protection offered by nuclear deterrence. It is argued, for instance, that even before the Indo-Soviet alliance of 1971, a strategic neutral nation such as India enjoyed *de facto* protection by the two superpowers against any threat from China because neither the United States nor the Soviet Union could afford to have Peking dominate the Indian subcontinent. The fact that both Washington and Moscow provided aid to India during the Sino-Indian border war of 1962 suggests that the theory may have some validity.

Whatever the merits of the alleged linkage between the existence of nuclear weapons and the dissolution of alliances—the issue can scarcely be considered settled less than thirty years following the first nuclear explosion—it should also be noted that strong dissenting views have been entered. For example:

Nuclear weapons do not reduce the value or number of alliances (I-10).

A closely related aspect of the problem focuses not on the *existence* of nuclear weapons, but on their *spread to alliance members* other than the superpowers. With a total of three cases—one of which has remained a steadfast ally and two that have not—from which to develop a theory, it is scarcely surprising that a sharp division of opinion exists.

The invention of a very cheap make-it-yourself all-purpose deterrent would invite every nation to be isolationist in military affairs, fragmenting such alliances as NATO and the Warsaw Pact. . . . (J-7; see also G-31).

As the possession of the technology of nuclear warfare spreads, such defections [from alliances] may well become more frequent (J-6).

Nuclear diffusion in the long run may stabilize alliances (D-2; also Q-27, but cf. G-27).

A measure of independent [nuclear] strength for each of the NATO allies is likely to contribute to the cohesiveness of the alliance (Q-1, but cf. G-28).

The view expressed in the first pair of propositions appears grounded in a strictly utilitarian view of alliances. The latter two seem to follow from the position that considerations other than pure expediency may be important considerations in the life of an alliance, and that sharing nuclear capabilities will add to the sense of equality and cooperation among allies. Advocates of the first position can point to the recent *de facto* defections of France and China from their alliances. It is not clear which came first, however, the decision to acquire an independent nuclear deterrent or strains between Paris and its NATO partners, and between Moscow and Peking. The latter viewpoint receives support from Britain's continued adherence to NATO two decades after becoming the world's third nuclear power.

Disarmament. Paradoxically, effective agreement on disarmament measures has also been associated with the dissolution of alliances (E-9). Any discussion of serious steps toward disarmament must, of course, be based on speculation about the future rather than evidence from the past. Given the premise of substantial disarmament, one might be led to any of several conclusions. Those who assume that present levels of military arsenals are the major source of international tensions might conclude that a disarmed world would be free of the kinds of external threat which have often given rise to alliance formation. This thesis foresees that disarmament would result in a markedly different type of international politics than that of any previous period in history. Alternatively, some might argue that with disarmament it would be possible, indeed likely, for nations to establish some sort of genuine collective security arrangement. Such a system would rule out alliances because it requires nations to give up all binding security agreements save one—the commitment to assist the victims of aggression and to punish the aggressors.

Conclusions that foresee the end of alliances are not the only ones that might be derived from the premise of disarmament, however. It might be equally reasonable to predict that because there will always be differences in the capabilities of political units—whether the relevant capabilities are those necessary to fight a world war or to bargain for finite resources—the weak will always perceive the necessity for collaborative action. Advocates of this view can point to earlier eras of history in which armament levels were infinitesimally small by present standards, and yet which were characterized by extensive alliance politics (A-1, A-8).

External Threat.   Earlier we noted that external threat is generally linked to both alliance formation and alliance cohesion. The logical extension of these observations is that as the bond of fear dissolves, so do alliances (J-2, J-3, J-8). A closely related view is that as the world becomes relatively war-free, it is also likely to become relatively alliance-free (A-9). Several qualifications to these propositions have also been offered. If, for example, a competitive solution—one which sets off the interests of one ally against another—presents itself, alliances are unlikely to survive (J-1). The Suez Crisis of 1956 and the Sino-Indian border conflict six years later appear to have been situations of this type. But, as will be shown in greater detail in Chapters Five and Six, the consequences of such divisive events have been quite different for NATO and the Sino-Soviet alliance. And, as students of the Anglo-American alliances have pointed out, when traditional friends are in alliance, their behavior often defies the purely utilitarian calculus of those who see alliances as nothing more than compacts of expediency (T-8).

Alliance Attributes.   Virtually all alliance theorists maintain that some types of alliances are likely to survive for a longer period of time than others. There is less agreement, however, on the attributes that contribute to longevity. Among the more popular propositions are those that examine the effects of size, structure, purposes, and ideology on the duration and termination of alliances.

Earlier we discussed the "size principle," the postulate that alliances will only be as large as necessary to win. Supporters of the "minimum winning coalition" theory are quick to point out that under some circumstances—for example, when information is inadequate—alliances will in fact exceed this optimal size (P-4, P-5, P-6). A natural extension of this theory is that when the size principle is violated, the alliance is unlikely to survive for long after the discovery of the violation (O-1). Others who start from quite different theoretical bases tend to agree (O-15). But the opposite conclusion emerges from a study of nineteenth and twentieth century alliances:

Alliances break up at a constant rate independent of size (O-6).

Internal structure has also been related to the durability and termination of alliances. Some of the more prominent propositions are the following.

A rigid alliance system is likely to suffer much greater disintegration than a loose one (O-2).

Political structures that are authoritarian tend in time to disintegrate as a result of pent-up frustrations exploding in violence (O-11).

The more extensive the formation of subcoalitions within an international alliance, the greater the likelihood of alliance disintegration (O-3).

In Chapters Five and Six we will return to this issue when we explore some of the possible relationships between alliance structure and disintegration.

Several propositions link alliance purposes to durability.

Offensive alliances tend to disintegrate easily (O-5).

Nonaggression and mutual defense alliances have a short existence (O-7).

There are at least logical reasons why redistribution alliances, those that seek substantial changes to the status quo, should break up more easily than those whose primary motives are deterrence and defense. The first is related to the observation that failure to achieve goals has a disintegrative effect (O-9). Other things being equal, it is easier for an alliance of deterrence to succeed; it is sufficient to deny the enemy a victory or to maintain the status quo. An offensive alliance, on the other hand, must not only be able to avert defeat, but must also win a victory if it is to be successful. Even if it achieves a victory there are elements in the situation which may operate to reduce its life span. The rewards of an offensive alliance can be shared noncompetitively only when the goals of each nation are limited and do not overlap with those of its allies. Often such allies find themselves in a zero-sum situation, however. Thus, when Germany and the Soviet Union aligned to devour Poland and the Baltic nations, they still faced the problem of dividing the spoils. They could not both have all of Poland or Lithuania, and whatever one received reduced by that amount the gains of the partner. In that instance the spoils were divided before the conquests, but we might expect even greater friction between allies when distribution of rewards is delayed until the end of the war. In contrast, the more security a defensive or deterrent alliance provides for one nation, the more secure all of the others are likely to feel. The latter non-zero-sum situation has a greater probability of evoking and sustaining sentiments on behalf of alliance maintenance.

Another widely articulated argument is that the generality or scope of an alliance is inversely related to its durability (O-17, O-8). It is easier to maintain cooperation for specific purposes in geographically limited areas than in global alliances that make a substantial claim on resources and freedom of action (N-21). This is quite consistent with the "realist" position which tends to argue that alliances are, and should be, instruments of policy entered into to achieve specific and limited goals. In direct contrast is the view that an alliance is more likely to endure through crises if it has a rationale for existence that goes beyond some immediate, concrete problem (T-8, S-4).

A very closely related issue is that of ideology in alliances. Our present concern is with the role that ideology may play in sustaining or dissolving alliance bonds, a question which has two facets. First, does a similarity in values add to the durability of alliances? On this point there is widespread affirmation, even by those who tend to minimize the importance of ideology in alliance formation (S-17, T-1, but cf. L-18).

The second question concerns the presence of ideology as a salient component of the *raison d'être* for the bloc. There is wide variation in views, as suggested by the three propositions that follow.

A purely ideological alliance cannot but be stillborn (T-5; see also S-18).

Ideology is a relatively minor factor in alliance cohesion, incapable of making or breaking the system, but ideological affinity is an asset (N-25).

Common ideology may provide a source of alliance unity in the absence of common interests (Q-8).

A thesis which is partly compatible with all but the second proposition is that ideology may sustain alliances, but only as long as its tenets do not themselves become an issue. When they do, alliances in which ideology is highly salient are far less likely to endure than those in which ideology is of marginal importance.

The greater the need to maintain ideological homogeneity in an alliance, the greater will be the tendencies toward disintegration (O-10).

When ideology is taken seriously, issues arising therefrom have a quality that makes them particularly likely to exacerbate relations between those who interpret the faith differently. Concrete alliance problems such as the level of military contributions can almost always be resolved by compromise; half of an army corps is, after all, better than none. It is a good deal more difficult for true believers to split their differences on questions of "fundamental truth" (L-28, Q-29). Alliances with an ideological orientation may therefore be particularly prone to breaking up into splinter groups (L-33).

National Attributes. Domestic instability is the national attribute most often associated with alliance disintegration. Unstable regimes may experience radical changes in elites which, in turn, result in shifting patterns of alignment (T-4, T-10). Cuba's jump from one alliance to another following the successful Castro revolution is a case in point. A related argument is that unstable regimes may be more willing to take risks for their own interests, but not for those of their allies, thereby weakening alliance bonds. The classic example is Austria-Hungary in 1914. Faced with the prospect that the multinational Dual Monarchy would be torn apart by demands for autonomy from various ethnic groups, Vienna pursued a punitive policy toward Serbia, initially with the full support of Germany, but later with little attention to advice emanating from Berlin.

Whatever the merits of these arguments, some of the most dramatic cases of realignment or alliance defection have occurred in nations with well-entrenched elites who appear to have had little to fear from domestic rivals. Nazi-Soviet relations offer numerous examples. Their pact in 1939 was inconsistent with the Franco-Soviet alliance of 1935 and the Anti-Comintern Pact. After Hitler turned on his erstwhile ally in 1941, the Soviet government agreed with its new allies—Britain and the United States—that it would not enter into a separate peace with Germany. Yet there is evidence that it attempted to do so in 1943.[40] We shall pursue the argument that stable regimes are better able to defect from alliances in Chapters Five and Six, within the context of Sino-Soviet and Franco-NATO relations.

International Effects of Alliances

The foregoing discussion has been concerned solely with the theories and findings about how and why alliances are formed, operate, and disintegrate. That is, alliances have been the dependent variable. In the concluding section we shall reverse our perspective. Instead of considering the causes and conditions of alliances and their performances, we shall turn our attention to their effects, both on the international system and on the nations which join or shun alliances. Questions about the effects of alliances are clearly important but, if anything, the literature on this topic is even more filled with contradictory propositions.

Alliances and the Balance of Power. Most balance of power approaches to international politics assign a central role to alliances; they provide the primary means of deterring or defeating nations or coalitions that seek to destroy the existing balance by achieving a position of hegemony. Examples which are adduced to illustrate how shifting alliances maintain a relatively peaceful equilibrium are often drawn from European history during the century between the Napoleonic Wars and World War I. Typical of the propositions which assign this critical role to alliances are the following:

The alliance is one of the most prominent means of putting the balance of power theory to work (U-13; see also U-21, U-43, U-50, U-51).

Alliances uphold the balance of power by facilitating alert responses to developing imbalances (U-15).

Whenever an aggressor arises, alliances are indispensable to avoid war (U-14).

But most analyses based on balance of power theories also attach a number of important qualifications. Alliances among great powers are regarded as contributing to instability (U-16). Not only are great power alliances potentially strong enough to destroy the existing balance; they also reduce the number of nations which may act in the role of "balancers," nations which, according to the theory, are supposed to remain uncommitted until there is a threat to the balance, at which time they are to join a coalition against any potentially dominant nation or group of nations. Another stipulation is that alliances must be *ad hoc* arrangements, formed for the purposes of meeting a specific problem, or to mitigate the consequences of inevitable shifts in the relative capabilities of nations (U-18, U-26).

Alliances are also said to perform other stabilizing functions (U-47). They reduce uncertainty, and nations that might pursue impetuous or aggressive policies may be restrained by their alliance partners (U-45). And it has been noted that internal pressures for acquisition of nuclear weapons have been stronger among nonaligned nations—for example, Sweden and India—than among those whose allies include at least one nuclear power.

According to balance of power theories, then, alliances are accorded a major function in conserving the system. The failure of nations to carry out their functions properly permits dangerous imbalances to occur. The outbreak of both World Wars during this century are often cited as illustrations of this point. Had Great Britain made it clear from the first that she would support France completely in case of war, according to this view, the Central Powers would have taken a more moderate stand on the Serbian question, thereby averting a catastrophic war. And during the 1930s, the nations committed to maintaining the existing system either failed to develop coalitions capable of deterring the revisionist powers—Germany, Japan and Italy—or they failed to carry out their responsibilities under existing alliances. Inability or unwillingness of the French, British, and Russians to form an alliance during the negotiations preceding the Nazi-Soviet Pact of 1939, and the Munich agreement of 1938 are cited as examples of these failures. It should be noted that students of international politics and diplomatic history are certainly not agreed on these interpretations of the genesis of World War I and World War II. They are offered only to illustrate one school of thought on the role of alliances in balance of power systems.

Alliances and War. In almost direct opposition to the line of reasoning summarized above are a number of writers who stress that balance of power systems always contain the seeds of their own destruction (a point which even the most sanguine will not completely deny), and that alliances are a major source of instability and war in all types of international systems, *including balance of power systems.* These arguments are certainly as venerable as those on behalf of beneficial consequences of alliances, but they have gained special favor during the past half century. In the aftermath of World War I, the revulsion against the ghastly and seemingly purposeless destruction of that conflict led many to point to the alliance system of prewar Europe as the primary cause of the war. Woodrow Wilson was the most prominent spokesman for this position, but he was not alone (U-12). Ironically, it was the fear that Article X of the League of Nations Covenant would permanently "entangle" the United States in the seemingly endless quarrels of Europe—just as would joining an alliance system—that led some senators to oppose Wilson's hopes that the League would act as a collective security system, rendering alliances unnecessary. After a hiatus of some twenty-five years (roughly 1940–1965), during which the stabilizing effects of alliances were often stressed,[41] there has been a rehabilitation of the thesis that alliances are a major source of international tensions and violence. It hardly need be added that this development has taken place against a background of: (1) a bloody war in Indo-China in which both South Vietnam and North Vietnam have received enormous support from their allies, the United States on the one hand, and the Soviet Union and China on the other; and (2), a continuing conflict in the Middle-East in which the major regional powers—Egypt and Israel—have been supported by the two superpowers, giving rise to fears that the United States and Soviet Union might be drawn into a major war as a result of their military assistance.

A number of specific propositions linking alliances to international violence have been developed. Perhaps the most popular is the argument that alliances merely breed counter-alliances (U-35, U-36, U-49), thereby leaving no nation more secure, while at the same time contributing to polarization and a rise in international tensions (U-4, U-11, U-28). For this reason Wright offers the suggestion that international stability is better served by efforts to break up dangerous coalitions, rather than merely opposing them with counter-alliances (U-17). This is surely one of the most difficult tasks which can be assigned to diplomacy. The Triple Entente powers were able to achieve the detachment of Italy from the Triple Alliance, ensuring Rome's neutrality in 1914 and its entry into the war against the Central Powers the following year. But efforts to split Mussolini from Hitler through a policy of appeasement failed completely. Moreover, the classical methods of detaching allies from a dangerous combination usually involve secret agreements of territorial compensation. For example, Italy was offered parts of the Austro-Hungarian empire for joining the Allies in World War I. But both secret diplomacy and territorial transfers, standard techniques in the repertoire of diplomats of an earlier era, have acquired such unsavory reputations—deservedly so in the latter case—that they can scarcely be used under any circumstances, even by the most cynical.

A second argument which finds wide expression in the literature is that alliances are incompatible with a system of collective security (U-3, U-7, U-8, U-9, U-10). The point is valid, because collective security requires every nation automatically to assist the victim of aggression; alliance commitments can place a nation in a position of having a conflict of interest. But it does not necessarily follow that in the absence of alliances nations of the world will develop an effective collective security system. Indeed, a more persuasive case can be developed for the proposition that alliances may arise from disappointed hopes for collective security (F-4), a thesis for which American diplomatic history would appear to offer some support. After an initial alliance with France in 1776, American statesmen took to heart warnings by Washington and Jefferson against "entangling alliances." During and after World War II a good deal of optimism about the outlook for the United Nations as a nascent collective security system was generated—perhaps in part as a result of the "hard sell" campaign to generate public support for a postwar international organization. Not until it was clear that an effective collective security system had not been established did the United States begin to construct a vast system of alliances. A good case might be made that alliances such as SEATO and CENTO have proved to be examples of less-than-inspired statecraft, but the argument that eliminating these and other alliances will give rise to an effective collective security system will hardly stand serious scrutiny. Elimination of alliances may be a necessary condition for collective security, but it is not sufficient.

A somewhat different line of reasoning has been developed by others who question the contributions of alliances to international stability. They point out that, like many other institutions, alliances, once formed, tend to develop their own policy imperatives. That is, they come to be valued as ends rather than as instruments, and the requirements for strengthening and maintaining alliances may be incompatible with simultaneous efforts at détente.

The greater the emphasis on strengthening alliances, the less the emphasis on achieving international détente (U-6).

The more the international system is polarized into competing alliances, the fewer the summit conferences (U-5).

The greater the cohesion of alliances on matters of substance and strategy, the more polarized the international system (U-39).

A more extreme statement of this relationship suggests that groups may seek, or even create, outside enemies where none exist in order to preserve internal cohesion (U-2).

Some very impressionistic evidence in support of these propositions can be adduced from the cold war alliances. At various times Secretary of State Dulles expressed fears that a premature or false sense of security about the state of international affairs would destroy NATO and other alliances. Even Winston Churchill, hardly the archetypical naive dove, had serious doubts about those aspects of Dulles' diplomacy that appeared to place the solidarity of the alliance ahead of efforts toward détente following Stalin's death. On the other hand, Soviet interests in sustaining the Warsaw Pact as well as the bilateral alliances that preceded it work against serious efforts to achieve a permanent détente in Europe. Without the spectre of "NATO aggression" or the "Bonn revanchists" it would be rather difficult to justify maintaining a vast military establishment in "friendly socialist" nations.

In summary, this line of reasoning suggests that, just as some degree of external threat may enhance alliance cohesion, some policies that are pursued with a view to maintaining alliances may exacerbate international tensions.

Still another closely related argument is that alliances act as conduits to spread conflict to regions previously free of it (U-25, U-27). Supporters of this position can point to historical instances in which alliances have had this result, as can those who stress that alliances serve a deterrent function. But Liska has come to the conclusion that alliances neither cause nor prevent conflict, nor do they expand or limit it (U-31). Aside from the contradictory conclusions, a serious difficulty with most of these theories about the consequences of alliances is that virtually all of them are based on limited evidence, sometimes only on a single case.

Recently, however, several rigorous studies of the systemic effects of alliances have been undertaken. The most comprehensive is an analysis of all international alliances during the period between the end of the Napoleonic Wars and the outbreak of World War II, as one part of a broader study of the "correlates of war." [42] This research stems from two premises. First, the greater the number of independent units, the more peaceful the international system, because nations can concentrate less of their attention on any other country.[43] Second, the maximum freedom of interaction between nations enhances international stability because cross-pressures on each country are increased. Hence, international cleavages tend to be cross-cutting rather than reinforcing, with the result that bargaining rather than war will be used to resolve differences. Very much in the spirit of classical free market economics, the theory goes on to suggest that alliances interfere with freedom of interaction and its beneficial effects. Nations that are allied militarily are also likely to cooperate economically, politically, culturally and in other areas, concomitantly discriminating against nonaligned nations or members of other coalitions. Conversely, nations in opposing military alliances are less likely to cooperate on other international issues. As a consequence, although at any given time there may be dozens of salient issues which divide nations, alliances increase the probability that the divisions will cumulate along a single axis. Or, to state this somewhat differently, instead of different groupings of nations arising on each issue, the opposing coalitions are likely to be identical on all questions, a situation that increases tensions and the likelihood of war (U-29).

The premises underlying the Singer-Small studies have an evident relationship to a number of prominent alliance theories. They are quite consistent with theories of integration which postulate that cooperative activity on one issue tends to nurture cooperation in others. They are also related to classical balance of power theories, the central argument of both being that entangling commitments tend to reduce the freedom of action necessary to maintain system stability. Moreover, the thesis that cross-cutting cleavages contribute to system stability by sustaining nonviolent means of conflict resolution has been shown to have significant explanatory power at the level of national politics. It is also of some importance that this theory is stated in terms that can be applied to all alliances and international systems.

Results based on a system-level analysis of 118 alliances indicate that alliance formation and international conflict are positively correlated for the twentieth century, but the relationship for the nineteenth century is negative. Although these studies have been subjected to an impressive critique on both logical and methodological grounds, the finding of some relationship between the level of alliance commitment in the system and the outbreak of war still emerges from a revised analysis of the data.[44]

The Singer-Small research stands as a notable exception to the general lack of empirical rigor in alliance studies. Moreover their data lend themselves to research on many other aspects of alliances—one extension of their pioneering work may be found in Chapter Two. However, despite the merits of these studies it may be too early to dismiss Liska's conclusion that "alliances neither limit nor expand conflicts any more than they cause or prevent them," [45] and to indict alliances as the progenitors of war.

In the first place, the finding that alliance commitments were *negatively* related to the outbreak of war during the nineteenth century should give rise to some second thoughts about why these results are so different from those for the years since 1900. As noted earlier, the nineteenth century is almost invariably cited as the classical era of balance of power politics, a period during which the system reputedly "worked" approximately as the theory indicates it should. Even a cursory look at history reveals that it was scarcely free from war, although it may seem quite peaceful by the standards of the seventeenth or twentieth centuries. The record also reveals no dearth of alliances. Is it conceivable that, for at least this short period of time, alliances functioned as the balance of power theorists say they should? The Singer-Small findings are consistent with this interpretation, but they do not prove it. Conversely, during much of the present century alliances have been rigid and global rather than limited *ad hoc* arrangements, precisely the type that even balance of power theorists consider dangerous. This was especially true during the decade preceding World War I and the fifteen years following World War II.

Secondly, we may not be in a position yet to rule out the possibility of a spurious relationship between alliances and war. That is, could both alliance commitments and international conflict be the product of some common underlying factor? Purely for the sake of illustrating the point, suppose that the outbreak of war tended to be associated with sharp changes in relative capabilities—arising perhaps from differential rates of growth in population, technology, or both—with some regularity.[46] It would not be surprising to find that the same shifts in relative capabilities would also give rise to a good deal of alliance formation. Indeed, according to most theorists, *this is precisely the function that alliances are supposed to perform* in order to prevent any nation or group of nations from gaining a position of hegemony. Were this reasoning valid for any period of time—and it bears repeating that it is presented only as a hypothetical illustration of the problem, not as a research finding—then any correlation between alliance formation and war would be spurious; that is, war would be related to alliances only because both are a response to some other condition.

Or, to illustrate the point further, consider the thesis that the prime source of international instability is to be located in the absence of internal stability.[47] As noted earlier, regimes seeking to enhance domestic stability may be motivated to do so by acquiring allies. Domestic instability might then be a source of both alliance formation and the outbreak of war. But this too is only a hypothetical argument to illustrate the point that correlations do not necessarily establish a causal link between alliances and war.

Finally, because these studies were undertaken at a systems rather than national level, the results do not lend themselves to inferences about state behavior. Even if the number of alliances in the international system is positively correlated to the level of international violence, this does not tell us whether the nations in alliance were also more likely to engage in war. That is, statistical relationships which exist for aggregates (the international system in this case) are not necessarily the same for smaller units (nations).[48] This point is especially germane to the Singer-Small studies because both alliance commitments and participation in war were, for the entire period under analysis, actions undertaken by nations, not by larger aggregates.

In summary, the Singer-Small studies are an impressive landmark in an area of international politics that is hardly overrun with rigorous research, but they also give rise to some intriguing questions that bear a good deal of further investigation.

Alliances and Integration.   Another strand of theory, not necessarily incompatible with either of the above, sees alliance as a possible step in the process of more enduring forms of integration. This view begins with the premises that effective cooperation among units in one sphere of endeavor gives rise to collaboration in others and, in the long run, to institutionalization of the arrangements. Propositions on this issue reveal a considerable lack of unanimity.

Alliances can be transformed into regional supranational organizations (U-34).

Only a very few alliances succeed in transforming themselves into federal unions (U-32; see also U-44, U-46, U-48).

Where there is an alliance, there tends not to be a community (U-33).

Presently available evidence appears to support those who doubt the integration potential of alliances. A study of ten political communities in the North Atlantic area revealed that alliances were neither necessary nor sufficient for integration.[49] A detailed study of NATO supports these findings. Not even in areas thought to be especially promising—armaments, infrastructure and science—was there evidence of integration.[50] Others have similarly concluded that cooperation in security-related matters has a lower potential for "spillover" than collaboration in issue-areas such as economic relations.[51]

Finally, there are a number of propositions which relate alliances to changes in the structure of the international system. One such hypothesis is that the more cohesive the alliances on matters of substance and strategy, the more polarized the international system (U-39). But propositions of this form are of fairly limited interest as they tend to be true by definition; that is, a polarized system is usually defined as one in which alliances are cohesive and rigid. Thus we are impelled to ask other questions. For instance, under what circumstances are alliances in balance of power or loose bipolar systems likely to become rigid, thereby transforming the nature of the system? Among the propositions that have been advanced are the following:

The more hierarchical the blocs, the greater the likelihood of transformation to a tight bipolar system (U-38).

When the issues that separate alliances are matters of ideology, alliances tend to become rigid.

In summary, the diversity that characterizes theories of alliance formation and performance is perhaps even more evident in discussions of the international effects of alliances. They have been portrayed at various times as prime causes of war, as vital balance-wheels in the always delicate stability of the international system, and as potential precursors of more enduring forms of collaboration among nations. Given the rather rudimentary state of research on the problem, it is perhaps not inappropriate to suggest that, pending badly needed further investigations, the verdict on each of these claims must remain "not proven."

National Effects of Alliances

An alliance has traditionally been regarded as an instrument of policy by means of which a nation may augment its own capabilities. Among the benefits that should accrue from alliance membership are enhanced security from external threat, reduced defense expenditures, and possible side benefits such as economic aid (V-4) and prestige (V-12, V-16). For a regime with shaky popular support a strong ally may be a necessary condition for survival. How long, for instance, would the present governments in South Vietnam, East Germany, Poland, Czechoslovakia, and many others remain in power without external support (V-11)?

But benefits rarely come without attending costs, and several students of alliances have placed considerable stress on some negative effects of external military ties. For instance, they may actually be a net drain on national resources (V-2, V-13); they may distort calculations of national interest because allies may become wedded to "inherent good faith" models of each other (V-1); and they may lead to a loss of decision making independence (V-3, V-17, V-18) and status (V-15). Most importantly, if alliances merely trigger off counter-alliances and arms races, they leave everyone poorer and less secure (V-5). Some of these arguments can almost certainly be documented in such cases as the Soviet alliance with Cuba, the American alliance with South Vietnam, and no doubt many others. But without accurate knowledge of "what might have been" (which, of course, we must always do without), net costs or benefits are rather difficult to assess. Consider, for example, the thesis that NATO has been a drain on the national resources of its constituent members, an argument which has recently gained some popularity. The point is valid if we accept the underlying assumption that NATO was never needed because it was a reaction against a phantom threat. But if one begins with the different premise that the threat was real, then surely NATO must be judged as the cheapest and most successful alliance in history. The validity of each argument is no better than the original premise about Soviet intentions in Europe, and it is not likely that the Kremlin archives will be opened to permit that issue to be settled.

A rather different argument is that alliances tend to have significant consequences for domestic politics, not all of which are beneficial. It scarcely needs to be stated that the American alliance with South Vietnam (through SEATO) has resulted in deep domestic divisions within both countries. Even the establishment of NATO during the later 1940s triggered an often bitter debate between the proponents of an isolationist "Fortress America" concept of defense and the internationalists who supported the implications of the Truman Doctrine.

It is not clear whether the domestic consequences of alliance participation will differ according to the nature of the political system. One hypothesis is that in an era of mass politics when there are widespread expectations that one's allies be ideologically purer than the driven snow, the internal consequences of alliances will continue to increase (V-7). There is no shortage of examples to illustrate the point. Demands that the military regime in Greece be expelled from NATO and isolated diplomatically are heard with increasing frequency, especially in Northern European democracies. Or, consider the probable consequences if the United States were to suggest admitting the autocratic Spanish regime into NATO. Loud applause from some domestic groups would be matched by passionate denunciation from others. Conversely, proposals to readmit the equally authoritarian Cuban government into the OAS would no doubt find the roles of supporters and critics being reversed, but with no diminution of passions. These examples would suggest that democratic nations are likely to be more sensitive to feedback from alliance politics. There are also advocates of the opposite position, however, who suggest that the domestic effects of alliances are likely to be especially intense in hierarchical coalitions composed of authoritarian regimes (V-6, V-9, V-10).

A further examination of the linkages between alliance relations and domestic politics appears in Chapters Five and Six. At that time we shall consider how these linkages are likely to differ, depending on the nature of the alliance and the attributes of its member nations.

Conclusion

The most obvious conclusion that emerges from this survey is that the literature on alliances is marked by competing explanations, none of which appears sufficient for a general theory, and contradictory findings: [52] Whether discussing the formation, performance, termination, or effects of alliances, we have repeatedly cited propositions which allegedly explain some fundamental issue, only to find that its exact opposite has been proposed in another source. Indeed, it is not impossible to find contradictory propositions coexisting in the same source.

This is not to say that all areas of alliance theory are equally marked by disagreement. We appear to know more about the cohesion of alliances, for instance, than about their international consequences. Nor is lack of complete agreement among writers necessarily a sign of theoretical chaos. The existence of the "Flat Earth Society" does not lead us to conclude that the disciplines of astronomy and geography are inadequate. Yet even where contradictions about alliances are most apparent, it is not easy to identify explanations that are the equivalent of the flat earth theory. Thus, even a generous appraiser must conclude that the alliance literature taken as a whole falls short of being satisfactory.

Given the universality of alliances throughout the history of international politics, why should this state of affairs exist? Certainly it cannot be attributed to an absence of interest. The number of books, monographs, essays, and articles on the subject is enormous, especially if we include those that deal with one specific alliance or another. It becomes even larger if we add general texts on international politics and foreign policy, virtually all of which include some discussion of alliances. The problem, then, is not the lack of attention.

One obvious explanation is that the student of alliances has relatively few cases to observe. For example, Singer and Small uncovered only 118 peacetime alliances in their exhaustive survey of the century and a quarter between 1815 and 1939. Even if we include those contracted in wartime, the total for the entire period is only 130 (see Chapter Two). How much would we know about the correlates of voting, one might ask, if the total electorate throughout the world were equally small? Suppose, for example, that we wished to assess the effects of national attributes, international system, situation, and type of alliance on some aspect of alliance performance. To simplify the task we might decide to use classifications in which variables can take only two or three values. Thus a nation might be placed into one of eight categories, depending upon its political system (open-closed), size (large-small), and development (developed-underdeveloped). International systems could be classified as balance of power, loose bipolar and tight bipolar. Situations could be simply distinguished between high threat and low threat, and we could classify alliances as defense pacts, neutrality and nonaggression pacts, or ententes.[53] Although a design of this type is clearly vulnerable to the charge of oversimplification, it yields 144 different possibilities (8 nation types × 3 systems × 2 situations × 3 alliance types), exceeding by a considerable margin the total number of alliances that existed between 1815 and 1939.

The obvious difficulty presented by the limited number of cases needs to be acknowledged, but it is not a wholly satisfactory explanation for the state of the literature on alliances. A comparative study of only two alliances can yield rich theoretical returns if it is designed with this aim in mind. Indeed, study of a single case need not be barren of more general implications.[54] Even a cursory examination of the literature reveals a distinct shortage of research that is designed to shed light on central issues of alliance theory and is *also* documented with data derived by explicit and systematic methods. Instead a vast majority of the studies falls into one of two categories. In the first we find essays of a general nature, usually sustaining a broad-gauge theory of alliances with selected historical examples. The most incisive of these are indispensable reading for any serious student of alliances, but the idiosyncratic nature of the supporting evidence usually renders it difficult to assess either the generality of the proposed theory, or its potency relative to competing explanations of the same events. On the other hand there are large numbers of studies that tell us a great deal about one alliance or another, but usually with a degree of specificity that underscores the *unique* aspects of that coalition. As a consequence they make a limited contribution to a more general understanding of alliances.

If the foregoing survey reflects with any accuracy the state of the literature on alliances, it gives rise to the suspicion that we may have to settle for something that falls short of a "general theory of alliances"—at least for the foreseeable future. Indeed, the present review strengthens the suspicion that one source of difficulty in the literature is the widespread tendency to assume the existence and sufficiency of *a* theory of alliances, be it derived from models of the international system, the theory of N-person games, or whatever. In the chapters that follow we begin with the opposite premise, from which it follows that our major task is not to demonstrate the irrefutable superiority of one theory over another; it is, rather, to identify the scope and limits of alternative explanations. In adopting this approach we are aware that there is a price to pay: the end result must be considerably more modest than a general, integrated theory. And because we attempt in each case to subject hypotheses to the test of systematic evidence, using multiple indicators where possible, the effort is necessarily focused on a few central aspects of alliances rather than diffused among all of the many issues discussed in the present chapter. This choice, too, involves costs as well as benefits. In the concluding chapter we shall attempt an assessment of our research strategy.

Notes

1. George Modelski, "The Study of Alliances: A Review," *Journal of Conflict Resolution,* 7, 1963, p. 773.
2. For example, Edward Vose Gulick distinguishes *alliances* from *coalitions* by the number of nations involved; Kautilya states that in an *alliance* the rewards are shared equally, whereas in a *pact* they are not; Edwin Fedder regards *alliances* as a subcategory of *coalitions.*
3. Julian R. Friedman, Christopher Bladen, and Steven Rosen, *Alliance in International Politics,* Allyn and Bacon, Inc., Boston, 1970, p. 232.
4. Edwin H. Fedder, "The Concept of Alliance," *International Studies Quarterly,* 12, 1968.
5. Exceptions occur when a nation joins and remains in an alliance because of coercion by its partners. This appears to be the case with some members of the Warsaw Pact. For this reason it is sometimes asserted that the Warsaw Pact is not a true alliance. Malcolm Mackintosh, *The Evolution of the Warsaw Pact,* Institute for Strategic Studies, London, Adelphi Papers, No. 58, 1969, p. 18.
6. The plural is used here deliberately as the concept "balance of power" is characterized by a multiplicity of usages—descriptive, conceptual and normative. For excellent summaries, see Ernst B. Haas, "The Balance of Power: Prescription, Concept, or Propaganda," *World Politics,* 5, 1953, pp. 442–477; Dina A. Zinnes, "Coalition Theories and the Balance of Power," in Sven Groennings, E. W. Kelley, and Michael Leiserson, eds., *The Study of Coalition Behavior: Theoretical Perspectives From Four Continents,* Holt, Rinehart and Winston, New York, 1970; and Inis L. Claude, Jr., *Power and International Relations,* Random House, New York, 1962, pp. 11–39.

Although alliances are an integral part of balance of power theories, the latter have purposes that go beyond explanations of alliances—for example, to explain how the international order is preserved.

7. Codes that appear in the text within parentheses refer to entries in Appendix C. For more details on the propositional inventory, consult the Preface and the introductory section of Appendix C.

8. Nicholas Spykman, *America's Strategy in World Politics,* Harcourt, Brace & Co., New York, 1942, pp. 103–104.

9. These rules are formally spelled out (without normative overtones) in Morton Kaplan, *System and Process in International Politics,* John Wiley & Sons, Inc., New York, 1957.

10. See, for example, Edward Vose Gulick's excellent study of *Europe's Classical Balance of Power,* Cornell University Press, Ithaca, 1955.

11. This point is well illustrated in Raymond Dawson and Richard N. Rosecrance, "Theory and Reality in the Anglo-American Alliance," *World Politics,* 19, 1966.

12. For a further discussion, see Haas, *op. cit.*

13. For example, Kautilya's *Arthasastra.*

14. The basic applications of these theories to politics are in William H. Riker, *The Theory of Political Coalitions,* Yale University Press, New Haven, 1962. A review of experimental findings may be found in Jerome M. Chertkoff, "Socio-psychological Theories and Research on Coalition Formation," in Groennings, *et al., op. cit.* For an excellent comparison of coalition and balance of power theories, see Zinnes, *op. cit.*

15. Coalition theorists are not alone, however, in relating size to alliance formation; see (K-2), for example.

16. This point is derived from Zinnes, *op. cit.,* p. 366.

17. There is a lack of unanimity among balance of power theorists on the role of moderation and self-restraint, but maintenance of the system for any extended period would seem to require that statesmen act from these motives as well as those of self-aggrandizement. For a further discussion, see Haas, *op. cit.,* pp. 454–455.

18. But, as Chertkoff, *op. cit.,* points out, the experimental results have often yielded contradictory results.

19. See, for example, Riker, *op. cit.* and the effort to apply the "size principle" to the Nazi-Soviet Pact in Bruce M. Russett, "Components of an Operational Theory of International Alliance Formation," *Journal of Conflict Resolution,* 12, 1968.

20. This point is usually acknowledged by coalition theorists. See propositions P-4, P-5, and P-6.

21. A partially contradictory hypothesis predicts that the capabilities of adversaries will be underestimated, whereas those of allies are likely to be overestimated (I-3).

22. Doing so may, however, be viewed by the adversary as an invitation to attack the "nonessential" areas. This appears to have been the case in Korea, when Dean Acheson's "perimeter" speech in early 1950—in which he

appeared to place South Korea outside the defense perimeter of the West —may have been misinterpreted by North Korea and its allies.

23. For a different assessment, however, see Russett, *op. cit.*

24. For impressive evidence that virtually all nations view themselves as playing a multiplicity of international roles that bear on alliance policies, see K. J. Holsti, "National Role Conceptions in the Study of Foreign Policy," *International Studies Quarterly*, 14, 1970.

25. Philip M. Burgess, *Elite Images and Foreign Policy Outcomes*, The Ohio State University Press, Columbus, 1967.

26. For evidence on 137 twentieth-century alliances, see Bruce M. Russett, "An Empirical Typology of International Military Alliances," *Midwest Journal of Political Science*, 15, 1971.

27. A somewhat different, but not necessarily contradictory, hypothesis is that in a bipolar system competing alliances will tend to resemble one another (B-4), a proposition drawn from an examination of the two cold war alliances. However, at least one student of the Warsaw Pact has challenged this, suggesting that the similarities are superficial and reflect little of the realities underlying intra-bloc relations within NATO and the Warsaw Pact. Mackintosh, *op. cit.* A partial test of this hypothesis appears in Chapter Four.

28. Pluralism is usually associated with fragmented authority, multiple centers of power, and the legitimacy of diversity among component parts of the whole. Thus a pluralistic alliance is marked by recognition that the ultimate locus of decision making authority resides with the nation—rather than in the alliance as a whole, or with its leading member(s)—and acceptance of diversity in ideology, institutions, and other salient attributes. We consider pluralistic alliances and their polar opposite, monolithic ones, to be "ideal types" that define two ends of a continuum on which we may locate all alliances, rather than as dichotomous attributes.

29. This is not to say that nations in pluralistic alliances will always refrain from interference in the internal affairs of their allies. Secretary of State Dulles' efforts to influence the West German election of 1953 and General DeGaulle's blatant interference in the politics of Canadian federalism in 1967 were hardly models of diplomatic etiquette. But inappropriate as such actions were, they can scarcely be equated with the invasions of Hungary in 1956 and Czechoslovakia in 1968. These examples are used to restate a point that has relevance for the present discussion as well as that in Chapter Five: Although no alliance is totally pluralistic or monolithic, it is nevertheless useful to make distinctions along this continuum.

30. The third usage of cohesion is discussed in the next section on alliance termination.

31. Philip M. Burgess and James A. Robinson, "Alliances and the Theory of Collective Action: A Simulation of Coalition Processes," *Midwest Journal of Political Science*, 13, 1969; and Mancur Olson, Jr. and Richard Zeckhauser, "An Economic Theory of Alliances," *The Review of Economics and Statistics*, 48, 1966.

"Collective goods" are those that cannot be withheld from any member of a group, whether or not he pays for them; "private goods" can be selectively withheld. Protection provided to citizens by armed forces is an example of the former, whereas postal service illustrates the latter. For a further discussion, see Mancur Olson, Jr., *The Logic of Collective Action: Public Goods and the Theory of Groups,* Harvard University Press, Cambridge, 1965.

32. The impact of ideology and nuclear weapons on alliance cohesion has also received considerable attention, but we shall defer discussion of these topics until the next section.

33. Samuel R. Williamson, Jr., *The Politics of Grand Strategy: France and Britain Prepare for War, 1904–1914,* Harvard University Press, Cambridge, 1969, p. 317; and Gordon Craig, "The World War I Alliance of the Central Powers in Retrospect: The Military Cohesion of the Alliance," *The Journal of Modern History,* 37, 1965.

34. Mackintosh, *op. cit.,* p. 3.

35. See, for example, Dawson and Rosecrance, *op. cit.;* and Richard E. Neustadt, *Alliance Politics,* Columbia University Press, New York, 1970.

36. Quoted in Norman J. Padelford and George A. Lincoln, *The Dynamics of International Politics,* 2nd ed., The Macmillan Co., New York, 1967, p. 402.

37. Quoted in Robert L. Rothstein, *Alliances and Small Powers,* Columbia University Press, New York, 1968, p. 125.

38. See, for example, Graham T. Allison, *Essence of Decision: Explaining the Cuban Missile Crisis,* Little, Brown & Co., Boston, 1971; Neustadt, *op. cit.;* and Alexander L. George, "Political Decision-Making: Problems of Stress and Coping in Individual, Group, and Organizational Contexts," mimeo., Stanford Univ., 1970.

39. For example, Samuel R. Williamson's forthcoming study of the alliance between Germany and Austria-Hungary, cited in Neustadt, *op. cit.,* p. 141.

40. Drew Middleton, "British Book Says German and Soviet Officials Met in '43 to Discuss Peace," *New York Times,* Jan. 4, 1971, 1–6.

41. The leaders of nonaligned states have, of course, never ceased to maintain that most alliances tend to increase the dangers of war.

42. J. David Singer and Melvin Small, "Formal Alliances, 1815–1939," *Journal of Peace Research,* 1, 1966; and Singer and Small, "Alliance Aggregation and the Onset of War," in Singer, ed., *Quantitative International Politics: Insights and Evidence,* Free Press, New York, 1968.

43. This aspect of the theory is spelled out in Karl W. Deutsch and J. David Singer, "Multipolar Power Systems and International Stability," *World Politics,* 16, 1964.

44. Dina A. Zinnes, "An Analytical Study of the Balance of Power Theories," *Journal of Peace Research,* 3, 1967.

45. George Liska, *Nations in Alliance: The Limits of Interdependence,* Johns Hopkins Press, Baltimore, 1962, p. 138.

46. Answers to questions of this type are emerging from an extensive study of

the period 1870–1970 being conducted by Robert C. North and Nazli Choucri. See their forthcoming *Nations in Conflict*. The Singer group is also examining this question. See J. David Singer and Melvin Small, *The Power of Nations: Comparative Capabilities Since Waterloo*, forthcoming; and J. David Singer, Stuart Bremer, and John Stuckey, "Capability Distribution, Uncertainty, and Major Power War, 1816–1965," in Bruce M. Russett, ed., *Peace, War, and Numbers*, Sage, Beverly Hills, 1972.

47. See, for example, Richard N. Rosecrance, *Action and Reaction in World Politics*, Little, Brown & Co., Boston, 1963.

48. The classical statement of this problem is W. S. Robinson, "Ecological Correlations and the Behavior of Individuals," *American Sociological Review*, 15, 1950. Some preliminary evidence that this problem may exist in the Singer-Small alliance studies appears in William Moul, "The 'Level of Analysis Problem': Spatial and Temporal Aggregation in International Relations," paper read at the Canadian Political Science Association meeting, 1972.

49. Karl W. Deutsch *et al.*, *Political Community and the North Atlantic Area: International Organization in the Light of Historical Experience*, Princeton University Press, Princeton, 1957.

50. Francis A. Beer, *Integration and Disintegration in NATO: Processes of Alliance Cohesion and Prospects for Atlantic Community*, Ohio State University Press, Columbus, 1969, pp. 239–240.

51. Amitai Etzioni, "The Dialectics of Supranational Unification," *American Political Science Review*, 56, 1962.

52. Other reviews have arrived at the same conclusion. Edwin H. Fedder, "The Concept of Alliance," *International Studies Quarterly*, 12, 1968; and Philip M. Burgess and David W. Moore, "Inter-Nation Alliances: An Inventory and Appraisal of Propositions," in James A. Robinson, ed., *Political Science Annual*, Vol. III, Bobbs-Merrill Publishing Co., Indianapolis, 1972.

53. The categories for types of nation, system, and alliance are drawn from James N. Rosenau, "Pre-Theories and Theories of Foreign Policy," in R. Barry Farrell, ed., *Approaches to Comparative and International Politics*, Northwestern University Press, Evanston, 1966; Morton A. Kaplan, *System and Process in International Politics*, John Wiley & Sons, Inc., New York, 1957; and Singer and Small, "Formal Alliances, 1815–1939," *op. cit.*

54. On this point, see Glenn D. Paige, *The Korean Decision*, Free Press, New York, 1968, pp. 3–18; and James N. Rosenau, "Moral Fervor, Systematic Analysis, and Scientific Consciousness in Foreign Policy Research," in Rosenau, *The Scientific Study of Foreign Policy*, Free Press, New York, 1971.

CHAPTER TWO

Sources of Alliance Performance: National and International Factors

Introduction

As we have seen in the first chapter, alliances are pervasive in international politics. They have been considered important both for the behavior of individual nations and for stability and conflict within the international system. Nations have resorted to alliances as devices for deterring or repelling the threatening words and deeds of third parties or to reduce the likelihood of conflict among themselves. In addition, alliances have been thought to have consequences for the functioning of the international system. The existence of alliances has been linked to the frequency and intensity of war and certain alliance configurations—such as bipolarity and multipolarity—have been thought to affect other aspects of nation-state behavior such as patterns of trade relations and the sharing of scientific and technological innovations.

While alliances are crucial devices for achieving national goals, they also present nations with a number of problems. The realization that some goals cannot be reached by individual action and that some form of collective effort is necessary does not insure a viable coalition. Nor does it mean that such collective action as an international alliance will be free from internal strains and stresses. The fact of coming together presents nations with problems which may persist for the life of the alliance and may ultimately be a factor in its breakdown. On the one hand, they will have to come to agreement as to the range and extent of their relationship. On the other hand, they will have to devote some time to the assessment of alliance performance especially in terms of the goals which originally led them to such an arrangement. Thus, while alliances are formed, in part, to further the goals of the members, they also present those nations with intra-alliance problems.

Our concern in this chapter will be with problems which arise at the point of alliance formation or which occur with respect to the performance of the alliance during its existence. We will assess the impact of national attributes, members of the alliance, of the alliance itself, and of the international system on alliance performance. We will consider as independent variables attributes from the three levels of analysis—nations, alliances, and the international system. Measures of alliance performance will be employed as dependent variables.

The two *national characteristics* to be employed here as independent variables are the *ideological similarity* of alliance members and the *regime stability* of those nations. These variables will be aggregated for members of each alliance in order to produce ideological homogeneity and regime stability scores for each alliance. The three *alliance characteristics* we will examine are the *number of nations* in the grouping, the *geographical dispersion* of those nations, and the *number and ambiguity of alliance goals*. Finally, we will look at the impact of two aspects of the international system. We will divide the 124 years into subperiods that appear to differ in significant ways. Secondly, the presence or absence of war in the system will be used as a measure of the amount of threat with which nations are faced.

Performance is used here to refer to the following alliance characteristics: type of alliance, alliance effectiveness, mode of alliance termination, alliance renewal, and the actual and proposed length of alliances. It is assumed that these variables include many of the problems faced by decision-makers in forming and maintaining alliances. The independent and dependent variables are summarized in Table 1.

A word is in order concerning our selection of independent and dependent variables. Our concern is with factors which affect decisions made at the point of alliance formation and with the performance of the alliance subsequent to its formation. As independent variables, we have selected those factors which are thought to be related to alliance performance. Thus, domestic stability of the alliance members, potential ideological disputes among the members, and the size and dispersion of the members can all be hypothesized to affect alliance performance. We have, in addition, identified the number and ambiguity of alliance goals as factors which may affect alliance performance. Alliance goals are generally formalized at the time of alliance formation and it is useful to indicate why we draw a distinction between alliance goals as an independent variable and type of alliance as a dependent variable.

Our focus is on factors which affect the performance of an alliance. The number of members in the alliance, their dispersion, and the stability of their regimes are all factors which are distinct from the alliance itself. It

TABLE 1. National and International Factors Affecting Alliance Performance

Variable	Description
Ideological Similarity	Degree of difference among the members of each alliance in ideological orientation
Regime Instability	Number of changes in political regimes experienced by alliance members
Size, Distance, Goals	
Alliance size	Number of members in each alliance
Geographical dispersion	Average distance among the members of an alliance
Ambiguity of alliance goals	The extent to which the alliance focuses on specific targets and political problems
Number of alliance goals	The number of different goals specified in the treaty formalizing the alliance
Impact of the International System	
Nature of the international system	Comparison of pre- and post-World War I systems; Comparison of pre- and post-Bismarckian systems
Amount of threat in the international system	Years under study in which wars of a certain magnitude occurred and those in which no wars or wars of a lesser magnitude occurred

can be hypothesized, however, that they will affect certain aspects of alliance performance. We consider alliance goals in a similar light. Nations are led to seek alliance partners because of problems they face and goals they wish to achieve. These problems and goals existed *prior* to the alliance itself and, in part, gave rise to its formation. Further, the nature of these goals, as we will see below, may have an impact on the alliance both at the point of formation and during its existence.

It is important to make clear that in this chapter we are discussing only one aspect of alliance formation. In considering the formation of an alliance, nations must reach some decision as to the exact form that the alli-

Aspects of Alliance Performance

Variable	Description
Type of alliance	Commitment class: defense pact, non-aggression pact, entente *
Alliance effectiveness	Whether the alliance was honored if invoked
Mode of alliance termination	Manner in which the members terminated the alliance
Alliance renewal	Number of times alliance renewed
Length of alliance	
Actual length	Number of years the alliance actually existed
Proposed length	Number of years specified in the treaty

* The types of commitment are derived from J. David Singer and Melvin Small, "Alliance Aggregation and the Onset of War, 1815–1945," in J. David Singer, ed., *Quantitative International Politics,* The Free Press, New York, 1968, p. 266. Their definitions are as follows: "Class 1, which will be called a *defensive pact,* commits each signatory to intervene with military force on behalf of the other(s). Class II, which is called here a *neutrality or non-aggression pact,* commits each to refrain from military intervention against any of the other signatories in the event that they become engaged in war. Class III, labeled *entente,* merely requires that the signatories consult with one another in the contingent eventuality."

ance will take. In part, forming an alliance involves the specification of the nature of the subsequent relationship. We take this to be an important part of alliance formation and consider this to be one of our independent variables. It will be discussed below in more detail when we consider the various aspects of alliance performance.

One final word should be said about the way in which the various scores used in this study will be developed. All scores will represent *alliance* characteristics or factors in the international system. These alliance characteristics are composed of two types of factors. On the one hand, there are those which are initially *national* in nature, such as ideology. On the other hand, there are factors which are *relational* in character—such as the distance between the members of an alliance—and which refer to a geographical or size factor of the alliance. In both cases, alliance scores will be computed but, for the sake of comparison, a distinction will be drawn between factors which are national and those which are relational.

The data in this chapter are derived from the formal alliances concluded during the period from 1815 to 1939, as identified by Singer and Small.[1] These alliances are formal arrangements among the nations involved specifying the kinds of rights and obligations each is to assume. The next section will discuss in greater detail the nature of the various factors employed in this study as well as the specific hypotheses to be confronted with our data. The following section will present the findings of the analyses and their theoretical implications. The final section will present an overall assessment of the findings of this chapter.

National and International Factors Affecting Alliance Maintenance

A nation seeking alliance partners must consider factors which will affect the reliability and trustworthiness of any potential ally. If a potential partner appears in some way to be unreliable, the nation seeking to form an alliance may anticipate future conflict and dissent. If a nation, for whatever reason, fails to live up to its alliance obligations, this decreases the probability that the alliance will be successful in attaining its goals. We consider here a set of factors which are thought to be important for maintaining alliance commitments.

Ideological Similarity.　　The period after the Congress of Vienna in 1815 witnessed a gradual breakup of the coalition which formed in response to Napoleon's imperialistic adventure. The eastern regimes, Austria, Prussia, and Russia, slowly began to move away from the western nations of France and England. In 1836, British Foreign Secretary Palmerston noted that this separation was "not one of words, but of things, not the effect of caprice or of will, but produced by the force of circumstances. The three and the two think differently and therefore they act differently." [2] The three eastern nations tended, in general, to be conservative and to be opposed to popular sovereignty. France and England, on the other hand, shared a more liberal orientation and favored some degree of popular participation in government.

In 1894, France and Russia concluded a defensive pact. There appeared to be very little basis for such a pact. There were no common ideological orientations shared by both countries. Furthermore, France was a republic, the only one among the major European powers, whereas Russia was ruled by an autocratic monarchical regime. As Albrecht-Carrié puts it, "Godless Marianne and Holy Russia stood at opposite poles of belief." [3] Yet, these two quite dissimilar nations did form a military alliance, one which was of the highest commitment class. The main impetus for the alliance was France's fear of Germany and her desire for support should Germany attack her. Thus, considerations of power and security overrode the problems created by the ideological gulf which separated these two powers.

These examples illustrate the principle and expediency theories of explaining alliance maintenance discussed in Chapter One. Expediency theory assumes that abstract ideological principles or cultural similarities matter little when national leaders are considering forming alliances. The premise is that nations are primarily concerned with gaining power sufficient to attain their national objectives and that they will align with other nations whenever it is deemed necessary, regardless of the ideological orientation of the other nations.

This position has been identified mainly with Morgenthau and the balance of power school: "Whether or not a nation shall pursue a policy of alliances is, then, not a matter of principle but of expediency." [4] Similarly, Liska has suggested that alliances are primarily the result of concerns for security and do not result from a "sense of community." [5] Proponents of the expediency theory thus argue that the main impetus for alliance formation is a concern for power or security and has little to do with ideological or cultural similarities. This approach additionally implies that ideological factors ought not to affect alliance maintenance or other aspects of its performance. As long as the problem which gave rise to the alliance exists and as long as the needs of the member nations remain the same, cultural, ideological, or other differences should present no great problems for the alliance.

Proponents of this approach do not deny that a common ideology may play a role in alliance formation. Morgenthau, for instance, has suggested that an alliance does require some basic community of interests or common interests for its existence.[6] Liska has maintained that ". . . ideological affinities among regimes are merely the immediate impetus to such alignments or their consequence." [7] Although some writers imply that such common interest may range from ideological similarity to something as specific as the existence of a common enemy,[8] the expediency approach assumes that ideological similarities by themselves play little or no role in the formation and functioning of alliances.

Opposed to this position is the principle theory, which argues that ideological, cultural, or other similarities are crucial to alliances. This position argues that similar nations are more apt to form an alliance and are also likely to coordinate their intra-alliance behaviors more effectively than are ideologically dissimilar nations. Allen has argued, for instance, that the Triple Alliance and Triple Entente "were in some respects illogical and neither of them stood the strains of war or its termination . . ." because the member governments were too dissimilar.[9] Teune and Synnestvedt, employing the notion of cultural or psychological penetration, have hypothesized that the ". . . alignment of a country . . . is . . . a direct function of the saliency or the degree of psychological penetration of the major powers . . ." in referring to the Soviet and American blocs.[10] Holsti has noted that ideological incompatibilities do not often inhibit alliance formation, but that strains within an alliance are produced by the ". . . incompatibility of the major social and political values of the allying states." [11] The principle theory therefore argues that power is not the sole consideration in alliance formation; ideological factors play an important —perhaps crucial—role, especially in maintaining an alliance.

The first national characteristic we will consider will be the ideological similarity or dissimilarity of the members of an alliance. In our analyses we will compare the two theories just discussed. The hypothesis to be tested is:

In alliances which are ideologically homogeneous, there will be fewer problems of performance than in those that are ideologically heterogeneous.

We thus expect that ideologically heterogeneous alliances will be of a lower commitment class, shorter duration, broken prior to termination date, and less effective than homogeneous alliances.

Regime Instability. When William II acceded to the throne of Germany in 1888, he was strongly influenced by German military men who felt that a war on two fronts was possible and who desired to plan a campaign against Russia. Bismarck disagreed with this policy and attempted to dissuade William from this path. In 1890, the conflict between Emperor and Chancellor over a domestic issue reached a climax and the latter resigned. The issue which gave rise to Bismarck's resignation was *primarily domestic* but his departure had important effects on German foreign policy.

The Russians had been attempting to renew the so-called Reinsurance Treaty with Germany. Bismarck favored such a move but his successors had decided on a "new course" for German foreign policy.[12] This new course, in the judgment of A. J. P. Taylor, ". . . seemed to have erased the entire Bismarckian period and reverted to the foreign policy of the shortlived 'liberal era' between 1858 and 1862." [13] The system of alliances which Bismarck had spent twenty years constructing was drastically altered by William's accession to the throne, their subsequent dispute, and Bismarck's retirement from office.

The impact of Bismarck's retirement, however, was not limited to German foreign policy. Russia had sought to have the Reinsurance Treaty renewed, partly to avoid an alliance with France. "The conservative party at St. Petersburg, with Giers at their head, were convinced that only Bismarck stood between them and the French alliance that they dreaded." [14] After Bismarck's removal from office, France and Russia began to move towards an alliance despite limited enthusiasm in Paris and St. Petersburg for such an arrangement.

This example illustrates the impact that a single change in leadership in one nation may have for foreign policy and international politics. In this case, the foreign policies of Germany, Russia, and France were altered as a result of changes in German policy following the accession of William II and the subsequent retirement of Bismarck. In addition, the "new course" in German policy began a process of polarization between the groupings that became known as the Triple Alliance and the Triple Entente. The culmination of this process was World War I.

Nations enter an alliance in order to increase their military capability, and anything which weakens an alliance has the same effect on the capabilities available to its members. Changes in national leadership might affect alliances in two ways. As nations seek alliance partners, they attempt to estimate the reliability of potential allies. Nations with a history of political instability are less likely to be sought as alliance partners, unless the perceived need for an alliance is great and the availability of partners is limited. Then we might expect that the resulting alliances have a limited scope. Stability may also have an impact on the maintenance of formal commitments. Changes in national leadership may result in a re-evaluation of goals, strategy, and tactics. As a result members of an alliance may attempt to renegotiate the treaty or to break the commitment completely, as happened with Russia in 1917 and with Cuba after Castro's victory.

We will assess the impact that regime instability has on patterns of alliance maintenance, testing the hypothesis that:

The more regime instability experienced by one or more members of an alliance, the more that alliance will experience problems of performance.

Thus, we expect that, in contrast to alliances with stable members, those composed of one or more unstable nations will be of a lower commitment class, shorter duration, less effective, and will tend to be broken prior to termination date.

If both ideological similarity and national stability have an impact on alliances, the question arises as to any interaction or cumulative effect. From the expediency and principle theories we can derive competing hypotheses about the relationship between ideology and stability on the one hand and patterns of alliance maintenance on the other.

The expediency theory would argue that because stability is an important element of national power, stable regimes would be more likely to align and effectively maintain an alliance than would unstable nations, regardless of ideology. The expediency theory would thus predict that there is no interaction between ideology and stability with respect to alliance formation and alliance maintenance. On the other hand, the principle theory would hypothesize that ideology and stability interact with respect to alliance maintenance. Ideologically similar and stable nations are considered more likely to align and to maintain an alliance than are ideologically dissimilar and unstable nations. Ideology and stability taken together are thus better predictors of alliance activity than are either of these attributes alone.

Size, Distance, and Goals.   The act of forming an alliance places the members in a formal and relatively structured relationship. The ability to maintain that relationship may depend on factors such as ideology and the amount and nature of threat in the international system. It may also be affected, however, by various aspects of the relationships themselves. Forming an alliance requires that the nations in question come to an agreement as to the goals and ends that are to be embodied in the formal treaty. It then becomes important to undertake activities that maintain the alliance. Three alliance characteristics are hypothesized to be crucial to maintenance: geographical dispersion of the members, the size of the alliance, and the number and ambiguity of alliance goals.

Alliances generally presuppose that nations perceive a common set of problems. A dispute is apt to arise among the members as to whether or not a particular goal or problem faced by one member is in fact one that should concern all members of the alliance. In a widely dispersed alliance each member may face problems unique to its own location. Nations seeking assistance may be refused on the grounds that the problem is a "local" one and not of concern to the alliance as a whole. Wolfers has illustrated this problem in his discussion of the western alliance.[15] He characterizes that alliance as a wheel with the United States at the hub and the other allies spread out along the rim. When a nation at some part of the rim is faced with threat, the United States is likely to respond with a strong reaction. Nations on other parts of the rim, Wolfers suggests, are likely to view such strong reactions as unnecessary diversions of American attention. To the extent that dispersion contributes to a disparity of interests, it may increase problems of alliance performance and actually cause disruption of the alliance prior to attainment of its stated goals.

As noted in Chapter One, the size of an alliance may play a similar role. The more members in an alliance, the more likely it is that they will be unable to agree on the direction that the alliance ought to take and the less effectively will they be able to maintain it. In large alliances, there may be a tendency for the members to make demands on their partners which are not perceived as relevant to the entire alliance. These demands may become points of contention, leading to difficulties in coordinating strategy and, ultimately, to the disruption of the alliance.

The nature of the goals for which the alliance was formed can also be a source of intra-alliance conflict and disruption. If members have limited goals which are clear and unambiguous, they may maintain their alliance relationships with relative ease. Numerous and ambiguous goals may become points of contention, perhaps ultimately affecting survival of the alliance. Thus, the purpose which brought the nations together in the first place may become a source of friction.

We will explore the impact of these three factors with our data. The hypotheses to be tested are:

The more dispersed the members of an alliance, the less effective it will be.

The larger the number of nations in alliance, the less effective it will be.

The greater the number and the more ambiguous the goals of an alliance, the less effective it will be.

Thus, we expect that large, dispersed alliances with ambiguous goals will tend to be of a lower commitment class, shorter duration, less effective, and to be broken prior to termination date. The opposite should be true of small localized alliances that are formed to achieve a few clearly specified goals. We will also investigate whether certain combinations of them seem to be related to patterns of alliance maintenance. Two types of analyses will be made: the joint impact of the size of an alliance and the nature of the goals of the alliance will be assessed; the impact of size, the dispersion of alliance members, and the nature of the goals will be investigated.

To this point we have identified a set of national and alliance characteristics which are hypothesized to be related to the performance of an alliance. These variables are summarized in Table 1. As this figure indicates, we hypothesize that certain national and international factors affect alliance maintenance and performance.

The Impact of the International System. The international environment within which decision-makers act establishes constraints on their behavior and, to a certain extent, determines how they will respond to each other, within or outside of alliances. In order to examine the impact of the international system on alliance behavior, we will look at patterns of maintenance in different time periods. We will divide the 1815–1939 period into sections which will permit us to explore the impact that system characteristics have on alliance maintenance. We assume that the time periods employed in the analysis represent different systemic characteristics. It is impossible to measure all of these attributes directly, nor is it possible to assign any kind of weights to many factors for each time period. It is possible, however, to specify the ways in which the time periods are different and to determine whether the patterns of alliance maintenance also differ.

We can, however, develop at least one measure: the amount of threat in the international system. As we noted in the first chapter, the impact of threat on alliance cohesion has received extensive treatment in the literature; [16] it is widely assumed that alliance cohesion decreases as the amount of danger and threat in the international system declines. There is reason to think that the various aspects of alliance maintenance will also be affected by variations in threat. During periods of considerable international threat, we might expect to find more military pacts than other types of commitments, as well as alliances of longer duration. As one measure of threat we will utilize the presence or absence of a major war in the international system. We will look at patterns of maintenance in years when a major war was in progress as contrasted to years in which there was no major war.

It is also possible to describe other ways that historical periods differed and then to explore the patterns of maintenance in those periods. It can be argued, for instance, that World War I represented a major turning point in international politics. The system which emerged after that was significantly different from that of the nineteenth century. The prewar balance of power arrangements ceased to exist despite French efforts to ensure that her security would never again be threatened by Germany. The League of Nations represented a significant departure with respect to peace-keeping activities. The actors also changed in important ways. Towards the end of the nineteenth century, Germany emerged as the major continental power. World War I left her defeated and subjected to a peace treaty which attempted to prevent her re-emergence as a major power. France and England were also left weakened and exhausted by the war. Finally, the United States and the Soviet Union emerged as major international actors. Thus, World War I represented a shift from a Europe-centered balance of power system to one in which there were at least modest efforts to replace balance of power politics. Moreover, within less than a generation the international system came to be dominated by the United States and the Soviet Union instead of the traditional powers of Western and Central Europe.

World War I also represented a shift in the attitudes of many decision-makers towards war as an instrument of policy. The nineteenth century was characterized by the widespread belief that "war could be profitable." [17] The experience of World War I, however, had a profound effect on this belief. During the interwar period, the victors of World War I "were willing to tolerate great and unfavorable changes in the balance of power before judging war to be necessary." [18]

But World War I was not the only major turning point during the 1815–1939 period. The departure of Bismarck from office was perhaps equally important. Bismarck's successors were unable to maintain the balance of power system he had developed, and Europe soon polarized into two competing alliance systems. It could be argued that the balance of power system broke down in 1890 rather than in 1914. Thus it is worth while examining alliance patterns before and after the departure of Bismarck as well as before and after the war.

It is important to stress again that, with the exception of threat, we will not be able to measure directly any of the system characteristics discussed. We will, however, be able to examine patterns of maintenance in the various periods to observe if there are differences. If such differences do emerge, we can attribute them to the mix of system characteristics without singling out any particular one as of more importance.

Aspects of Alliance Performance

TYPE OF ALLIANCE. Those who decide to seek allies must decide at the point of alliance formation what type of commitment is appropriate to their concerns and goals. Because different levels of commitment create varying expectations among alliance members, the matter is not trivial. Following Singer and Small [19] we will consider three types of military alliance: defense pact, neutrality-nonaggression pact, and entente. These types of alliances can be considered a rank order scale, with the first requiring the most extensive assistance (aid in the event of war).

ALLIANCE EFFECTIVENESS. Effectiveness of alliances can be examined in a variety of ways. One might consider their deterrent effects, the extent to which they permit nations to avoid increases in military budgets, or the extent to which nations in an alliance honor the alliance if it is invoked. In this chapter, the latter aspect of alliance effectiveness will be examined. We will consider factors which affect the likelihood that an alliance will be honored if it is invoked.

MODE OF ALLIANCE TERMINATION. The manner in which alliances are terminated is an indication of how effectively the member nations are maintaining their relationships. We will consider three modes of alliance termination: permitting the alliance to lapse, merging of alliances into larger groups, and breaking of alliances prior to the termination date.

ALLIANCE RENEWAL.   When nations are faced with long-term problems and they believe that their alliance relationships are satisfactory, they might be expected to renew those relationships. We will consider factors which result in the renewal of alliances with specified termination dates.

LENGTH OF ALLIANCE.   In the process of forming an alliance, nations have the option of specifying its duration. In many past cases, the length of the alliance was left unspecified. Alliances of a specified duration will be examined in order to determine what national and alliance attributes, if any, affect the determination of proposed length.

Findings

The formation of an alliance creates for the actors involved a new set of relationships and obligations. We have identified above a set of factors which are believed to affect the formation and maintenance process. In this section we shall explore the various relationships and assess the theoretical implications of the results.

Data.   The data used to test our hypotheses and the procedures employed are described in detail in Appendix A. In order to set the context for the discussion of our findings, however, a brief description of the data will be useful. As noted above, the basic set of alliances employed in this study is that collected by Singer and Small.[20] Since their study excluded alliances formed during war years, these alliances have been added and are identified in Appendix A.

Three kinds of additional data were collected. First, a code sheet specifying information relevant to each variable was developed and used to select information from each of the alliance treaties on size, duration, and goal structure, and the maintenance variables. The number of changes in chief executive and in sovereign were counted for each nation for a period of one decade prior to the formation of the alliance and for the duration of the treaty. Each pair of nations in every alliance was judged in terms of ideological similarity and an alliance homogeneity score computed. The final step involved the identification of years in which a major war occurred. For this purpose, the list developed by Singer and Small [21] was employed. The fourteen wars with more than a total of 4,000 battle deaths were included in the analysis. They are listed in Appendix A.

For subsequent analyses each variable was divided into categories generally representing high and low groups. Every effort was made to use the median value or categories of roughly equal number as the dividing point so as to avoid highly skewed marginal distributions.

Ideological Homogeneity. Ideological orientations of nations have long been felt to be crucial to international interactions. We have discussed above the presumed impact of this factor as specified by two contending approaches, the principle theory and the expediency theory. To explore these alternative explanations, the ideological orientations of the nations in each alliance were assessed, and ideological homogeneity scores for each alliance were developed.

Table 2 reveals that the impact of ideology on alliance maintenance appears to be quite small. At the point of alliance formation when nations must decide upon the type of relationship they wish to develop, ideology does play some role. Ideologically similar nations tended to form military pacts more frequently than did dissimilar nations, whereas the latter predominately formed nonaggression pacts. After the alliance was formed, however, the impact of ideological differences was minimal. There was no tendency for heterogeneous alliances to experience such problems as short duration or to be broken prior to termination. There was, however, a slight tendency for dissimilar nations to agree to renew their treaty arrangements while the same was less true for similar nations. This relationship is quite weak, however.

It is important to stress that ideological differences were evident during this whole period. Europe during the period from 1789 to 1815 experienced a revolution and subsequent international upheavals that profoundly affected the relations among states. The legitimacy of the eighteenth century balance of power system was challenged by Napoleon who used the forces unleashed in France by the Revolution.[22] The defeat of Napoleon presented the victorious states at the Congress of Vienna with the problem of reordering the international system. The Napoleonic period and the Congress of Vienna reflected and institutionalized ideological issues which were to divide the European states for the remainder of the nineteenth century.

The powers which had joined in order to defeat Napoleon soon found themselves at odds. Furthermore, France was soon accepted back into the European system. The major European powers, including France, subsequently became divided over two main issues: the nature of the international order and the nature of domestic regimes.[23]

The conservative regimes—Austria, Prussia, and Russia—profoundly feared the principles of the French Revolution and the ideas of popular sovereignty. They were committed to resist change in European nations

TABLE 2. Ideology and Alliance Maintenance *

Ideology and Type of Alliance	Ideologically Homogeneous Alliances	Ideologically Heterogeneous Alliances
Military Pacts	35 (54%)	21 (33%)
Nonaggression Pacts	15 (23%)	30 (48%)
Ententes	15 (23%)	12 (19%)
	65	63
Cramer's V = 0.26		

Ideology and Alliance Effectiveness	Ideologically Similar Alliances	Ideologically Dissimilar Alliances
Invoked and Honored	23 (88%)	19 (86%)
Invoked and Not Honored	3 (12%)	3 (14%)
	26	22
Phi = 0.03		

Ideology and Mode of Termination	Ideologically Similar Alliances	Ideologically Dissimilar Alliances
Not Broken Prior to Termination Date	21 (32%)	23 (37%)
Broken Prior to Termination Date	44 (68%)	40 (63%)
	65	63
Phi = 0.02		

Ideology and Alliance Renewal	Ideologically Similar Alliances	Ideologically Dissimilar Alliances
Number Not Renewed	51 (78%)	39 (62%)
Number Renewed Once Or More	14 (22%)	24 (38%)
	65	63
Phi = 0.16		

Ideology and Proposed Length

Proposed Length	Ideologically Homogeneous Alliances	Ideologically Heterogeneous Alliances
Up to 49 Months	6 (21%)	10 (25%)
49 to 360 Months	23 (79%)	30 (75%)
	29	40
Phi = 0.01		

Ideology and Actual Alliance Length

Actual Length	Ideologically Homogeneous Alliances	Ideologically Heterogeneous Alliances
Actual Length Up to 81 Months	35 (55%)	27 (43%)
Actual Length 82 to 619 Months	29 (45%)	36 (57%)
	64	63
Phi = 0.10		

* A Phi coefficient measures the strength of association between two variables. It varies between 0 and 1 and a value of 0 indicates complete independence between the two variables while a value of 1 indicates complete association. Cramer's V has the same interpretation but is used on contingency tables larger than 2 × 2. See William L. Hays, *Statistics for Psychologists,* Holt, Rinehart and Winston, New York, 1953, pp. 604–605. The total number of alliances in this study is 130. In some cases it was not possible to collect appropriate data on one or more alliances and these alliances had to be dropped from certain analyses. Thus, in some of the tables in this chapter, the marginal totals will equal less than 130.

and to uphold existing, "legitimate" governments. Their opposition to revolutionary or constitutional reform led the conservative powers to espouse the principle of "intervention"—the right to intervene in any nation threatened by revolutionary forces.

The two western powers, France and England, adhered to liberal and constitutional principles and opposed the principle of intervention. They rejected the notion of a "legitimate" regime and were willing to tolerate and encourage governments which had constitutional and liberal bases. These ideological divisions tended to persist through the end of the nineteenth century.

During the period between the two world wars the European nations continued to be concerned with the nature of domestic regimes. The issues that divided nations after 1918, however, were not those of autocratic, "legitimate" regimes versus liberal, constitutional democracies. Rather, the European international system began to split along democratic-totalitarian lines. The success of the Russian Revolution in 1917, the rise of fascism in Italy in 1922, and the inception of nazism in Germany in 1933 provided a nucleus of totalitarian regimes. While totalitarian regimes of the right and left were opposed to each other, they did share in common a number of doctrinal positions.

Loosely aligned against the totalitarian systems were the liberal democracies of Western Europe and the United States. In principle they tended to be opposed to the ideological doctrines and expansionist international policies of the Communist and the Fascist regimes. Thus, the period under study did witness considerable ideological conflict among the major and frequently the minor powers.

The findings summarized in Table 2 give rise to many questions. We noted in Chapter One that ideology is considered an important factor by those who espouse an "affiliational" theory of alliances. Writers such as Liska and Osgood have argued that ideology is the impetus to and the "cement" of an alliance while the opposite view has been just as strongly held.[24] Our findings for the period 1815 to 1939 suggest that neither view is completely valid. Rather, it appears that ideology is a factor in alliance *formation* insofar as it affects the strength of the commitment which nations are willing to make to each other. Once the alliance is formed, however, it appears that ideological heterogeneity does not have many disruptive effects. Furthermore, at the point of inception, ideology plays no role in determining if nations set some time limit to their arrangement. Thus, whether ideology does or does not play a role in alliance formation seems not to be important for alliance performance. In specifying the role of ideology, then, it is important to establish the conditions under which it is to be operative.

Regime Stability. Domestic politics cannot be divorced from foreign policy. Thus we have argued that the regime stability will have an impact on alliance performance. In order to assess this factor, two types of analyses were performed. First, regime instability of alliance members for the decade preceding the signing of the treaty was related to decisions made at the time of formation. Second, the impact of regime instability during the existence of the alliance on patterns of maintenance was explored.

An examination of Table 3 reveals that instability prior to forming the alliance has no impact on their decision as to what type of alliance to form. There is a slight tendency for unstable nations to form nonaggression pacts but it is extremely weak. No significant pattern emerges with proposed length.

When we turn to alliance performance, it is also clear that stability has little or no impact on alliance performance. Except for renewals, none of the relationships in Table 3 exhibit a very strong degree of association.

We now turn to consider the joint impact of ideological similarity and national instability on alliance performance. Recall that the expediency and principle theories presented different conclusions on this point; the expediency theory maintains that there should be no joint impact while the principle theory holds that there will be some joint relationship between these two factors. As the data presented in Table 4 are a departure from the form of presentation used earlier, a word of explanation is useful. The table compares alliances which are ideologically similar to those which are dissimilar with respect to the impact of instability on type of alliance and on proposed length of alliances. Total instability here refers to the sum of the changes of sovereign and chief executive for the decade prior to the formation of the alliance.

The data indicate that there is some joint effect at the point of alliance formation. Regardless of instability, nations with similar ideological orientations are more likely to form alliances of higher commitment class than dissimilar nations as indicated by the positive relationship. This suggests that shared ideological orientations mitigate somewhat the impact of instability on the tendency for nations to make a commitment to a military pact as opposed to a nonaggression pact or an entente.

Ideology and instability also jointly affect the willingness of nations to commit themselves for an extended period of time. Alliances with ideologically similar nations are slightly more likely to have long proposed durations, whereas there is a fairly strong tendency for dissimilar alliances to have shorter proposed durations, as indicated by the negative Phi coefficient. Ideology appears to reduce the impact of instability for homogeneous alliances and to reinforce the impact of instability for dissimilar alliances.

Turning to patterns of alliance performance, the data in Table 5 indicate that the combination of ideological similarity and stability has no impact on either alliance effectiveness or the mode of alliance termination. We cannot examine the impact of stability, either alone or in combination with other variables, on the actual length of the alliance because the measure of instability is, in effect, spuriously related to length of alliance. Hence, this variable is omitted from Table 5. It is clear from the table that the combination of these two variables has no effect on the remaining aspects of alliance performance.

Ideology thus has its main impact at the point of alliance formation with

TABLE 3. Regime Stability and Alliance Maintenance

	Stability and Type of Alliance	
	0–8 Changes First Decade	9–49 Changes First Decade
Military Pacts	23 (42%)	21 (36%)
Nonaggression Pacts	22 (39%)	22 (37%)
Ententes	11 (19%)	16 (27%)
	56	59
Cramer's V = 0.09		

	Stability and Alliance Effectiveness	
	4 or Less Changes During Alliance	5–49 Changes During Alliance
Invoked and Honored	18 (86%)	19 (86%)
Invoked and Not Honored	3 (14%)	3 (14%)
	21	22
Phi = 0.00		

	Stability and Mode of Termination	
	4 or Less Changes During Alliance	5–49 Changes During Alliance
Not Broken Prior to Termination Date	17 (30%)	21 (35%)
Broken Prior to Termination Date	40 (70%)	39 (65%)
	57	60
Phi = 0.03		

respect to the type of alliance formed. The data indicate that ideologically homogeneous alliances are more likely to form pacts of a high commitment level than are heterogeneous alliances. The role of trust identified by the principle theory seems to be important. After the alliance is formed, however, ideology appears to play no role, suggesting that the members of an alliance are guided primarily by the dictates of the problem with which they must cope. Instability affected the length of alliances but in a manner opposite from that expected. It was suggested that unstable regimes may

	Stability and Alliance Renewal	
	0–8 Changes First Decade	9–49 Changes First Decade
Number Not Renewed	47 (85%)	34 (57%)
Number Renewed Once or More	8 (15%)	26 (43%)
	55	60
Phi = 0.31		

	Stability and Proposed Length	
	0–8 Changes First Decade	9–49 Changes First Decade
Up to 48 Months	8 (25%)	8 (24%)
49 to 360 Months	24 (75%)	26 (76%)
	32	34
Phi = 0.01		

seek to maintain their alliance relations both to insure stability in their international relations as well as to free resources to cope with their domestic problems. Finally, the impact of instability on alliance maintenance was reduced somewhat when ideology was introduced as a control. Ideologically similar nations tended to have longer alliances than dissimilar nations at the same levels of domestic instability.

The analysis indicates that neither approach—the expediency or the principle theory—with which we began this analysis is sufficient by itself to account for the observed patterns of alliance formation and alliance maintenance. The data tend to support the expediency approach with re-

TABLE 4. Ideology, Stability, and Alliance Formation *

	Similar Ideology and Total Instability	Dissimilar Ideology and Total Instability
Type of Alliance	.19 **	.01 **
Proposed Length	.10	.35 (−)

* (−) indicates a negative relationship.
** Indicates Cramer's V for 3 × 2 table or larger. Remaining values are Phi coefficients.

TABLE 5. Ideology, Stability, and Alliance Maintenance *

	Alliance Effectiveness	Mode of Termination
Similar Ideology—Sovereign Change	.07	.07
Dissimilar Ideology—Sovereign Change	.05 (−)	.02
Chief Executive Change—Similar Ideology	.07	.05
Chief Executive Change—Dissimilar Ideology	.01	.21 (−)

* Entries are Phi coefficients. (−) indicates a negative relationship.

TABLE 6. Distance and Type of Alliance

Distance and Type of Alliance		
	0–947 mi	948–9800 mi
Military Pacts	30 (48%)	26 (40%)
Nonaggression Pacts	20 (32%)	25 (39%)
Ententes	13 (21%)	14 (22%)
	63	65
Cramer's V = 0.08		

Distance and Alliance Effectiveness		
	0–947 mi	948–9800 mi
Invoked and Honored	16 (80%)	26 (93%)
Invoked and Not Honored	4 (20%)	2 (7%)
	20	28
Phi = 0.17		

Distance and Mode of Termination		
	0–947 mi	948–9800 mi
Not Broken Prior to Termination Date	21 (33%)	23 (35%)
Broken Prior to Termination Date	42 (67%)	42 (65%)
	63	65
Phi = 0.02		

spect to the impact of ideology on alliance performance. However, as we indicated above, we cannot test the direct impact of expediency and can conclude only that the analyses of the role of ideology in alliance maintenance suggested by the expediency theory received more support from the data than that suggested by the principle theory.

Size, Distance, and Goals. This section deals with the impact on alliance maintenance of various characteristics of the alliances themselves. It is hypothesized that increases in size, in the dispersion of the members, or in the number or ambiguity of goals will create problems of coordination and other aspects of performance.

The impact of dispersion, summarized in Table 6, appears to be minimal. The exception is its effect on alliance effectiveness. But so few alliances were invoked and not honored that this result must be viewed with caution.

These results are somewhat puzzling at first glance. There seemed good reason to expect that different geographical locations would give rise to

Distance and Alliance Renewal		
	0–947 mi	948–9800 mi
Number Not Renewed	43 (69%)	45 (70%)
Number Renewed Once		
or More	19 (31%)	19 (30%)
	62	64
Phi = 0.01		

Distance and Proposed Length		
Proposed Length	0–947 mi	948–9800 mi
Up to 48 Months	7 (21%)	9 (26%)
49 to 360 Months	27 (79%)	26 (74%)
	34	35
Phi = 0.02		

Distance and Actual Alliance Length		
Actual Length	0–947 mi	948–9800 mi
Up to 81 Months	33 (53%)	29 (45%)
82 to 619 Months	29 (47%)	36 (55%)
	62	65
Phi = 0.08		

differences among the members as to goals and priorities of the alliance. That this proved not to be the case can possibly be explained by the political context during the period under consideration. A very large proportion of the nations in these alliances were European powers. This was especially true for the nineteenth century. Although the number of non-European powers increased after World War I, the former still predominated.[25]

International politics during this whole period was also primarily "European" in character. Up to World War I, most of the alliances formed were designed to affect the balance of power in Europe in some fashion. The same was in part true for the inter-war period. In the aftermath of war, many of the European powers searched for new ways to organize

TABLE 7.   Size

Size and Type of Alliance		
	Two Members	Three or More Members
Military Pacts	41 (41%)	15 (52%)
Nonaggression Pacts	41 (41%)	5 (17%)
Ententes	19 (19%)	9 (31%)
	101	29
Cramer's V = 0.209		

Size and Alliance Effectiveness		
	Two Members	Three or More Members
Invoked and Honored	31 (89%)	11 (85%)
Invoked and Not Honored	4 (11%)	2 (15%)
	35	13
Phi = 0.05		

Size and Mode of Termination		
	Two Members	Three or More Members
Not Broken Prior to Termination Date	37 (37%)	8 (28%)
Broken Prior to Termination Date	64 (63%)	21 (72%)
	101	29
Phi = 0.079		

their relationships and to deal with conflicts. The League of Nations was an important if unsuccessful effort in this direction. At the same time they did not forsake traditional means such as alliances to regulate their foreign affairs and, as before the war, much of this activity was concerned with Europe. France was especially active in attempting to establish a network of alliances directed toward containing Germany. Thus, while there was dispersion among the members of alliances during this whole period, much of the focus of their activities was European international politics. To be sure, issues arose relating to countries far from Europe, and many of the major powers, such as England, France, and Germany before World War I, had extensive colonial interests. A significant portion of their alliance activities was directed, however, to anticipating and responding to European

	Size and Alliance Renewal	
	Two Members	Three or More Members
Number Not Renewed	67 (67%)	21 (81%)
Number Renewed Once or More	33 (33%)	5 (19%)
	100	26
Phi = 0.12		

	Size and Proposed Length	
	Two Members	Three or More Members
Up to 48 Months	14 (23%)	2 (29%)
49 to 360 Months	48 (77%)	5 (71%)
	62	7
Phi = 0.043		

	Size and Actual Alliance Length	
	Two Members	Three or More Members
Actual Length Up to 81 Months	44 (44%)	20 (69%)
Actual Length 82 to 619 Months	56 (56%)	9 (31%)
	100	29
Phi = 0.208		

developments. Thus, the lack of impact of dispersion on alliance performance may be due to the fact that many of the alliances analyzed here had
the rather single-minded European focus which overrode problems raised
by the geographical distance.

As the data in Table 7 indicate, the size of an alliance has some impact
on alliance performance. A greater percentage of the large alliances tend
to be military pacts than is true for the small alliances. As expected, small
alliances tend to last longer than large ones. The relationship between size
and type of alliance was unexpected, however. The level of threat in the
international system may be an important factor. Nations that perceive a
significant international threat may prefer to conclude military pacts rather
than other types of commitment. The data provide some support for this
hypothesis. Of the fourteen large alliances in existence during war years,
nine were military pacts whereas only six of the fifteen large alliances in

TABLE 8.   Goal Ambiguity

Goal Ambiguity and Type of Alliance		
	Ambiguous	Nonambiguous
Military Pacts	17 (27%)	39 (57%)
Nonaggression Pacts	27 (44%)	19 (28%)
Ententes	18 (29%)	10 (15%)
	62	68
Cramer's V = 0.305		

Goal Ambiguity and Alliance Effectiveness		
	Ambiguous	Nonambiguous
Invoked and Honored	16 (89%)	26 (87%)
Invoked and Not Honored	2 (11%)	4 (13%)
	18	30
Phi = 0.03		

Goal Ambiguity and Mode of Termination		
	Ambiguous	Nonambiguous
Not Broken Prior to Termination Date	22 (35%)	23 (34%)
Broken Prior to Termination Date	40 (65%)	45 (66%)
	62	68
Phi = 0.017		

existence during peacetime were military pacts. Thus, although the data are somewhat limited, threat and size appear to have a joint effect on the level of alliance commitment.

These results are interesting in view of our earlier speculation that large alliances would be less cohesive than small ones.[26] The present results provide only partial support. Small alliances do last longer but are no less likely than large alliances to be broken early. Thus, it appears that size does permit an alliance to persist but it does not affect the manner in which it is brought to a conclusion. Finally, the impact of size on the nature of alliance commitments is overcome by threat in the international system. During periods of high threat, large alliances tend to be defense pacts rather than lesser commitments.

We shall next consider the hypotheses that alliances with many different goals or ambiguous goals will experience maintenance problems.[27] It is

Goal Ambiguity and Alliance Renewal		
	Ambiguous	Nonambiguous
Number Not Renewed	44 (73%)	44 (67%)
Number Renewed Once or More	16 (27%)	22 (33%)
	60	66
Phi = 0.09		

Goal Ambiguity and Proposed Length		
	Ambiguous	Nonambiguous
Up to 48 Months	6 (19%)	10 (27%)
49 to 360 Months	26 (81%)	27 (73%)
	32	37
Phi = 0.098		

Goal Ambiguity and Actual Alliance Length		
	Ambiguous	Nonambiguous
Actual Length Up to 81 Months	28 (45%)	36 (54%)
Actual Length 82 to 619 Months	34 (55%)	31 (46%)
	62	67
Phi = 0.086		

clear from Table 8 that nations entering an alliance with relatively unambiguous goals will tend to form defensive pacts. This may be due, in part,
to the fact that when nations are able to identify specific goals with respect
to targets and third-party relations, they are more willing to undertake a
higher level commitment—that is, a military pact. These data indicate,
however, that aside from the impact on type of alliance, the ambiguity of
alliance goals has no impact on alliance maintenance. With one exception
the data indicate that there is no association between goal ambiguity of an
alliance and the alliance performance; there is a slight tendency for alliances with ambiguous goals to survive for longer periods than alliances
with unambiguous goals. One possible explanation is that in alliances with
ambiguous goals, disagreements take place in the context of possible
"trade-offs" in interpreting the nature of the alliance purposes. That is,
perhaps, alliances with ambiguous goals provide their members with considerable "bargaining space" for reaching some form of agreement on the

TABLE 9. Number of Goals

Number of Goals and Type of Alliance		
1–3	4–5	6+

	1–3	4–5	6+
Military Pacts	28 (55%)	16 (37%)	12 (33%)
Nonaggression Pacts	10 (20%)	20 (47%)	16 (44%)
Ententes	13 (25%)	7 (16%)	8 (22%)
	51	43	36

Cramer's $V = 0.10$
Gamma $= 0.15$

Number of Goals and Alliance Effectiveness		
1–3	4–5	6+

	1–3	4–5	6+
Invoked and Honored	12 (80%)	17 (89%)	13 (93%)
Invoked and Not Honored	3 (20%)	2 (11%)	1 (7%)
Cramer's $V = 0.05$	15	19	14

Number of Goals and Mode of Termination		
1–3	4–5	6+

	1–3	4–5	6+
Not Broken Prior to Termination Date	15 (29%)	17 (40%)	13 (36%)
Broken Prior to Termination Date	36 (71%)	26 (60%)	23 (64%)
Cramer's $V = 0.01$	51	43	36

purposes of the alliances. Aside from the impact on the type of commitment and on the actual length of alliance, however, goal ambiguity does
not affect alliance maintenance.

The number of alliance goals also effects alliance performance. Table 9
reveals a weak relationship between the number of goals and the type of
alliance. These data suggest that nations forming an alliance with many
goals perhaps anticipate problems and hence are inclined to prefer a pact
of lower commitment. Given the possibility of conflict over the importance
and merit of alliance goals, nations may tend to avoid undertaking alliances of the highest commitment class.

An interesting relationship emerges between the number of alliance
goals and the tendency for the alliance to be broken prior to its termination date. As Table 9 indicates, the relationship is very weak. However,
compared to alliances with few goals, more of those with four or more
goals tended *not* to be broken prior to the specified termination date. Brief
reflection may give a clue as to the reasons. In an alliance with few goals there
may not be much leeway for "trade-offs" among alliance members with
regard to those goals should disagreements arise. The result may be disrup-

Number of Goals and Alliance Renewal		
	1–3	4–5	6+
Number Not Renewed	6 (55%)	34 (74%)	47 (69%)
Number Renewed Once or More	5 (45%)	12 (26%)	21 (31%)
	11	46	68
Cramer's V = 0.11			

Number of Goals and Proposed Length		
	1–3	4–5	6+
Up to 48 months	1 (15%)	5 (20%)	10 (28%)
49 to 360 months	6 (85%)	20 (80%)	27 (72%)
	7	25	37
Cramer's V = 0.10			

Number of Goals and Actual Length		
	1–3	4–5	6+
Up to 81 months	3 (25%)	23 (50%)	36 (52%)
82 to 619 months	9 (75%)	23 (50%)	33 (48%)
	12	46	69
Cramer's V = 0.15			

TABLE 10. Size, Distance, Goals, and Type of Alliance *

Size

	Two Members				Three or More Members			
	Distance				Distance			
	Up to 947 mi		947 mi to 9800 mi		Up to 947 mi		947 mi to 9800 mi	
	Goals		Goals		Goals		Goals	
	1–4	5+	1–4	5+	1–4	5+	1–4	5+
Military Pact	15 (48%)	7 (39%)	18 (54%)	1 (5%)	3 (33%)	5 (100%)	5 (72%)	2 (33%)
Nonaggression Pact	11 (35%)	8 (44%)	9 (27%)	13 (68%)	1 (11%)	0 (0%)	1 (14%)	2 (33%)
Entente	5 (16%)	3 (17%)	6 (18%)	5 (26%)	5 (56%)	0 (0%)	1 (14%)	2 (33%)
	31	18	33	19	9	5	7	6
	Cramer's V = .09		Cramer's V = .59		Cramer's V = .64		Cramer's V = .38	

* The percentages in some columns do not sum to 100% because of rounding.

tion of the alliance. In an alliance with many goals, on the other hand, there may be more room for bargaining if nations are not intensely and inflexibly committed to a single outcome for each issue. In short, alliances with many goals, like alliances with ambiguous goals, may provide members with more "bargaining space." [28]

Although we cannot test this explanation directly, we can offer an illustrative example. As part of his strategy to unite Germany without including Austria, Bismarck formed an alliance with Italy.[29] The "cement" was Bismarck's promise that Italy would get Venetia—a long-term goal that Italy had been unsuccessful in attaining by other means—if she would bind herself to join Prussia should war break out with Austria. It appears that Bismarck cared little for the disposition of Venetia. His main concern was to unite the German Duchies and exclude Austria from the arrangement—the "small Germany" solution. When war broke out between Prussia and Austria, the latter easily defeated the Italians. But Prussia won a decisive victory in the battle of Königgratz, and as part of the peace settlement Bismarck insured that Italy received Venetia, but not South Tyrol. In this case, the goals of each party were of no interest to the other and yet they did provide a basis for an arrangement, despite the defeat of one of the partners. This example illustrates how nations with multiple goals, about which none has equally intense feelings, coordinate their behaviors.

At this point we turn to an examination of the cumulative effect of size, membership dispersion, and goal structure. We will focus on the type of alliance formed as the dependent variable. The data in Table 10 reveal no clear cumulative effects. Interpretation of the results is somewhat difficult because of the limited number of cases in some categories. It is clear, however, that there is no support for the hypothesis that these three variables have an additive effect. For two-nation alliances, a fairly clear pattern emerges. When alliance members are proximate and the goals are few in number, there is a very slight tendency to prefer military pacts. This tendency becomes even stronger when the members are dispersed. The opposite is true for alliances with many goals; the preferred mode of commitment is a nonaggression pact, regardless of dispersion.

The scanty data on alliances with three or more members are even more difficult to interpret. In proximate alliances there is a tendency for ententes to predominate when goals are few in number, whereas defense pacts predominate when there are many goals. The opposite seems to be true for dispersed alliances.

A clearer pattern emerges from the Table 11 data on size, distance, and goal ambiguity. Alliances with unambiguous goals tend to be of the highest commitment class, regardless of size or dispersion. Alternatively, there is a

TABLE 11. Size, Distance, Goal Ambiguity and Type of Alliance

Size

	Two Members				Three or More Members			
	Proximate		Dispersed		Proximate		Dispersed	
	Distance				Distance			
	Goal Ambiguity		Goal Ambiguity		Goal Ambiguity		Goal Ambiguity	
	Yes	No	Yes	No	Yes	No	Yes	No
Military Pact	3 (18%)	19 (59%)	9 (31%)	10 (43%)	1 (20%)	7 (78%)	4 (44%)	3 (75%)
Nonaggression Pact	9 (52%)	10 (31%)	13 (45%)	9 (39%)	1 (20%)	0 (0%)	3 (33%)	0 (0%)
Entente	5 (29%)	3 (9%)	7 (24%)	4 (18%)	3 (60%)	2 (22%)	2 (22%)	1 (25%)
	17	32	29	23	5	9	9	4
	Cramer's v = 0.41		Cramer's V = 0.13		Cramer's V = 0.59		Cramer's V = 0.37	

strong tendency for alliances with ambiguous goals to be either nonaggression pacts or ententes. In summary, the data exhibit some interesting trends but do not support the hypothesis that the three variables have a cumulative effect.

Systemic Characteristics. The final factor to be considered is the impact of the international system on alliance performance. While we will be able to determine any differences in alliance maintenance for different international systems, it will not be possible to attribute those differences to any particular system characteristic. As we noted earlier, it is possible to identify certain points at which the international system did change significantly, but we cannot separate the consequences of the many changes.

As Table 12 indicates, there are two ways in which the pre-1919 and the inter-war systems differed with respect to alliance formation. There was a very strong tendency for nations in the nineteenth century to form

TABLE 12.   Pre-1919 and Post-1919 System

Type of Alliance		
	Before 1919	After 1919
Military Pacts	38 (60%)	18 (27%)
Nonaggression Pacts	8 (13%)	37 (56%)
Ententes	17 (27%)	11 (17%)
	63	66
Phi = 0.458		

Alliance Effectiveness		
	Before 1919	After 1919
Invoked and Honored	33 (89%)	9 (82%)
Invoked and Not Honored	4 (11%)	2 (18%)
Phi = 0.09	37	11

Mode of Termination		
	Before 1919	After 1919
Not Broken Prior to Termination Date	25 (40%)	20 (30%)
Broken Prior to Termination Date	38 (60%)	46 (70%)
	63	66
Phi = 0.098		

Table 12. (*Continued*)

Alliance Renewal

	Before 1919	After 1919
Number Not Renewed	50 (81%)	37 (59%)
Number Renewed Once or More	12 (19%)	26 (41%)
	62	63
Phi = 0.23		

Proposed Length

	Before 1919	After 1919
Up to 48 Months	5 (36%)	11 (20%)
49 to 360 Months	9 (64%)	43 (80%)
	14	54
Phi = 0.146		

Actual Length

	Before 1919	After 1919
Actual Length Up to 81 Months	35 (56%)	28 (43%)
Actual Length 82 to 619 Months	28 (44%)	37 (57%)
	63	65
Phi = 0.125		

TABLE 13. Pre-1890 and Post-1890 System

Type of Alliance

	Before 1890	After 1890
Military Pacts	26 (68%)	30 (33%)
Nonaggression Pacts	6 (16%)	39 (43%)
Ententes	6 (16%)	22 (24%)
	38	91
Cramer's V = 0.332		

Alliance Effectiveness

	Before 1890	After 1890
Invoked and Honored	15 (83%)	27 (90%)
Invoked and Not Honored	3 (17%)	3 (10%)
	18	30

Phi = 0.09

Mode of Termination

	Before 1890	After 1890
Not Broken Prior to Termination Date	16 (84%)	29 (60%)
Broken Prior to Termination Date	3 (16%)	19 (40%)
	19	48

Phi = 0.228

Alliance Renewal

	Before 1890	After 1890
Number Not Renewed	31 (82%)	56 (64%)
Number Renewed Once or More	7 (18%)	31 (36%)
	38	87

Phi = 0.17

Proposed Length

	Before 1890	After 1890
Up to 48 Months	4 (50%)	12 (20%)
49 to 360 Months	4 (50%)	48 (80%)
	8	60

Phi = 0.228

Actual Length

	Before 1890	After 1890
Actual Length Up to 81 Months	22 (58%)	41 (46%)
Actual Length 82 to 619 Months	16 (42%)	49 (54%)
	38	90

Phi = 0.113

defense pacts, whereas the preferred mode of alignment in the inter-war years was the neutrality pact. There was, in addition, a slight tendency for both the proposed and the actual duration of alliances to be longer in the inter-war years and for pre-1919 alliances not to be renewed.

It is clear from Table 13 that patterns of alliance formation and mainte-nance were different in the two periods. The nineteenth-century system was characterized by a tendency for defense pacts to predominate and for alliances to be of rather short duration. The post-World War I period, on the other hand, was marked by a predominance of neutrality pacts. It is also interesting to examine the differences between the system which ex-isted prior to Bismarck's departure from office with that which developed after 1890. The relationships are similar to those found for the pre- and post-war periods, but they are not quite as strong. The data suggest that the system seemed to be moving away from a reliance on military pacts and that, for whatever reasons, there seemed to be a need for the members

TABLE 14.   Impact of War

	War	Peace
Type of Alliance		
Military Pacts	32 (54%)	24 (34%)
Nonaggression Pacts	20 (34%)	26 (37%)
Ententes	7 (12%)	21 (30%)
	59	71
Phi = 0.246		
Alliance Effectiveness		
Invoked and Honored	24 (92%)	18 (82%)
Invoked and Not Honored	2 (8%)	4 (18%)
	26	22
Phi = 0.15		
Mode of Termination		
Not Broken Prior to Termination Date	18 (30%)	27 (38%)
Broken Prior to Termination Date	41 (70%)	44 (62%)
	59	71
Phi = 0.079		

of alliances to maintain their connections for longer periods.

The data thus indicate that patterns of alliance behavior are at least in part responsive to systemic attributes. We can only speculate on the causes of these different patterns. Perhaps one is the shift from a balance of power system to a more multipolar system. Both after Bismarck, when the classical nineteenth-century balance of power system began to break down, and after World War I, when it can be said to have finally ended, we observe significant changes in patterns of alliance behavior.

The second systemic factor to be considered is the level of international threat. Recall that our measure of threat is the occurrence in any year of a war magnitude of 4,000 battle deaths or higher. The data in Table 14 indicate a clear impact of threat on the type of alliance formed. Alliances formed in years of a major war tend to be defensive pacts whereas alliances formed in peacetime were of all three types. This suggests that in the presence of significant perceived threat, nations forming an alliance are led to seek a relationship of the highest commitment level. The pres-

Alliance Renewal		
	War	Peace
Number Not Renewed	48 (87%)	40 (56%)
Number Renewed Once or More	7 (13%)	31 (44%)
	55	71
Phi = 0.17		

Proposed Length		
	War	Peace
Up to 48 Months	7 (25%)	9 (22%)
49 to 360 Months	21 (75%)	32 (78%)
	28	41
Phi = 0.035		

Actual Length		
	War	Peace
Actual Length Up to 81 Months	44 (76%)	20 (28%)
Actual Length 82 to 619 Months	14 (24%)	51 (72%)
	58	71
Phi = 0.475		

ence of international threat has little effect on either the manner of termination or alliance effectiveness, but there is a strong relationship between threat and the actual length of an alliance. Alliances formed during nonwar years tend to be of longer duration than those formed in war years. Perhaps this supports the view that wartime alliances rarely survive the end of the conflict.

Conclusion

This chapter has explored one aspect of alliance formation and several aspects of performance. After identifying several theoretical approaches to these aspects of alliances, we considered some national, alliance, and system factors that may affect alliance performance. Alliances formed between 1815 and 1939 were used to test several hypotheses.

Our investigation revealed several national, alliance, and systemic factors that appear to have an impact on alliance formation and performance. The results do not, however, provide unambiguous support for any single theory of alliances. Moreover in several cases variables that were thought to be important—for example, dispersion of alliance members—proved to have little effect on alliances during the period under study. In other cases, the results are rather mixed. Some aspects of alliance formation are affected by ideological homogeneity, for example, but not others. In several instances we attempted a *post hoc* analysis to explain the findings. For instance, it was suggested that the notion of a "bargaining space," that is, a relationship in which there are many goals not highly valued by all members of the alliance or in which the goals are ambiguous, may be important for the functioning of alliances.

Finally, the analyses demonstrated the importance of the systemic context within which international decision-makers must operate. In particular, we demonstrated that the characteristics of different systems seemed to produce different patterns of alliance performance. While we could not attribute those differences to any particular systemic characteristics, the differences were significant. In addition, we explored the impact of threat in the system, as measured by years in which a major war occurred, on alliance functioning. Again, it was quite clear that this type of threat did have an impact, at least on certain aspects of alliance performance. Similarly, size of alliance had an unusual effect which was accounted for when threat was introduced as a control.

In summary, the data presented in this chapter do not completely support or reject assertions made about alliances which can be derived from the two theoretical approaches which were the focus of this chapter. Rather, the picture which emerges is rather complex and suggests that neither of these competing theories of alliances can claim to be universally valid.

Notes

1. J. David Singer and Melvin Small, "Alliance Aggregation and the Onset of War, 1815–1945," in J. David Singer, ed., *Quantatative International Politics,* The Free Press, New York, 1968, pp. 268–271. Singer and Small excluded alliances formed just prior to or during a war; these have been added to the present list of alliances and they appear in Appendix A.

2. Quoted in Gordon Craig, "The System of Alliances and the Balance of Power," *The New Cambridge Modern History,* Cambridge University Press, Cambridge, 1960, p. 246.

3. Rene Albrecht-Carrié, *A Diplomatic History of Europe Since the Congress of Vienna,* Harper and Row, New York, 1958, p. 209.

4. Hans J. Morgenthau, "Alliances in Theory and Practice," in Arnold Wolfers, ed., *Alliance Policy in the Cold War,* The Johns Hopkins Press, Baltimore, Maryland, 1959, p. 185. See also, Joseph Frankel, *International Relations,* Oxford University Press, London, 1964; Ernst B. Haas and Allen S. Whiting, *Dynamics of International Relations,* McGraw-Hill Book Co., New York, 1956; Bruce M. Russett, "Components of an Operational Theory of International Alliances," *Journal of Conflict Resolution,* 12, 1968; and John D. Sullivan, "Cooperation in International Politics," in Michael Haas, ed., *Behavioral International Politics,* Chandler and Company, San Francisco, Forthcoming.

5. George Liska, *Nations in Alliance,* The Johns Hopkins Press, Baltimore, 1962, pp. 12–13.

6. Morgenthau, *op. cit.;* Morgenthau, "Sources of Tension between Western Europe and the United States," *The Annals of the American Academy of Political and Social Science,* 312, 1957, pp. 24–28; Morgenthau, *Politics Among Nations,* 3rd ed., Alfred A. Knopf, New York, 1962.

7. Liska, *op. cit.*

8. See, for instance, Morgenthau, *Politics Among Nations,* p. 183.

9. S. H. Allen, *International Relations,* Princeton University Press, Princeton, 1920, p. 450.

10. H. Teune and S. Synnestvedt, "Measuring International Alignment," *Orbis,* 9, 1965, p. 188.

11. K. J. Holsti, *International Politics: A Framework for Analysis,* Prentice-Hall, Englewood Cliffs. New Jersey, 1967, pp. 117–118. See also Herbert S. Dinerstein, "The Transformation of Alliance Systems," *The American Political Science Review,* 59, 1965; and Harold Guetzkow, "Isolation and Collaboration: A Partial Theory of Inter-Nation Relations," *Journal of Conflict Resolution,* 1, 1957.

12. This summary is based on A. J. P. Taylor, *The Struggle for Mastery in Eu-*

rope, *1848–1918*, Oxford University Press, London, 1954, pp. 326 ff. See also, Albrecht-Carrié, *op. cit.*, pp. 194–206.

13. Taylor, *op. cit.*, p. 329.
14. *Ibid.*, p. 327.
15. Arnold Wolfers, "Stresses and Strains in 'Going It with Others,' " *op. cit.*
16. See pp. 17–18, for the discussion of the role of threat in alliance cohesion.
17. Dinerstein, *op. cit.*, p. 598.
18. *Ibid.*, p. 590.
19. J. David Singer and Melvin Small, "Formal Alliances, 1815–1939," *Journal of Peace Research*, 1, 1966, pp. 1–32.
20. Singer and Small, "Alliance Aggregation and the Onset of War, 1815–1945," pp. 268–271.
21. *Ibid.*, pp. 262–266.
22. Henry Kissinger, *A World Restored*, Houghton Mifflin Co., Boston, 1957.
23. This brief summary is based on: Albrecht-Carrié, *op. cit.;* Kissinger, *op. cit.;* Taylor, *op. cit.;* and William L. Langer, *European Alliances and Alignments, 1871–1890,* 2nd ed., Vintage Books, New York, 1950.
24. See Chapter One and the propositions cited there.
25. Singer and Small, "Alliance Aggregation and the Onset of War, 1815–1945," pp. 252–255.
26. See Chapter One, p. 21.
27. In order to clarify the subsequent analysis, a few comments on the nature of the data and the analysis will be useful. The main independent variables here are the number and ambiguity of goals. The types of themes which were counted in determining the number of goals that an alliance had are presented in Appendix A. The main types of goals were military problems, nonmilitary problems, and target nations. An index of the number of goals was constructed by summing across each of these categories for each of the alliances. Thus the independent variable in the first part of this analysis is the number of different types of military and nonmilitary goals contained in a treaty.

In coding these treaties, it was originally planned that the goal or problem statements would be coded both for number and for ambiguity. As the code sheet in Appendix A indicates, most of the categories listed under the three types of problems are rather specific and, as coded, could not be used in this analysis. As the code sheet also suggests, there are two indicators which might be taken to refer to a state of ambiguous goals or, alternatively, to index the "tightness" of the alliance.

These are the following: 1) the presence in the treaty of a prohibition on treaties with third parties without consulting with the members of the present alliance; 2) the presence in the treaty of some provisions for the supply of troops and military equipment in the event of war (either specification of number of troops or specification of a military commission to meet in the event of war). It seems reasonable to use these treaty clauses as one way of measuring goal ambiguity. The reasoning is the following: in all alliances in which one or more of these matters are specified, one could assume that the treaty partners had a clear conception of the problems and goals and, perhaps more important, of their expectations of each other. On the other hand, if these matters were left unspecified, it could be argued that the alliance goals and the mutual expectations of the members were rather ambiguous. Thus, the initial assumption is that these two items provide one measure of goal ambiguity.

28. Cyert and March have made a parallel argument regarding goals in an organization, and James Coleman had suggested this approach as grounds for a theory of coalition or "constitutional" formation. Richard M. Cyert and James G. March, *A Behavioral Theory of the Firm*, Prentice-Hall, Inc., Englewood Cliffs, New Jersey, 1963, Chapter 3. James S. Coleman, "A Theory of Collective Action," *Sociological Inquiry*, 34, 1964, pp. 166–181.

29. This discussion is based on Taylor, *op. cit.*, pp. 158–170.

CHAPTER THREE

Effects of International Conflict and Détente on Alliance Cohesion

Changing Postwar Alliance Patterns

Probably the most widely held belief about alliances found in the extensive literature surveyed in Chapter One is the proposition that alliances exist to provide institutions within which nations may combine their capabilities in defense against a common external enemy. From this premise it follows that alliances are generally formed in response to external threat, that their cohesion is largely dependent upon the intensity and duration of that threat, and that one major cause of their disintegration may be the reduction or disappearance of the external threat against which they were initially formed.

This hypothesis has been widely applied not only to alliances but to many different kinds of social groups. For example, nations have often exhibited increased cohesion during periods of conflict with an outside enemy, as was generally the case within the United States during World War II. In some cases nations have even found it useful to create external enemies to provide a source of domestic unity. For instance, in 1861 Secretary of State Seward suggested to President Lincoln that it might be useful to provoke a quarrel with England in order to save the union from the ravages of civil war. This hypothesis has also been applied to the behavior of small groups. For example, in experiments with children, groups have been found to increase internal solidarity in response to competition with other groups.[1]

Since alliances are groups of nations rather than individuals, it is important to examine whether this hypothesis, which has often been tested in small groups, is also valid at the international level of analysis. Therefore, this chapter primarily involves a systematic test of this simple but crucial hypothesis concerning the effects of external conflict and détente on alliance cohesion.

To test this hypothesis we will focus on the effects of East-West conflict and détente on cohesion within the Communist system and NATO throughout the postwar years. In so doing we will concentrate on two opposing alliances during one historical period in contrast to the more general, long-range survey of alliance behavior found in Chapter Two. Our analysis will thus sacrifice a level of generality in the explanations in order to augment the depth of analysis of these two alliances. A brief historical summary of postwar relations between the Communist system and NATO may provide some background for the analysis of this period.

The world system which emerged in the late 1940s was characterized by substantial bipolarity. Two superpowers emerged after the war, the United States and the Soviet Union. As is often the case when power is divided approximately equally between two major powers, these two nations were in conflict on a large number of issues. One consequence of this conflict was the formation of two major alliance systems dominated by each of the superpowers. These two alliances, in turn, dominated the international system, forming the poles of the bipolar system.

The level of conflict between these alliances has varied substantially. Conflict developed in the late 1940s over Berlin, Iran, Greece, and Turkey. These events were met in the West by the formation of the North Atlantic Treaty Organization (NATO) as the major western alliance. At the same time the Soviet Union was consolidating its control over the countries of Eastern Europe which were occupied by the Soviet armed forces after the war. A Communist coup in Czechoslovakia in 1948 represented the final step in the extension of Soviet influence throughout the region. Simultaneously, the Chinese Communists seized control of mainland China in 1949, extending Communist influence throughout the heartland of Asia. This provided an additional source of East-West conflict, especially after the outbreak of the Korean War in 1950. In addition, a continuous conflict developed over the islands controlled by the Nationalist Chinese government located on Taiwan. The Communist system was initially unified through a series of bilateral "Treaties of Friendship and Mutual Assistance." In 1955, however, following the rearmament of West Germany and its entry into NATO, the Warsaw Treaty Organization was formed, bringing together the Soviet Union and the Communist nations of Eastern Europe in a military alliance. Alignments involving the Asian members of the bloc remained on a bilateral basis.

Despite formation of these two competing alliance systems, tensions appeared to relax slightly following the end of the Korean War and the death of Stalin in 1953. This relaxation was exemplified by the first meeting between Soviet and western heads of state since the end of World War II at the Geneva Summit Conference of 1955. The "Big Four" leaders met to discuss the reunification of Germany and disarmament. Despite the failure of this conference to produce any significant results and the Soviet military response to the uprising in Hungary in 1956, a partial détente was maintained tenuously throughout the remainder of the 1950s. This culminated in a visit by Soviet Premier Khrushchev to the United States in 1959 and the scheduling of another summit conference for 1960.

This conference was never held, however, as the Soviet Union shot down an American U-2 plane carrying out high altitude aerial reconnaissance over the Soviet Union in 1960. Khrushchev used this incident to justify the breakup of the summit conference. A renewed series of tension-producing events developed over Berlin in 1961, climaxing in the erection of the Berlin Wall in August of that year. There were widespread expectations of renewed Soviet pressure on Berlin following the congressional elections of 1962. But three weeks prior to the elections the United States detected a Soviet nuclear buildup on the island of Cuba. President Kennedy responded by declaring a naval "quarantine" of Cuba, preventing the shipment of strategic materials to the island. This action eventually forced the Soviet Union to withdraw their missile bases from the island. This confrontation between the superpowers, however, probably brought the world closer to nuclear war than at any other time in its history.

As a result of the Cuban missile crisis Soviet and American leaders both recognized the dangers of nuclear war. This realization was apparently reflected in the signing in 1963 of the Partial Nuclear Test Ban Treaty, the first in a series of limited but nevertheless significant arms control agreements between the great powers. The partial détente which followed the Cuban missile crisis was highly tenuous, being broken by events such as the Arab-Israeli conflict in the Middle East which escalated in June 1967, and which threatened to involve the great powers directly, the intervention of Soviet armed forces in Czechoslovakia in 1968, the Soviet and American decisions to build and deploy antiballistic missile defense systems (ABM's) and more advanced offensive missile systems (MIRV's), and finally the war in Vietnam. Probably the most clear-cut escalation of that war occurred in February 1965, when the United States commenced regular bombings of North Vietnam. These raids, which lasted on a fairly regular basis until March 1968, were accompanied by a rapid buildup of American ground combat troops in Southeast Asia, reaching almost a half million men by 1968. Thus, while the general trend throughout the last two-thirds of the 1960s appeared to be toward coexistence between the two major alliance systems, the Vietnam War and several other conflictual incidents and military decisions remained as continuing sources of conflict.

The strength of the general trend toward détente throughout the 1960s, however, was illustrated by the major efforts toward improved East-West relations taken in the first few years of the 1970s. Soviet-American arms control negotiations continued on an expanded basis in the Strategic Arms Limitation Talks, culminating in a visit by President Nixon to Moscow in May 1972. Even more striking was the improvement in relations between the United States and the Chinese People's Republic which grew out of President Nixon's trip to mainland China and his personal negotiations with Mao Tse-Tung and Chou En-Lai in February 1972.

In short, the period since the end of World War II has been characterized by changing levels of conflict in the relations between the two great power blocs. The overall trend toward increased détente on a number of issues has been accompanied by a change in the structure of the international system. The tight bipolar system which emerged in the late 1940s has become looser, as evidenced especially by the increasing role of international actors such as the United Nations and its various agencies as well as the increasing power of a bloc composed mostly of newly independent and nonaligned nations. One probable consequence of this has been a reduction of the unity of the two great power alliances and the emergence of a system described by Togliatti, the former Italian Communist Party First Secretary, as "polycentrism," the development of multiple, independent centers of power throughout the international system.

Perhaps the greatest transition occurred during the period of relative détente in the mid and late 1950s. In the Communist alliance, Khrushchev attacked Stalin at the Twentieth Congress of the Communist Party of the Soviet Union in 1956; at the same time he acknowledged the possibility of multiple roads to socialism. Whereas in the past the Soviets had always insisted upon the superiority of the Soviet revolutionary model as the basis for the development of all Communist societies, now a degree of diversity would be tolerated. These events opened up a major schism between the Soviet Union and the Peoples' Republic of China. While taking advantage of this tolerance of diversity, the Chinese Communists also attacked the new doctrines of Soviet "revisionism" and argued for the superiority of the Chinese revolutionary model, especially as applied to the less developed countries. An ideological conflict thus developed between the two leading powers within the Communist system which spilled over into other substantive areas and drastically curtailed Sino-Soviet cooperation, especially in the economic and military spheres. The suspicion with which Soviet leaders viewed the Chinese-American rapprochement of 1972 was further dramatic evidence of the deepening split in the political and diplomatic arena. At the same time the Eastern European members of the Communist system also sought greater independence from Soviet domination, leading to violence in the cases of Hungary in 1956 and Czechoslovakia in 1968, while taking less violent forms in countries like Poland and Rumania. The overall impact of these events, however, was a substantial reduction in the cohesion of the Communist system.

Similarly, in the NATO alliance a conflict between the United States and France was at the heart of the reduced cohesion which appeared within the alliance throughout the 1960s. Soon after De Gaulle's return to power in France in 1958, he began to attack Anglo-American domination of the NATO alliance. De Gaulle contended that American commitments to use nuclear weapons to defend Europe in the event of a Soviet attack were not reliable. Thus, increased French autonomy was a necessity in the military sphere. He asserted French independence from the American nuclear deterrent by speeding up the French nuclear weapons program begun in 1957 under the government of Premier Guy Mollet. These policies led to the withdrawal of French forces from the integrated NATO command in 1966. Throughout the dispute De Gaulle insisted on a distinction between the North Atlantic alliance as a mutual defense commitment, which still served a significant function, and the military pact including an integrated NATO military force, which in his view had no future. He thus committed France to continued membership in NATO beyond its renewal in 1969, unless there was a very basic change towards détente in East-West relations, a policy generally continued in a slightly moderated form under President Pompidou. Limited though this conflict was in scope, it did significantly affect NATO's cohesion, especially since it was mirrored by other less dramatic but still significant disputes among NATO members. For example, limited disputes developed between the United Kingdom and France, the Federal Republic of Germany and France, Norway and the United States, among others. The consequence of these events was an overall decline in NATO's cohesion, roughly parallel to the development of polycentrism within the Communist system.

This brief summary provides a background for the problems analyzed in this chapter and in Chapter Four. Our major task, therefore, will be to test hypotheses concerning the effects of East-West conflict or détente on the internal cohesion of NATO and the Communist system.

Theory and Hypotheses

In Chapter Four we will be testing one hypothesis about the effects of conflict and détente on alliance cohesion and two corollaries to that hypothesis. These may be stated as follows:

HYPOTHESIS: *The greater the inter-alliance conflict, the greater the intra-alliance cohesion; conversely, the greater the inter-alliance détente, the less the intra-alliance cohesion.*

COROLLARY 1: *Inter-alliance conflict will exert symmetrical effects on the cohesion of competing alliances.*

COROLLARY 2: *The tighter the polarity of the international system, the greater the cohesion of component alliances; conversely, the looser the polarity, the less the alliance cohesion.*

The general hypothesis may be derived from a simple model of rational decision making by alliance members. As Liska has noted using economic terminology, "alliances aim at maximizing gains and sharing liabilities." [2] Therefore, alliances can remain cohesive only if they are able to maintain a favorable balance of gains to liabilities for their members. We may assume that, other things being equal, national decision-makers prefer to act independently since collaboration inevitably involves a number of liabilities, including restrictions on their latitude for decision. Therefore, alignment becomes a rational policy when an external force threatens the nation with greater liabilities than those entailed by collaboration.[3] The primary collective benefit which an alliance can provide its members is through the aggregation of group resources in defense against the common enemy. Thus, alliance members are more likely to engage in collaborative behavior and exhibit consensus with their allies on basic issues during times of external threat than during periods of relative détente. If the threat expressed between alliance systems is relatively symmetrical, one would also expect the effects to be felt relatively similarly in both alliances. Corollary 1 consequently predicts that increased conflict between alliances will produce symmetrical increases in the cohesion of both alliances; conversely, decreasing conflict and increasing détente should be related to a decline in the cohesion of both coalitions. Finally, since a tight bipolar structure within the international system involves a rigid division of the world between two competing systems, conflict between alliances is likely to be greater than in less tightly organized systems. Therefore, Corollary 2 predicts that alliance cohesion will decline as the tight polarity of the international system is reduced over time.

At this point we must clarify our definition of the dependent variable, alliance cohesion. Definitions of cohesion have generally emphasized both attitudinal and behavioral components. Behavioral definitions of group cohesion emphasize the direct nature of relations and information flow between members of the group. Furthermore, they assume that actors are collaborating in such a way as to coordinate their individual behaviors within some kind of group or organizational context.

Behavioral definitions of cohesion alone are not satisfactory, however. While behavior must be coordinated in any cohesive group, it does not follow that cohesive groups will necessarily be characterized by similarity of behavior. Indeed, different members of a group may be expected to perform specialized roles in response to the demands and needs of the group, so that a division of labor may contribute to alliance cohesion. Hence we need to add an attitudinal component to our definition of cohesion.

This attitudinal component of cohesion has often been defined in social-psychological studies as the shared attractions or consensus among the members of a group. For example, Festinger and his colleagues have defined cohesiveness as the "total field, or resultant, for forces acting on members to remain in a group, or, in other words, as the attraction of a group for its members." [4] In this case, cohesion may be viewed as attitudinal consensus among alliance members about alliance objectives and targets. Some writers in international relations have suggested that the behavioral and attitudinal components of cohesion ought to be related to one another. Scott has suggested that, "when the perceived *interests* of actors *conflict,* their *attitudes* will tend to be *hostile,* and their *behavior* will tend to involve *conflict.* Conversely, it suggests that when the perceived *interests* of actors are held in *common,* their *attitudes* will tend to be *friendly* and their *behavior* will tend to be *collaborative.*" [5]

Some of the small group research on cohesiveness, however, raises at least some doubts about whether these two sets of components will actually be closely related. Eisman has attempted to operationalize the concept of cohesiveness through the use of five operational measures: 1) a sociometric index based on friendship; 2) a direct rating of group attractiveness; 3) average number of reasons given by group members for belonging to the group; 4) number of same reasons for group membership given by a majority of members; and 5) the degree of similarity existing among group members with respect to their values.[6] Finding no significant correlations among any pair of these five indices, she concluded that "we have been mistaken in considering cohesiveness as a unitary concept. As a reflection of the total field of forces to remain in a group, it may be best measured not by one instrument but by a composite instrument that attempts to sample all of the forces, or at least the major ones." [7]

We may, therefore, assume that cohesion is composed of some mix of both behavioral and attitudinal components, although the relationship between these two sets of components is not at all clear. This consideration has been taken into account in developing empirical measures. The extent to which cohesion is a unitary concept when applied to international alliances remains an open question to be taken up later in this chapter.

One further problem with cohesion in international alliances is that it may be derived either from group consensus or from coercion. While a definition might exclude cohesion based on coercion, this type of behavior is often extremely difficult to differentiate empirically from that based on consensual acceptance of group norms. This distinction may be made by a determination of the source of liabilities for alliance members. Presumably most consensual alliances are based upon an attempt to minimize liabilities which threaten the group from outside, and the alliance thereby provides benefits for its members in the form of protection against an external threat. Conversely, in coercive alliances, one major source of liabilities for noncohesive behavior may be the dominant member within the coalition instead of, or in addition to, the external enemy. In this case, at least one benefit of membership is a reduction of the threat from one's own allies. For example, when Czechoslovakia began to deviate from the Communist system in 1968, Soviet action was designed to make clear the severe liabilities which nonconformity would entail.

Whether based on coercion or consensus, however, there appears to be validity in Liska's argument that alliances can remain cohesive only insofar as they are able to "maintain the initial balance between the gains and liabilities which can be attributed to the alliance," [8] regardless of the source of those liabilities. Therefore, while recognizing the significance of the distinction between alliances based on consensus and coercion, we shall treat both as cohesive so long as members maintain similar attitudes about objectives and targets and continue to behave in a collaborative manner.

We may now turn to a more thorough discussion of our hypothesis that alliance cohesion is a direct function of the degree of conflict or cooperation between alliances. Among the most important discussions of this hypothesis as applied to many different kinds of groups is found in the work of the nineteenth-century German social scientist, Georg Simmel.

A basic hypothesis in Simmel's work is that, as long as the basic values of a group remain intact, inter-group conflict tends to strengthen the internal unity of the group. Groups at peace can allow antagonistic members to exist, since they can go their own way without creating severe internal schisms. On the other hand, conflict "pulls the members so tightly together and subjects them to such a uniform impulse that they either must completely get along with, or completely repel, one another." [9] Simmel further asserts that in the absence of a central sovereign power a coalition will tend to break apart unless all members share a common external danger. Thus, conflict increases the concentration of an existing group, blurring boundaries between individual group members; conflict may even bring actors together who would otherwise have little or no contact with one another.

Coser has expanded Simmel's theory, hypothesizing that "outside conflict will strengthen the internal cohesion of the group and increase centralization." [10] Coser's argument suggests that external conflict has a variety of unifying effects on a group. It enhances the group's sense or self-perception of identity by clarifying the boundaries separating it from the surrounding world.[11] Conflict also mobilizes the energies of the group and causes it to increase its efforts in its own defense, again requiring enhanced cohesion. This does not mean, however, that all components of the group will respond by performing the same functions in the face of a common enemy or that their behavior will be identical. In highly complex groups there is likely to be a high degree of role differentiation and a related division of labor in the face of the external threat. Substantial centralization may be required to coordinate the various group components which are performing their own specialized functions.[12] Therefore, the major impact of the external threat may be evidenced in the realm of attitudes and values, inasmuch as conflict frequently affects a group by creating a "reaffirmation of their value system against the outside enemy." [13] Another aspect of the effect of external conflict is that the group tends to be more intolerant of internal dissent. This may even be carried so far as to search for internal enemies in the form of dissenters who may then be removed, either voluntarily or involuntarily, from the group.[14]

Perhaps the most important point is that external conflict may bring together unrelated units when their pragmatic interests coincide. Since the formation of one alliance may be perceived by the units with which a competitive relationship exists as a threatening act in itself, this may lead to the formation of counter-alliances. The result is a tendency toward bipolarity. Alliances which exist only for the purpose of a specific conflict are likely to be highly unstable. They will either dissolve after accomplishing the purposes for which they were created or they will develop new purposes to provide for their continued existence.[15]

Coser also suggests one major qualification for the hypothesis that external conflict increases internal cohesion. Conflict may enhance the cohesion of a group only when it concerns values, beliefs, and goals which do not contradict the basic assumptions or consensual values upon which group unity is based. The preexisting structure of conflict within the group is an essential variable. If the group is divided by crosscutting cleavages, conflict may help alleviate or reduce the intensity of these internal conflicts. On the other hand, if the group is divided by a single issue, especially when that embraces its consensual values, then external conflict may split rather than unify that group. Thus the degree of consensus prior to the outbreak of a conflict seems to be an important factor affecting group cohesion. If a group lacks consensus, outside threat leads not to increased cohesion but to general apathy and disintegration.[16]

Propositions relating inter-group conflict and intra-group cohesion have also been suggested, but infrequently tested, by many students of international relations. For example, Kaplan suggests that conflict between actor systems produces greater needs for cooperation within each system.[17] Similarly, Liska argues that a common enemy is perhaps the single most important cause for the formation of an alliance. In the absence of an external threat, small powers are unlikely to attempt to ally with large powers out of fear that their identity will be abridged. Greater powers will normally be unlikely to seek out allies so as not to overextend their commitments and resources. However, when an external threat appears, smaller powers may rally around the larger states to obtain protection against the common enemy. At the same time stronger states may seek out the weaker states in order to keep their resources out of the control of the adversary. Therefore, both large and small states may perceive common benefits from alliance membership in the face of an external threat.[18]

There is a limit to this phenomenon, however, particularly when there is a disparity between the willingness or the capability of the bloc leader to protect various allies from the external threat and its willingness and capability to defend itself. The ability of a major power to defend its lesser allies may rise as its own homeland becomes more invulnerable to an enemy attack. However, this may mean that the lesser allies will remain relatively more vulnerable to enemy attacks than the bloc leader. Therefore, this may lead to a situation in which the lesser powers resent this disparity among alliance members, even though it enhances the ability of the superpower to defend them. Given both the political resentment and the relatively increased vulnerability to enemy attack on the part of the lesser members of an alliance, this situation may, at times of external threat, lead to reduced rather than augmented alliance cohesion.[19]

There are also several significant modifications and additions to this hypothesis. First, inter-bloc conflict will tend to increase the hierarchical nature of alliances, increasing centralization. This implies that external threat will increase the organizational rigidities of alliances, whereas détente might be accompanied by a reduction in the hierarchical organization.[20] It has also been suggested that second-ranking allies during periods of relative détente may not only refuse to be dependent upon the bloc leader, but they may increase their contacts across alliances to enhance their negotiating positions vis-à-vis the hegemonic power of their own alliance leader.[21] Diplomatic and economic exchanges between France and Rumania are perhaps illustrative of the type of cross-alliance interaction which may be possible during periods of détente.

Second, alliances which derive their cohesion from the threat of a common enemy may disintegrate rapidly when that threat is removed. There may be a certain spill-over if integrative habits are learned during the period of external conflict and are then carried on even after that threat has disappeared. However, when the initial basis for an alliance is defense against an external enemy, "any diminution of the external threat or of the will to meet it will tend to undermine cohesion and render futile any attempts to save the alliance by inward-directed 'diversions.' " [22]

Third, external conflict may not necessarily have an integrative effect on an alliance if the threat is perceived as directed at only one or a few members of the alliance so that other members perceive no threat to themselves. Liska, for example, has suggested that the problems for decision making in alliances like NATO are greatest when the external threat is directed at only one or several countries rather than at the entire alliance. [23] In such a case it is possible that the allies, in the spirit of mutual commitment, may come to one another's assistance even though there is no direct danger to themselves. However, in some cases, they may fall back on their own self-interest and leave the threatened ally to shift for itself. Thus when the alliance entails an uneven distribution of liabilities, cohesion may be disrupted.

Fourth, the relationship suggested by the hypothesis does not necessarily operate in one direction alone. Not only may international conflict be treated as a cause of increased alliance cohesion, but that cohesion may itself contribute to intensified international conflict. The increased unity of alliances may tend to enhance the polarity and rigidity in the international system, thereby increasing the degree of inter-alliance distrust and conflict and sometimes leading to war. [24] Some empirical support for this proposition can be found in the twentieth century in the research of Singer and Small reported in Chapter One, although this was contradicted by their data for the nineteenth century when alliance aggregation and war were inversely related. [25]

With the exception of the study by Singer and Small, the before mentioned literature on our hypothesis and its qualifications has generally been supported only with impressionistic examinations of historical events. This points to a need to organize these propositions in a more systematic fashion and to test them rigorously.

Indeed, the only systematic tests of these propositions have been in the small group. A brief examination of that literature also yields some interesting possible areas for further exploration at the level of the international system. Two experimental studies may be cited to illustrate this point. The "Robbers' Cave" experiment involved the observation of two competitive groups of children. The researchers concluded that, when the two groups met in competitive engagements, "in-group solidarity and cooperativeness increased." [26] A study of the effects of two conditions, crisis and noncrisis, on the cooperative behavior of groups playing an experimental game suggested several qualifications to this conclusion, however. In this study, group integration decreased during a crisis if either a likely solution to the crisis was unavailable or if a likely competitive solution was available. On the contrary, group integration increased during a crisis if a likely cooperative solution of the crisis was available.[27]

These findings suggest that, if a common solution to a crisis is available, the external threat will tend to integrate a group as an obvious way to defend against that common threat. However, if no solution is available, there is little to be gained or lost either by increasing collaboration or going it alone, so that no increase in integration was exhibited. In addition, if the only solution to the crisis is a competitive one, usually resulting from the kind of situation suggested by Coser in which the group lacks a basic consensus, then these findings suggest that external threat will tend to split a group apart.

In summary, we have hypothesized that conflict between alliances will tend to bring about increased cohesion in competing alliances, provided that the values of the alliance are intact and that the mutual threat is distributed relatively evenly among all members of both alliances. The resulting increase in the cohesion of both coalitions may provide increased mutual threat between alliances, thereby intensifying the inter-alliance conflict. These variables are hypothesized to be in a mutually reinforcing relationship, which may tend to produce patterns of spiralling interactions either between more intense conflict and increased cohesion or conversely between reduced conflict and declining cohesion.

Corollary 1 to the hypothesis stated that conflict between alliances will tend to have a symmetrical effect on both alliances. This hypothesis may be applied to the postwar interactions between the Communist system and NATO, which have been formed and have changed over time in response to the actions of each other. Thus, NATO was formed in response to a perceived threat from the Communist bloc, and this in turn was followed by the formation of the Warsaw Pact, which in some respects is a mirror image of NATO.[28]

Corollary 2 to the hypothesis stated that tight bipolar international systems are likely to be characterized by highly cohesive alliances; as the international system moves towards a loose bipolar system, then the cohesion of the component alliances is likely to decline. Thus conflicts which occur after bipolarity has declined may not be as integrative as in previous periods when bipolarity within the international system was relatively tight.

In some ways this proposition may appear to be a tautology in that one characteristic of declining bipolarity may be a reduction in the cohesion of component alliances. However, there are other characteristics of the international system which may affect a change from relatively tight to relatively loose bipolarity, including an increased role for mediating and nonaligned actors. These general differences may be clarified by examining definitions of tight and loose bipolar systems.

A tight bipolar system is one in which there are two major blocs in the international system, organized hierarchically and dominated by the two major actors in international politics. Each bloc acts at least to match the unity and capability of the opposing bloc. There are no significant universal actors such as a neutral bloc or an international organization in such a system to mediate between the opposing blocs. Each bloc is prepared to go to war to prevent the other from achieving a position of preponderant strength or from dominating the entire international system.[29]

A loose bipolar system operates according to the same rules, except that a universal actor plays a more important role in trying to reduce the incompatibilities between blocs, and nations belonging to neither bloc act to "coordinate their national objectives with those of the universal actor and to subordinate the objectives of bloc actors to those of the universal actor." [30]

A major feature of the postwar period would seem to be a transition from an international system approximating the tight bipolar system in its essential structures to one more representative of the loose bipolar system. The increasingly important role of the less developed countries, many of which have become independent nations during this period, has been a major change in the international system since about 1950. This change is expected to have an impact on the cohesion of the two postwar alliances. In a tight bipolar system communications are almost entirely restricted to the blocs themselves, whereas in a looser bipolar system communications between blocs are likely to increase and bloc cohesion is likely to decline.[31] As the tight bipolar system declines, multiple centers of power are likely to appear in competing alliances, and secondary allies may attempt to establish improved relations with members of the other bloc to increase their negotiating power against their major ally.[32]

One further phenomenon which may occur following the decline of bipolarity in the international system is an increase in the number of viable competing alternative alignments available to an alliance member. Hence an increase in the frequency of realignment is likely. In a bipolar system in which there are great differences in power between bloc leaders and followers, alliances cannot easily be reshuffled.[33] On the other hand, as the system becomes more multipolar the opportunities for realignment or for remaining outside the framework of alliances increase.[34] The decline of bipolarity thus increases substantially the degree of uncertainty present in the international system concerning the patterns of alliances.[35] This phenomenon in itself may have a disintegrative effect on alliances.

There may be some exceptions to this corollary, however. For example, even in a tight bipolar system local conflicts may arise between members of the same alliance or involving secondary states in both alliances. This may result in a situation in which "local adversaries seek great-power support by aligning on different sides of the larger, dominant conflict." [36] The split between Greece and Turkey over Cyprus may serve as an example of how a local conflict can contravene the alliance configuration created by the dominant international cleavage.

In summary, the hypothesis under investigation in this and the next chapter asserts that cohesion of alliances is in large part a function of the degree of conflict or cooperation between alliances. Thus conflict may bring alliances into existence and preserve their cohesion, whereas détente may reduce the cohesion of alliances or lead to their disintegration. This relationship between conflict and cohesion implies that two conflicting alliances will generally tend to behave symmetrically vis-à-vis one another. Finally, cohesion may also be a function of the degree of polarity in the international system; if polarity is tight, then conflict is likely to produce very cohesive alliances, whereas in a loose bipolar system conflict may no longer produce as much cohesion in competing alliances.

A Design for Empirical Research

To test this hypothesis and its corollaries we must be able to measure three sets of variables. The dependent variable in all hypotheses is the degree of alliance cohesion, defined in both behavioral and attitudinal terms. The independent variable in the main hypothesis is the degree of conflict between alliance systems and the perceptions by members of each alliance of the threat emanating from the opposing alliance. Corollary 2 has as its independent variable the relative tightness or looseness of the polarity in the international system. We shall next develop measurement models for each of these three variables, and then we shall discuss briefly the major research techniques required to collect data called for in these models.

Separate measurement models must be developed for the analysis of behavioral and attitudinal components of alliance cohesion. For the behavioral component we are interested in measuring the direct interactions among alliance members. Because this aspect of alliance cohesion has been defined as behavioral collaboration among members, the cohesion of an alliance may be measured on the basis of the mean proportion of cooperation relative to conflict in all dyads connecting all alliance members. The number of dyads always equals $\frac{N^2 - N}{2}$, where N is the number of alliance members. Thus, to measure the cohesion in NATO at any one point in time it would be necessary to determine the proportion of the total interactions among all fifteen members (105 dyads) which was characterized by cooperative as contrasted to conflictual behavior.

The attitudinal component of cohesion is considerably more complex to measure. The optimal research strategy might be to measure the mutual attraction of all members of a coalition for one another, such as by measuring the positive attitudes expressed by each towards all others. This procedure entails several difficulties, however. There are few publicly available communications exchanged among members of the Communist system and NATO. This problem is severe since the number of references which would be necessary for this type of model is $N^2 - N$, that is, 110 for the Communist system and 210 for NATO. Even those public communications which do exist are often very misleading; until very recently, allies seldom made direct criticisms of one another. For example, even one of the most serious disputes, that between the Soviet Union and the Chinese Peoples' Republic, was carried on until about 1963 through indirect attack, allegory, obscure jargon, and even omission of key concepts.[37] The problem of missing data would be even more severe for two countries which never referred to one another because they were not very closely related to each other, as for example Iceland and Turkey within NATO.

As a result of these difficulties, we have employed an indirect research strategy for measuring the attitudinal component of alliance cohesion. Cohesion was measured using a model of the co-orientation of decision-makers toward an external actor which is perceived by all members of the alliance. Thus, the consensus about the external enemy has become our indicator of the attitudinal aspect of cohesion. In other words, the differences in the perceptions of the enemy by various alliance members will serve as an indicator of intra-alliance conflict. This assumes that the more similarly the alliance members perceive the same object, the greater will be the cohesion among them.

Our model for measuring cohesion is derived from Newcomb's A-B-X model, a simple model of interpersonal communication.[38] A and B are treated as interdependent actors who have simultaneous orientations toward an external object, X. The three parts of this model are interrelated in a system characterized by a balance of forces which creates " 'strains' toward preferred states of equilibrium." [39] Equilibrium exists when the number of negative bonds connecting the three actors is either two or zero; in other words, if A and B agree in their perceptions of X, then they should be positively related, whereas if they disagree about X then they should be negatively related. These four possible balanced states of the triad are depicted in Figure 1.

If one assumes that a given triad is balanced, then one may be able to infer relations between two actors, A and B, from their joint relations with a third actor, X. This triangular relationship may be characterized by a strain toward balance which exists only if three scope conditions are met:

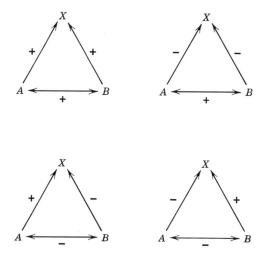

Figure 1. The *A–B–X* triangles constitute the four possible balanced configurations of the model; any other configuration is unbalanced with pressures to return to one of these balanced states.

the members of the system must be highly salient to one another; the object of reference must be important to all members; and the object must have joint relevance for all members. If these conditions are met and balance may be assumed to exist, then the *A-B-X* model suggests that attitudinal consensus may be a valid indicator of direct relationships between two actors, *A* and *B*.[40]

The implications of this model for the study of alliance cohesion are apparent. If cohesion is defined in terms of co-orientation toward salient external objects or events, then symmetry of orientations may be assumed to be a valid indicator of cohesion. Deutsch refers to this process as the establishment between actors of "mutual relevance" and "responsiveness", similar evaluations, by enhancing mutual responsiveness, tend to enhance cohesion.[41] Thus, co-orientation by actors in an international coalition toward an external actor or event would be likely to enhance cohesion among those actors. This may be summarized by the following postulate, upon which our attitudinal measurement of cohesion was based:

The greater the similarity of orientations toward a common external object by the decision-makers in all member nations of an international alliance, the greater the cohesion of the alliance, at least with regard to that object.

We may attempt to determine the direction and intensity of *A*'s and *B*'s and all other alliance members' attitudes towards the same *X* along a positive-negative dimension. We may treat relations between each pair of allies separately, and an alliance with more than two members may be depicted as a system of multiple triangles around one common X.

The configuration for a five-member alliance is illustrated in Figure 2. In such an alliance there are $\dfrac{N^2 - N}{2}$ (ten in this case) dyadic relationships connecting the member countries. We may employ the notion of "distance" between nations in each pattern.[42] These distances may be measured as differences in orientations toward X. For example, if nation A perceives X with an average score of -1.0 and B perceives the same as -2.0, the difference, 1.0, is an index of the distance between A and B. Thus, comparisons of interaction patterns in each period may be made on the basis of the sum of internal differences.[43] If the sum of internal differences was greater at time $t+1$ than at t, we could conclude that cohesion within the system as a whole had declined. Thus, this model provides a basis for comparing the degree of cohesion in one alliance at different points in time, for comparing differences between any two or more dyadic interactions between allies within an alliance at any given period of time, and for

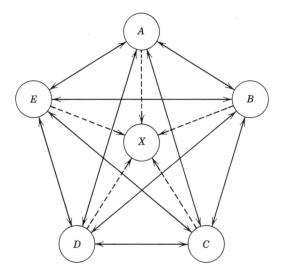

Figure 2. A model of the co-orientation of five actors (A, B, C, D, and E) towards an external object (X) is depicted above. This model is composed of ten individual A–B–X triangles. Thus the balance of the entire system is considered to be a function of the extent to which all ten individual triangles are balanced. If balance within the entire system is assumed to exist, then the ten dyadic relations (represented by solid two-way arrows) linking these five actors may be inferred from the similarity of their perception of the common X (represented by the dotted one-way arrows).

comparing the degree of cohesion in different alliances at the same period of time.

The degree of conflict or cooperation between alliance systems, the independent variable in the main hypothesis, also has an attitudinal and a behavioral component. The behavioral component may also be measured as the direct interactions among members of opposing alliance systems. We may assume that conflict between alliances will increase when the proportion of all interactions characterized by cooperation relative to conflict declines; conversely, an increase in the proportion of cooperation between alliances may be taken as an indicator of increased détente.

The attitudinal component of inter-alliance relations refers to perceptions by members of one alliance of the threat stemming from the opposing alliance. Increased perceptions of threat may be measured as a composite of perceptions of the other alliance as negative, strong, and active. Conversely, less threatening nations are likely to be perceived as more positive, weaker, and/or more passive. This aspect of inter-alliance conflict will be measured by the perceptions of threat in the actions of the other alliance.

A third variable is the degree of tightness or looseness of the polarity of the international system, the independent variable in Corollary 2. The distinction between a tight and a loose bipolar system as defined previously is so crude that precise measures were virtually impossible to obtain. However, we may assume that the international system was characterized by relatively tight bipolarity immediately after World War II. By 1967, however, the world more closely approximated a loose bipolar system. The presence of more nonaligned nations in the international system and the expanded function performed by international organizations indicated the appearance of a looser bipolar system. We may also make the simplifying assumption that this transition has proceeded in one general direction over the twenty-year period from 1948 through 1967. This is not to say that inter-bloc relations have consistently improved; data to be presented later will indicate that this is not the case. We are merely assuming here that the role of the nonaligned nations and international organizations in mediating between the great power blocs has generally increased over this period of time. Thus, the passage of time may serve as our empirical indicator of loosening polarity.

These indicators may then serve as measures to test our hypotheses. We have employed two research techniques to collect the data required by these indicators: computer content analysis and events interaction data.

For the attitudinal measures of cohesion and perceived external threat we have used computer content analysis of documents authored by decision-makers in eleven Communist countries and eight NATO countries during four postwar periods. These data were thus used as attitudinal yardsticks against which perceptions of hostility or threat could be compared, against which the attitudinal consensus within different alliances could be compared, and against which changes in the consensus within both alliances could be compared at different points in time. Content analysis was used to measure the responses of both major postwar alliances to four significant events in order to determine the amount of threat which each alliance member perceived to be emanating from the other alliance and their consensus about their enemies. In our choice of periods, we wanted to be able to distinguish events on two variables, time passage and the degree of intersystem conflict or détente. In this sense we have developed a quasi-experimental design, which gives us approximate control over two independent variables through the use of time series data.[44] Therefore, we selected documents representing the first reaction of each country as soon as possible after the following four dates:

June 25, 1950, the date of the outbreak of the Korean War;
July 17, 1955, the opening of the Geneva Summit Conference;
July 25, 1963, the signing of the Partial Nuclear Test Ban Treaty;
February 7, 1965, the first day of regular American bombing missions over North Vietnam.

In order to account for the time variable, we selected two events before and two after the crucial period from 1956 to 1958 when most scholars seem to agree that significant changes got underway in both the Communist system and NATO. In 1956, Khrushchev made his famous "secret speech" on de-Stalinization to the Twentieth Congress of the Communist Party of the Soviet Union which was followed in the same year by revolts in Poland and Hungary, all marking a transition point in the structure of the Communist system. Similarly, De Gaulle assumed power in France in 1958, and shortly thereafter he began to assert France's independence from NATO.

To account for the degree of conflict, two events of relatively high inter-alliance conflict and two events of détente were selected before and after this transition period. The outbreak of the Korean War in 1950 and the escalation of the Vietnam War in February 1965 were chosen as two comparable conflict events spread over this time span. Both were wars in Asia involving conflicts between divided countries, with the United States actively involved militarily in both. Similarly, the 1955 Geneva Summit Conference and the 1963 Test Ban Conference represent perhaps the most significant attempts at East-West negotiations on each side of the transition period mentioned above. Although we cannot attribute any differences between the first two and the last two events to time alone, we have attempted to select the most comparable events possible in an historical, non-experimental situation. Thus, while other factors may play a role in influencing any changes from the earlier to the later sets of periods, time may certainly be considered to be an important factor.

We have then compared the responses of the members of NATO and the Communist system to these events. For the Communist system, the responses of eleven countries, including the Soviet Union, the Peoples' Republic of China, Albania, the German Democratic Republic, Czechoslovakia, Hungary, Poland, Rumania, Bulgaria, the Democratic Republic of Korea, and the Democratic Republic of Vietnam, were content analyzed. Three countries ruled by the Communist party—Yugoslavia, Outer Mongolia, and Cuba—were excluded for different reasons.[45] Although North Vietnam was included in this list, it did not become a Communist country formally until 1954, when Vietnam was divided by the Geneva agreements. For the 1950 period we used documents monitored from the official radio of the Viet Minh under the command of Ho Chi Minh, and this exception must be taken into account in evaluating the results reported later.

NATO is composed of fifteen nations, including the United States, the United Kingdom, France, Canada, the German Federal Republic, Norway, Denmark, Iceland, the Netherlands, Belgium, Luxembourg, Portugal, Italy, Greece, and Turkey. In the NATO case problems of obtaining documents were far more serious than for the Communist system since systematic records of official positions are not always made available publicly in standard sources. Therefore, for the attitudinal measures we were restricted to a complete set of documents for all four periods from only eight countries: the United States, the United Kingdom, Canada, France, the German Federal Republic, Italy, Norway, and Denmark. While behavioral data for NATO was collected for all fifteen nations, the results from the attitudinal data must be limited to only these eight countries. As was the case for North Vietnam in 1950, West Germany was not at that time really a sovereign nation. For the document included from 1950 we have thus had to include a statement authored by the office of the Western High Commissioners for Germany, comprised of representatives of the United States, the United Kingdom, and France, although it also included numerous statements from native West German officials and press. These special circumstances must be taken into account in interpreting the results.

The first reaction to each event, authored by the decision-makers in each country, was analyzed if it contained references to the common external object, the *X*, toward which we wanted to measure co-orientation. For the Communist system this was the entire western bloc and the United States alone, and for NATO it was similarly the entire Communist system and the Soviet Union alone. The first document written after each date listed above which met this criterion was selected, in accordance with procedures summarized in Appendix B.

These documents were then content analyzed. Content analysis such as that employed in this study has been defined as "any research technique for making inferences by systematically and objectively identifying specified characteristics of messages." [46] As applied in this analysis, we have used a computer program with a standard dictionary coded on basic dimensions of human attitudes in order to analyze and compare the various texts collected by the methods just described.[47] The Stanford version of the General Inquirer was used, including a dictionary which contains over 4000 English words coded on three dimensions of the "semantic differential" found by Osgood and his colleagues to be basic to human attitudes in many cultures: [48]

Evaluative: (Positive) $+3, +2, +1, 0, -1, -2, -3$ (Negative)

Potency: (Strong) $+3, +2, +1, 0, -1, -2, -3$ (Weak)

Activity: (Active) $+3, +2, +1, 0, -1, -2, -3$ (Passive)

This procedure assumes that many relevant discriminations in individuals' perceptions of objects are made in terms of these three attitudinal dimensions. Furthermore, when all dictionary words are scaled on these three dimensions, comparisons among document authors' perceptions of events can be made against a constant yardstick.

To test our hypotheses we determined where each nation in both alliances rated the opposing alliance and its leading member on the evaluative dimension. We then computed the differences between each pair of nations in their perceptions of the enemy, and these differences were averaged across all pairs of nations within each alliance. In other words, we were able to compare the degree of attitudinal consensus in each alliance in different time periods on the basis of the average differences in perceptions of the opponent among members of each alliance. For example, to test our hypothesis about the effects of high conflict versus détente on alliance coorientation, we wanted to compare the differences between the high tension periods (1950 and 1965) and the low tension periods (1955 and 1963) to see if the countries in each coalition were significantly closer together during the periods of crisis than during periods of relaxed tensions. This hypothesis predicted that the average differences among the members of the Communist system in their perceptions of the United States and NATO would be greater in 1955 and 1963 than in 1950 and 1965; similarly, it predicted greater distance among the members of NATO in their perceptions of the Communist system and the Soviet Union in the years of détente compared to the years of greater conflict. In order to complement the inferences based on attitudinal orientations toward the enemy, we have also developed a behavioral indicator of alliance cohesion. We employed events interaction data to scale interactions among nations along a dimension ranging from conflict to cooperation. Thus the basic postulate upon which our behavioral measure of alliance cohesion was based is as follows:

The greater the cooperation and the less the conflict among members of an alliance, the greater the cohesion within the alliance.

Events interaction data simply entail the recording of a series of discrete events, including the bilateral and multilateral interactions of nation-states. These interactions are drawn from chronologies of events and then scaled along some relevant dimension, such as conflict and cooperation. In all cases events are treated as dyadic interactions at discrete points in time, and frequencies of interaction are tabulated in the analysis. This technique enabled us to scale interactions within and between both coalitions for both frequency and intensity on a dimension ranging from conflict to cooperation, thereby serving as a measure of the relations suggested in the hypotheses.

For this study interactions among twelve members of the Communist system, among all fifteen members of NATO, and between both blocs were recorded from July 1, 1948, through December 31, 1967, a period of time encompassing the four events analyzed through the content analysis procedures. Approximately 9000 bilateral and multilateral interactions among these actors were recorded from *Keesing's Contemporary Archives* for the 19½ year period. These 9000 events were then scaled for intensity of conflict and cooperation on a thirty-point scale by four judges, whose ratings of each event were averaged.[49] Results provided data on the average scores for every dyad within and between alliances for six-month and twelve-month periods as well as summaries for total intra-bloc and inter-bloc interactions. These data provided measures of the degree of conflict or cooperation within each alliance and between alliances over the 19½ year period, serving as a behavioral indicator of inter-alliance conflict and intra-alliance cohesion (cooperation).

In summary, our data were produced by two research techniques. Computer content analysis has been used to measure attitudinal consensus as a component of alliance cohesion and the perceived external threat to an alliance. Events interaction data were used to measure conflict and cooperation between alliance systems and within both competing alliances.

Notes

1. Muzafer Sherif *et al.*, "Intergroup Conflict and Cooperation: The Robbers' Cave Experiment," in J. David Singer, ed., *Human Behavior and International Politics*, Rand McNally, Chicago, 1965.
2. George Liska, *Nations in Alliance*, Johns Hopkins Press, Baltimore, 1962, p. 26.
3. *Ibid.*, pp. 29–30.
4. Leon Festinger, Stanley Schachter, and Kurt Back, *Social Pressures in Informal Groups*, Harper and Brothers, New York, 1950, p. 164.
5. Andrew M. Scott, *The Functioning of the International System*, The Macmillan Co., New York, 1967, p. 142.
6. Bernice Eisman, "Some Operational Measures of Cohesiveness and Their Interrelations," *Human Relations*, 12, 1959, p. 183.
7. *Ibid.*, p. 187.
8. Liska, *op. cit.*, p. 108.
9. Georg Simmel, *Conflict*, Free Press, New York, 1955, pp. 92–93.
10. Lewis Coser, *The Functions of Social Conflict*, Free Press, 1956, p. 88.
11. *Ibid.*, p. 38.
12. *Ibid.*, p. 95.
13. *Ibid.*, p. 90.
14. *Ibid.*, pp. 103–104.
15. *Ibid.*, p. 147.
16. *Ibid.*, pp. 92–93.
17. Morton A. Kaplan, *System and Process in International Politics*, John Wiley and Sons, New York, 1957, p. 130. Similar statements of this hypothesis may be found in Joseph Frankel, *International Relations*, Oxford University Press, London, 1964, p. 133; Hans J. Morgenthau, "Alliances in Theory and Practice," in Arnold Wolfers, ed., *Alliance Policy in the Cold War*, Johns Hopkins Press, Baltimore, 1959, p. 193; Ernst B. Haas and Allen S. Whiting, *Dynamics of International Relations*, McGraw-Hill, New York, 1956, p. 167; K. J. Holsti, *International Politics: A Framework for Analysis*, Prentice-Hall, Englewood Cliffs, New Jersey, 1967, p. 116; Kenneth Boulding, *Conflict and Defense: A General Theory*, Harper and Row, New York, 1962, p. 162; Amitai Etzioni, *Political Unification: A Comparative Study of Leaders and Forces*, Holt, Rinehart, and Winston, New York, 1965, pp. 30–31; Robert C. North, H. E. Koch, and Dina A. Zinnes. "The Integrative Functions of Conflict," *Journal of Conflict Resolution*, 4, 1960, p. 367; Andrew M. Scott, *op. cit.*, p. 117; and Arnold Wolfers, "Stresses and Strains of 'Going It With Others,'" in Arnold Wolfers, ed., *Alliance Policy in the Cold War*, Johns Hopkins Press, Baltimore, 1959, p. 3.

18. Liska, *op. cit.*, p. 13.
19. *Ibid.*, p. 93.
20. Kaplan, *op. cit.*, p. 45.
21. Herbert S. Dinerstein, "The Transformation of Alliance Systems," *American Political Science Review*, 59, 1965, p. 597.
22. Arnold Wolfers, *Discord and Collaboration: Essays on International Politics*, The Johns Hopkins Press, Baltimore, 1962, p. 29.
23. Liska, *op. cit.*, p. 129.
24. Kaplan, *op. cit.*, p. 145; M. M. Ball and H. B. Killough, *International Relations*, Ronald Press, New York, 1956, p. 176; and R. L. Buell, *International Relations*, Henry Holt & Co., New York, 1925, p. 483.
25. J. David Singer and Melvin Small, "Alliance Aggregation and the Onset of War, 1815–1945," in J. David Singer, ed., *Quantitative International Politics*, Free Press, New York, 1968, p. 283.
26. Sherif *et al.*, *op. cit.*, p. 428.
27. Robert L. Hamblin, "Group Integration During a Crisis," in J. David Singer, ed., *Human Behavior and International Politics*, Rand McNally, Chicago, 1965, p. 239.
28. Jan F. Triska and David Finley, "Soviet-American Relations: A Multiple Symmetry Model," *Journal of Conflict Resolution*, 9, 1965, pp. 38–39.
29. Kaplan, *op. cit.*, pp. 43–45.
30. *Ibid.*, p. 38.
31. *Ibid.*, p. 120.
32. Dinerstein, *op. cit.*, p. 597.
33. *Ibid.*, p. 596.
34. Kaplan, *op. cit.*, p. 130.
35. Hans J. Morgenthau, *Politics Among Nations*, 2d edition, Alfred Knopf, New York, 1959, p. 325.
36. Liska, *op. cit.*, pp. 18–19.
37. For an extensive discussion of this problem see the methodological introduction to Donald Zagoria, *The Sino-Soviet Conflict, 1956–61*, Atheneum, New York, 1964.
38. See T. M. Newcomb, "Communicative Behavior," in Roland Young, ed., *Approaches to the Study of Politics*, Northwestern University Press, Evanston, 1958; and Theodore Newcomb, "An Approach to the Study of Communicative Acts," in A. F. Hare, E. F. Borgatta, and R. F. Bales, eds., *Small Groups*, Alfred Knopf, New York, 1955.
39. *Ibid.*, p. 152.
40. A more thorough explication of the *A-B-X* model, especially of its relations to other cognitive consistency models and of its empirical foundations and limitations, may be found in Appendix B.
41. Karl Deutsch, "Communications Theory and Political Integration," in Philip E. Jacob and James V. Toscano, eds., *The Integration of Political Communities*, J. B. Lippincott, Philadelphia, 1964, pp. 66–70.
42. Alex Bavelas, "Communications Patterns in Task-Oriented Groups," in

Dorwin Cartwright and Alvin Zander, eds., *Group Dynamics,* Row, Peterson, & Co., Evanston, Illinois, 1956, p. 671.

43. *Ibid.,* p. 672.

44. Donald T. Campbell and Julian C. Stanley, *Experimental and Quasi-Experimental Designs for Research,* Rand-McNally, Chicago, 1963.

45. These reasons are explained in Appendix B.

46. Ole R. Holsti, Joanne K. Loomba, and Robert North, "Content Analysis," in Gardner Lindzey and Elliot Aronson, eds., *The Handbook of Social Psychology,* Vol. II, Addison-Wesley, Reading, Mass., 1968, p. 601; and Philip J. Stone, Dexter C. Dunphy, Marshall S. Smith, and Daniel M. Ogilvie, eds., *The General Inquirer: A Computer Approach to Content Analysis,* M.I.T. Press, Cambridge, 1966, p. 5.

47. A detailed description of the content analysis procedures employed in this chapter may be found in Appendix B.

48. Charles Osgood, George J. Suci, and Percy H. Tannenbaum, *The Measurement of Meaning,* University of Illinois Press, Urbana, 1959, pp. 72–73.

49. For a detailed description of the scale and the scaling procedures see Appendix B.

CHAPTER FOUR

Effects of East-West Conflict on Cohesion in NATO and the Communist System During the Postwar Period

General Findings

In this chapter we turn to an examination of the results when the methods discussed in Chapter Three were applied to test our hypotheses. A general examination of the statistical findings on our hypothesis and its two corollaries will be followed by a more detailed examination of the results within the context of a more qualitative analysis of the history of this period.

The hypothesis was: *The greater the inter-alliance conflict, the greater the intra-alliance cohesion.* If this hypothesis is confirmed, during periods of greater conflict when alliance members perceive high threat from the other alliance, they should tend to show greater consensus in their attitudes towards the enemy and greater cooperation in their behaviors. Conversely, during periods of lower threat perceptions and less conflict between alliances, the hypothesis predicts greater differences in the attitudes of each alliance member towards the opposing alliance and its leader and greater conflict in the behaviors among alliance members.

The attitudinal responses of the Communist system to their enemies, both the entire western bloc and the United States alone, are summarized in Tables 1 and 2. In the top half of the tables the perceptions by each individual member of the Communist system of the western bloc and the United States on the evaluative dimension are reported; scores in this part of the table may range from $+3$ (positive) to -3 (negative). In the bottom half of the table summary statistics for the Communist system are presented for four items. The hostility index serves as a rough indicator of the hostility perceived by the Communist system to be emanating from their enemies, the independent variable for the attitudinal component of our hypothesis. The bloc average refers simply to the average perception on the evaluative dimension of the enemies for the entire bloc. The average difference refers to the mean differences among these scores in the top half of the table on all fifty-five dyads connecting the eleven Communist states. This serves as our summary indicator of consensus, the attitudinal component of alliance cohesion, the dependent variable for all our hypotheses. The range between extremes indicates the differences in attitudes between the two most divergent members of the alliance.

Table 1 is based on responses of the eleven members of the Communist system to the entire western bloc. The larger scores on the hostility index at the time of Korea (1950) and Vietnam (1965) indicate the crisis levels reached at those times, in contrast to the other two periods which were

TABLE 1.   Attitudinal Responses of Eleven Members of the Communist System to the Western Bloc During Events of Crisis and Détente *

Nation	1950	1955	1963	1965
Soviet Union	− 1.76	0.23	− 0.09	− 1.71
Communist China	− 1.50	− 0.48	− 1.06	− 2.12
Albania	− 1.41	− 0.72	− 1.47	− 1.98
East Germany	− 1.75	− 0.05	0.28	− 1.71
Poland	− 1.31	0.30	− 0.69	− 1.60
Hungary	− 1.88	0.13	− 1.81	− 0.84
Rumania	− 1.73	− 0.71	0.00	− 1.55
Bulgaria	− 1.61	0.31	− 0.50	− 1.54
Czechoslovakia	− 1.17	− 0.14	− 0.45	− 1.77
North Korea	− 1.41	− 0.14	− 1.37	− 2.16
North Vietnam	− 1.05	0.57	− 1.97	− 2.33
Communist System Summary				
Hostility Index **	1.48	0.74	1.19	1.76
Bloc Average	− 1.51	− 0.06	− 0.83	− 1.76
Average Difference	0.32	0.50	0.91	0.45
Range Between Extremes	0.83	1.29	2.25	1.49

High Tension vs. Low Tension Periods: $U = 3667$, $z = 5.05$, $p < .001$
Early vs. Late Periods: $U = 4261$, $z = 3.79$, $p < .001$

* Scores are the average perceptions by each alliance member of the opponent on the evaluative dimension ranging from $+3$ (positive) to -3 (negative).
** The hostility index is a composite of the average scores for all alliance members across three dimensions—evaluative, potency, and activity—ranging from $+3$ (hostile) to -3 (friendly).

characterized by substantially greater détente. The average distance row indicates that the distances separating the attitudes of the Communist nations were considerably greater in the two periods of détente in contrast to the two periods of crisis. This difference was further confirmed when the distances for all fifty-five dyads in all four periods were rank-ordered from 1 for the closest dyad in all periods to 220 for the farthest apart. The differences among these rank-ordered dyads, divided between low and high tension periods, was significant on a Mann-Whitney U-test beyond the .001 level ($U = 3667$, $z = 5.05$). Thus, there was significantly greater consensus among the Communist nations in their attitudes toward the West at the time of the North Korean invasion and escalation of the Vietnam Wars compared to the negotiations at the Geneva Conference of 1955 and the Moscow Test Ban Conference of 1963.

TABLE 2. Attitudinal Responses of Eleven Members of the Communist System to the United States During Events of Crisis and Détente *

Nation	1950	1955	1963	1965
Soviet Union	−1.66	0.43	−0.08	−1.82
Communist China	−1.57	−0.69	−1.34	−2.39
Albania	−1.46	−2.00	−1.70	−2.14
East Germany	−1.81	−0.19	−0.28	−1.93
Poland	−1.14	0.30	−1.88	−1.56
Hungary	−2.08	0.13	−1.56	−0.84
Rumania	−1.52	−0.85	−1.00	−1.66
Bulgaria	−1.29	0.28	−1.20	−1.54
Czechoslovakia	−0.93	−0.21	−1.14	−1.74
North Korea	−1.66	−0.73	−1.58	−2.37
North Vietnam	−0.71	0.47	−1.99	−2.33
Communist System Summary				
Hostility Index **	1.55	0.74	1.49	1.79
Bloc Average	−1.44	−0.28	−1.53	−1.85
Average Difference	0.46	0.83	0.70	0.53
Range Between Extremes	1.15	2.47	1.91	1.55

High Tension vs. Low Tension Periods: $U = 4549$, $z = 3.18$, $p < .001$
Early vs. Late Periods: $U = 6018$, $z = 0.07$, $p > .10$

* Scores are the average perceptions by each alliance member of the opponent on the evaluative dimension ranging from $+3$ (positive) to -3 (negative).
** The hostility index is a composite of the average scores for all alliance members across three dimensions—evaluative, potency, and activity—ranging from $+3$ (hostile) to -3 (friendly).

Table 2 suggests the same conclusion when the United States alone rather than the entire NATO alliance served as the object of perception for members of the Communist system. The hostility index shows greater perceived threat from the United States during the two crisis periods, although there was a surprisingly high level of perceived hostility on the part of the United States at the time of the Test Ban Treaty. Once again the aggregate differences in consensus among the Communist states in low tension versus high tension periods was highly significant ($U = 4549$, $z = 3.18$, $p < .001$). Thus, when both the United States and the entire western bloc were the object of perception, there was greater consensus among the members of the Communist system during times of crisis as compared with times when the external threat was not so great.

The data from the NATO countries generally tended in the predicted direction, although the findings were not as clear as in the case of the Communist system. These data are summarized in Tables 3 and 4, which follow the same format as the preceding tables.

TABLE 3.   Attitudinal Response of Eight Members of NATO to the Communist System During Events of Crisis and Détente *

Nation	1950	1955	1963	1965
United States	−1.98	0.25	−0.61	−1.83
United Kingdom	−1.20	0.12	0.52	−1.56
France	−0.94	0.13	−0.83	−0.25
Canada	−2.80	−0.85	1.31	−1.27
Norway	−1.85	0.20	−0.38	−1.33
Denmark	−3.00	0.36	2.00	−0.44
West Germany	−1.28	0.07	−1.75	−1.23
Italy	−0.58	−2.00	1.40	−1.10
NATO Summary				
Hostility Index **	1.84	0.52	0.69	1.36
Bloc Average	−1.70	−0.22	0.21	−1.13
Average Difference	1.21	0.93	1.84	0.72
Range Between Extremes	2.42	2.36	3.75	1.58

High Tension vs. Low Tension Periods: $U = 1319$, $z = 1.45$, $p < .10$
Early vs. Late Periods: $U = 1397$, $z = 1.00$, $p > .10$

* Scores are the average perceptions by each alliance member of the opponent on the evaluative dimension ranging from +3 (positive) to −3 (negative).
** The hostility index is a composite of the average scores for all alliance members across three dimensions—evaluative, potency, and activity—ranging from +3 (hostile) to −3 (friendly).

Table 3 summarizes the perceptions by the eight members of NATO included in this study of the entire Communist system during each of the four periods. Clearly the Communist system was perceived to be far more hostile during the two crisis periods than during the two periods of détente. The mean differences among scores for the twenty-eight dyads connecting the eight countries, however, did not conform neatly to the pattern demonstrated by the Communist bloc. Indeed, the first two periods indicated a general reversal of the predicted trend. Here greater differences were found among the eight NATO countries in the period of the outbreak of the Korean War in 1950, whereas the Geneva Summit Conference of 1955 seemed to provide a source of somewhat greater consensus. When all twenty-eight dyads across all four periods were rank-ordered, the difference was in the predicted direction at better than the .10 level of significance ($U = 1319$, $z = 1.45$). Thus, even though the periods of 1950 and

TABLE 4. Attitudinal Responses of Eight Members of NATO to the Soviet Union During Events of Crisis and Détente *

Nation	1950	1955	1963	1965
United States	— §	0.50	− 0.57	—
United Kingdom	− 1.00	− 0.18	0.41	− 0.67
France	—	0.00	− 1.00	− 0.60
Canada	—	− 0.61	1.31	− 1.17
Norway	—	− 0.20	0.75	—
Denmark	—	0.50	2.00	—
West Germany	− 1.18	0.07	—	− 1.02
Italy	− 1.00	− 3.00	1.50	—
NATO Summary				
Hostility Index **	0.90	0.63	0.58	0.90
Bloc Average	− 1.06	− 0.32	0.63	− 0.87
Average Difference	0.68	1.30	1.49	0.66
Range Between Extremes	0.18	3.50	3.00	0.57

High Tension vs. Low Tension Periods: $U = 1001$, $z = 3.30$, $p < .001$
Early vs. Late Periods: $U = 1328$, $z = 1.39$, $p < .10$

* Scores are the average perceptions by each alliance member of the opponent on the evaluative dimension ranging from + 3 (positive) to − 3 (negative).
** The hostility index is a composite of the average scores for all alliance members across three dimensions—evaluative, potency, and activity—ranging from + 3 (hostile) to − 3 (friendly).
§ — indicates no perceptions of the target were recorded.

1955 did not correspond to the general pattern, the results from the later two periods were sufficiently close to our predictions to offset this reversal in the overall pattern.

This trend appeared more strongly when we considered the perceptions by these eight countries of the Soviet Union alone, as found in Table 4. Here almost exactly identical differences characterized the allies' perceptions of the Soviet Union for both crisis periods; similarly, in both low tension periods the differences were much greater, although there was little difference between the two periods of détente. The overall differences across all dyads based on perceptions of the Soviet Union alone showed greater consensus by the eight NATO members during the high tension than during the low tension periods, significant beyond the .001 level using the Mann-Whitney U test ($U = 1001$, $z = 3.30$). Thus, the measures of atti-

TABLE 5.   Conflict and Cooperation Within NATO, Within the Communist System, and Between All NATO and Communist Bloc Countries

Period	NATO *		Communist *		NATO–Communist *	
	6-month	12-month	6-month	12-month	6-month	12-month
1948 July–Dec.	7.66	7.66	10.62	10.62	14.04	14.04
1949 Jan.–June	8.87		7.36		13.96	
1949 July–Dec.	9.98	9.59	11.56	9.25	15.87	14.89
1950 Jan.–June	9.77		11.61		18.16	
1950 July–Dec.	10.00	9.98	9.81	10.46	15.28	17.35
1951 Jan.–June	9.79		10.10		15.20	
1951 July–Dec.	9.69	9.65	10.00	10.17	12.94	13.34
1952 Jan.–June	9.80		9.50		17.59	
1952 July–Dec.	10.01	9.94	9.44	9.47	15.76	17.16
1953 Jan.–June	10.00		9.00		15.36	
1953 July–Dec.	10.04	10.00	9.42	9.35	13.16	14.52
1954 Jan.–June	10.16		10.50		12.40	
1954 July–Dec.	9.68	9.86	10.23	10.24	13.42	12.74
1955 Jan.–June	9.91		7.64		13.34	
1955 July–Dec.	10.13	10.10	9.81	7.90	13.49	13.80
1956 Jan.–June	10.09		9.09		10.46	
1956 July–Dec.	10.13	10.09	11.23	9.24	14.05	11.76
1957 Jan.–June	10.01		9.84		12.87	
1957 July–Dec.	10.14	10.02	9.99	9.97	11.66	12.04
1958 Jan.–June	10.27		10.32		10.49	
1958 July–Dec.	10.08	10.16	10.51	10.32	11.88	11.78
1959 Jan.–June	10.25		9.95		12.84	
1959 July–Dec.	9.87	10.04	8.27	9.56	12.62	12.75

tudinal consensus tended to confirm the hypothesis about the effects of East-West conflict or détente on the cohesion of the Communist system in a clear fashion and in a somewhat more ambiguous manner for NATO.

We may next turn to the results obtained using events data as a measure of the behavioral component of cohesion, based on the degree of conflict or cooperation in interactions between alliances and within them. Our hypothesis would predict an inverse relationship between inter-alliance conflict and intra-alliance conflict. Consequently, greater conflict between the Communist system and NATO would be expected to produce greater cooperation within the blocs. For these data we have obtained average scores for the interactions within and between alliances on a continuum ranging from 1 (greatest cooperation) to 30 (greatest conflict). These data were then applied to test our hypothesis.

Period	NATO *		Communist *		NATO–Communist *	
	6-month	12-month	6-month	12-month	6-month	12-month
1960 Jan.–June	9.99		9.99		12.98	
1960 July–Dec.	10.06	10.02	9.91	9.94	13.72	13.20
1961 Jan.–June	10.01		11.11		13.81	
1961 July–Dec.	9.92	9.96	10.29	10.29	14.53	14.57
1962 Jan.–June	9.94		9.05		10.61	
1962 July–Dec.	9.93	9.93	8.69	8.97	13.71	11.36
1963 Jan.–June	10.11		10.21		15.06	
1963 July–Dec.	10.13	10.13	8.40	8.80	9.39	12.50
1964 Jan.–June	10.14		8.16		12.64	
1964 July–Dec.	10.06	10.10	11.64	8.33	11.05	11.67
1965 Jan.–June	10.05		11.09		12.12	
1965 July–Dec.	10.01	10.02	10.04	10.33	10.86	11.66
1966 Jan.–June	10.09		10.61		12.04	
1966 July–Dec.	9.99	10.05	11.74	11.54	11.97	11.89
1967 Jan.–June	9.98		10.68		11.90	
1967 July–Dec.	10.03	10.01	10.98	11.00	12.56	11.90
Mean	9.92	9.87	9.96	9.79	13.23	13.25
Standard Deviation	0.43	0.54	1.08	0.89	1.90	1.75
Time Correlation **	−.392	−.561	−.196	−.063	.612	.710

* Scores range from 1 (maximum cooperation) to 30 (maximum conflict).
** The time correlation is the Spearman rank-order correlation between the data and time.

Table 5 contains the data for the Communist system, NATO, and the interactions between them broken down on six-month and twelve-month intervals from July 1, 1948, through December 31, 1967. Table 6 summarizes the correlations among these variables.

The results for the Communist system indicate only very weak confirmation of our hypothesis. In direct relations the correlation between conflict/cooperation between the two alliances and conflict/cooperation within the Communist system was virtually zero for both six-month and twelve-month intervals. The only significant finding was for the six-month intervals where conflict in the Communist system lagged somewhat behind the inter-alliance interactions ($r_s = -.278$, $t = 1.74$, $p < .05$), although a twelve-month lagged correlation was not significant.

The NATO case, however, tended to support the hypothesis much more strongly. Looking first at unlagged correlations, the relationship between East-West conflict/cooperation and conflict/cooperation in NATO was significant both for data aggregated on a six-month basis ($r_s = -.455$, $t = 3.11$, $p < .005$) and on a twelve-month basis ($r_s = -.483$, $t = 2.34$,

TABLE 6. Correlations Between East-West Conflict and Conflict Within NATO and the Communist System, 1948–1967

Communist System			NATO		
Interval	No Lag	Lag	Interval	No Lag	Lag
6-months	−.010	−.278 *	6-months	−.455 *	−.378 *
12-months	.063	−.064	12-months	−.483 *	−.835 *

* These Spearman rank-order correlations are significant at the .05 level or better.

$p < .025$). These findings were even stronger when a twelve-month lag between cohesion within NATO and conflict/cooperation between NATO and the Communist system was introduced. For a lag of six months the correlation reached $-.378$ ($t = 2.45$, $p < .01$), and the twelve-month lag reached $-.835$ ($t = 6.26$, $p < .0005$). Thus, effects of East-West conflict on the cohesion of NATO seemed to be felt most strongly after some time interval had elapsed.

The behavioral data produced mixed results in testing our hypothesis. For NATO the hypothesis was clearly confirmed, but for the Communist system the expected relationship was found only when cooperation/conflict in the Communist system was lagged six months behind cooperation/conflict in relations between the Communist system and NATO.

There are several limitations to all of these findings, however. Because of the presence of some trends in these data, especially a trend toward increased East-West cooperation over time and toward increased conflict within NATO, as indicated by the time correlations at the bottom of Table 5, it is possible that our data are auto-correlated.[1] The sample of events included in this analysis may have been too small to be sensitive to all relevant changes in cooperative behavior. This may have been particularly true with respect to the relations among some of the smaller members of each bloc which were almost certainly underreported in the source from which these events were drawn. Finally, in any analysis of large numbers of events for a given time period many phenomena may appear simultaneously within any one set of data. This means that many different variables could have been influencing these data simultaneously, and all independent variables could not be isolated. For example, alliance cohesion was probably dependent on other variables in addition to external ones, including the nature of the alliance structure and decision making as well as domestic factors within the member nations. Yet it was virtually impossible to separate out all of the individual effects which these factors may have had in accounting for variations in cooperation within both NATO and the Communist system.

In spite of some differences between the events data and the content analysis data, the two sets generally tended to reinforce one another. This gave support to the notion that the attitudinal and behavioral components of cohesion are highly interrelated though not identical components of the same concept.[2]

The hypothesis may, therefore, be considered to be generally confirmed, although the confirmation was not strong in all cases. The hypothesis tended to hold more strongly for the Communist system when attitudinal data were employed and for NATO when behavioral data were analyzed. This would suggest that, in the presence of increased external threat, the Communist countries tended to exhibit greater attitudinal consensus, although overall there were only smaller increases in cooperative behavior, whereas NATO nations tended to cooperate more during times of crisis even though their attitudes did not change as radically. Yet, for both alliances and for both types of data there was at least some support for the hypothesis. While there are clearly other variables that also account for changes in the degree of alliance cohesion, the degree of conflict between alliances and the perceived threat resulting from that level of conflict does appear to affect significantly the overall degree of cohesion in competing alliances.

Corollary 1 to the hypothesis stated that: *Inter-alliance conflict will exert symmetrical effects on the cohesion of competing alliances.* For the attitudinal responses of the Communist system and NATO this hypothesis would predict that the changes in attitudinal consensus in response to the four events would vary directly between the two blocs. Comparing the data on consensus found in Tables 1 through 4, the hypothesis was supported only weakly. This was due largely to a few deviations from the expected patterns for the members of NATO, so that their attitudes did not correspond to those of the Communist system. The NATO countries tended to demonstrate greater consensus in response to the Communist system in 1955, during the Geneva Summit Conference, than in 1950, at the outbreak of the Korean War, contrary to the predicted pattern. When the four periods were rank-ordered for each alliance on the basis of mean differences in average scores for the perceptions of the opposing bloc, the Spearman rank-order correlation between the two blocs over time was .400; for the perceptions of the bloc leader of the two opposing blocs, the correlation was .600. With an N of four, tests of significance were not appropriate, and these results are reported for descriptive purposes only.

To compare the behavioral cohesion of the two alliances, the correlations between the average scores for the internal cooperation/conflict intensity in both the Communist system and NATO were computed. With a time interval of six months, the Spearman rank-order correlation was only .062, and for twelve-month periods it reached $-.245$. Neither finding was significant at the .10 level or better. Therefore, we must tentatively reject the hypothesis that changes in cohesion between NATO and the Communist system were generally symmetrical over the twenty-year period from 1948 through 1967.

Corollary 2 stated: *The tighter the polarity of the international system, the greater the cohesion of component alliances; conversely, the looser the polarity, the less the alliance cohesion.* We have assumed that the polarity of the international system has declined steadily throughout the postwar period. This assumption is partially supported by the events data, which indicate a significant trend toward increased cooperation between the two blocs throughout the twenty-year period from 1948 through 1967. Data analyzed on a six-month basis indicated a time correlation between time and inter-bloc cooperation (Table 5) of .612 ($t = 4.71$, $p < .0005$). On a twelve-month basis, the time correlation was even higher ($r_s = .710$, $t = 4.28$, $p < .0005$). Thus, Corollary 2 predicts that cooperation in both NATO and the Communist system should decrease with the passage of time throughout the postwar period.

This hypothesis may be tested first through the use of content analysis data to measure the attitudinal component of alliance cohesion. In this connection, the hypothesis would predict that, after controlling for the level of external conflict, there would be less attitudinal consensus among the members of both alliances in more recent periods compared to earlier periods. Thus, we would expect to find less consensus in 1965 compared to 1950 and in 1963 compared to 1955.

The data for the Communist system reveal significantly less consensus on the evaluative dimension in perceptions of the North Atlantic bloc (Table 1) in recent periods compared to earlier ones ($U = 4261$, $z = 3.79$, $p < .001$). By contrast, when the United States alone was the object of perception (Table 2) there was virtually no difference between early and late periods ($U = 6018$, $z = 0.07$, $p > .10$). This finding can be accounted for by one reversal in the predicted trend, since there was more consensus about the United States on the part of the Communist states in response to the Test Ban Conference of 1963 than to the Geneva Conference of 1955. Perhaps this may be accounted for largely by the substantially higher threat perceived emanating from the United States as indicated by a higher score on the hostility index for 1963 (1.49) compared to 1955 (0.74). This completely offset the greater differences found in 1965 compared to 1950.

The data for NATO indicate a slightly different pattern. When the entire Communist system was the object of perception (Table 3), the difference between earlier and later periods was in the predicted direction, though not quite statistically significant at the .10 level. In this case the deviations from the predicted patterns were in the crisis periods. There were smaller differences among the NATO countries in response to Vietnam compared to the early days of Korea, in spite of the fact that the Soviet Union and the Communist bloc as a whole were perceived as less hostile in 1965 than in 1950. When the Soviet Union alone was the object of perception (Table 4), the differences were significantly greater in the predicted direction. In this case differences in 1950 and 1965 were almost identical; however, greater diversity of perception of the Soviet Union in 1963 compared to 1955 was sufficient to make the predicted relationship statistically significant beyond the .10 level ($U = 1328$, $z = 1.39$). Thus, for both NATO and the Communist system there was a weak trend toward reduced consensus in the decade of the 1960s compared with events which occurred in the 1950s, as predicted by Corollary 2.

The hypothesis also predicts decreasing cooperation over time within NATO and the Communist system. In Table 5 we find that this hypothesis was not confirmed for the Communist system treated on six-month intervals ($r_s = -.196$, $t = 1.22$, $p > .10$) or on twelve-month intervals ($r_s = -.063$, $t = 0.27$, $p > .10$). Although there was some tendency toward reduced cooperation in the Communist system from 1948 through 1967, the trend was not statistically significant. Several factors may account for this result.

First, the news media from which our events data were obtained only reported the most obvious events of conflict in the Communist system prior to about 1963. Before that time most conflict events were carefully covered up within the Communist bloc. This assumption is supported by an analysis of the period from 1962 through 1967, analyzed for six-month intervals. In this case, there was a significant decrease in cooperation within the Communist bloc ($r_s = -.622$, $t = 2.51$, $p < .05$). Although Corollary 2 did not hold throughout the entire twenty-year period analyzed in this study, it was clearly supported by the most recent six years.

Second, the primary source of conflict in the Communist system over the twenty-year period involved the conflict of Albania and China versus the rest of the Communist system. In Table 7 data are presented for the Albanian-Chinese conflict with the rest of the Communist system, treated on six-month and twelve-month intervals. In these cases we find significant decreases in Sino-Albanian cooperation with their Communist allies over the entire twenty-year period for both six-month intervals ($r_s = -.547$, $t = 3.81$, $p < .005$) and twelve-month intervals ($r_s = -.554$, $t = 2.74$, $p < .01$). Thus, the hypothesis, which was not supported for the entire Communist system, was confirmed when relations of China and Albania with the rest of the Communist system were analyzed separately.

TABLE 7. Conflict and Cooperation Between Albania/Communist China and the Remainder of the Communist System

Period	6-Month Score *	12-Month Score *
1948 July–Dec. §	—	—
1949 Jan.–June	6.33	
1949 July–Dec.	13.08	9.45
1950 Jan.–June	11.33	
1950 July–Dec.	10.08	10.42
1951 Jan.–June	10.50	
1951 July–Dec.	—	10.50
1952 Jan.–June	—	
1952 July–Dec.	9.17	9.17
1953 Jan.–June	10.00	
1953 July–Dec.	9.69	9.69
1954 Jan.–June	8.00	
1954 July–Dec.	9.94	9.94
1955 Jan.–June	8.01	
1955 July–Dec.	9.50	7.85
1956 Jan.–June	9.14	
1956 July–Dec.	11.17	9.24
1957 Jan.–June	9.88	
1957 July–Dec.	9.99	9.98
1958 Jan.–June	9.96	
1958 July–Dec.	12.83	10.13
1959 Jan.–June	9.78	
1959 July–Dec.	9.50	9.78

Declining bipolarity thus had little overall impact on cooperation in the entire Communist system. However, decreased cooperation was found during the period from 1962 through 1967 for the entire Communist system and in Chinese and Albanian relations with the rest of the bloc throughout the entire twenty-year period. The increasing conflict appeared to be confined largely to the Chinese and Albanian actions prior to the early 1960s, after which it spread throughout the entire Communist system.

For the events data for NATO (Table 5), we find strong confirmation of Corollary 2. There were significant negative correlations between the passage of time and cooperation within NATO, analyzed for both six-month intervals ($r_s = -.392$, $t = 2.59$, $p < .01$) and for twelve-month intervals ($r_s = -.561$, $t = 2.88$, $p < .005$). Thus the declining bipolarity over time within the international system was significantly associated with decreasing cooperation within the NATO alliance.

In summary, the results gave general support to our hypothesis and one of its corollaries, but the other corollary hypothesis was not supported. Al-

Period	6-Month Score *	12-Month Score *
1960 Jan.–June	9.98	
1960 July–Dec.	9.95	9.96
1961 Jan.–June	11.79	
1961 July–Dec.	10.93	10.13
1962 Jan.–June	10.67	
1962 July–Dec.	10.56	10.57
1963 Jan.–June	11.27	
1963 July–Dec.	12.70	12.49
1964 Jan.–June	9.17	
1964 July–Dec.	13.42	9.35
1965 Jan.–June	16.29	
1965 July–Dec.	10.14	11.11
1966 Jan.–June	12.99	
1966 July–Dec.	15.88	14.52
1967 Jan.–June	18.50	
1967 July–Dec.	18.19	18.60
Mean	11.12	10.68
Standard Deviation	2.66	2.36
Time Correlation **	−.557	−.554

* Scores range from 1 (maximum cooperation) to 30 (maximum conflict).
** The time correlation is the Spearman rank-order correlation between the data and time.
§ — indicates that no interactions were reported for these periods.

though these two hypotheses alone cannot explain variations in alliance cohesion, they do tend to indicate that the international system does have some substantial impact on the cohesion of alliances. While other factors such as domestic politics in member nations and the structure of the alliance systems themselves probably have some impact on alliance cohesion, we have found a definite tendency for alliance cohesion to vary partly in relation to two aspects of the international system.

First, the relations between alliances within the international system appear to affect alliance cohesion. Specifically, greater conflict between alliances tends to exert an integrative impact on alliances, whereas reduced conflict tends to permit reductions in cohesion to become manifest in alliances.

Second, the structure of the international system appears to have an impact on the cohesion of alliances. In the postwar period, declining polarity of the international system was associated with decreasing cohesion of the two opposing alliance systems.

We may next attempt to explain these results by placing them in the context of the historical events which they were intended to measure. Special attention will be given in this analysis to the four periods on which we have focused in some detail. We shall examine the findings for each of the two alliances separately.

The Results for the Communist System

The Communist system emerged in its present form immediately following World War II, when the countries of Eastern Europe, occupied by Soviet troops at the end of the war, were integrated into the system and when the Chinese Communists under Mao Tse-tung defeated the Nationalist Chinese government under Chiang Kai-shek in 1949. Thus, by 1950 all countries included in this study except North Vietnam had entered the system, which at that time was tightly centered around the only country to have been ruled by a Communist government for more than a few years, the Soviet Union. By that time the Communist system had already engaged in substantial conflict with the West over Berlin, Iran, and more indirectly, over Greece and Turkey. However, the first overt military conflict began on June 25, 1950, when the Korean War broke out.

The events data for the first six months of 1950 indicated that East-West conflict reached the highest point for any six-month period during the 19½ years analyzed in this study (18.16).[3] This high level of conflict was generally perceived as such by the Communist nations which, on the average, perceived the West at 1.48 on the hostility scale (Table 1) while the United States alone was perceived at 1.55 on the same scale (Table 2).

In other words, the Communist countries clearly perceived a substantial threat from the West as a result of the outbreak of the Korean War.

These data also tended to indicate that at the same time nations in the Communist system exhibited a substantial degree of cohesion. In their behavior the bloc members increased from very little cooperation in the first six months of 1950 (11.61) to substantially greater cooperation (9.81) by the second half of the year, after the outbreak of the war.[4] In their attitudes the Communist states also exhibited substantial co-orientation in their perceptions of the West, with an average distance of only 0.32 on the seven-point scale among all fifty-five pairs of nations (Table 1). These average differences were the lowest for the four periods. Perceptions of the West ranged from Hungary, which was most negative (-1.88), to the Viet-Minh, which was least negative (-1.05), a range of only 0.83 out of seven possible points. Since North Vietnam was not a member of the Communist system at this time, forcing us to include a document broadcast by the Viet-Minh radio under the command of Ho Chi Minh, this most divergent case in 1950 was not surprising. If this case were eliminated, then Czechoslovakia remained the least negative (-1.17), reducing the total range for ten countries to only 0.71.

Thus, in this period at least ten of the eleven countries were fairly closely clustered around the Soviet Union. Even Communist China and the Soviet Union exhibited fairly high agreement in their evaluations of the West, with the Soviets being slightly more negative (-1.76) than the Chinese (-1.50). This difference in scores (0.26) was less than the mean difference for all dyads (0.32). In behaviors the Soviet-Chinese dyad was characterized by high cooperation (8) for the year 1950. Finally, Albania (-1.41) was quite close to Communist China in its perception of the West (0.09 difference in scores) and only slightly more divergent from the Soviet Union (0.35 difference) than was average for the Communist system (0.32). Soviet-Albanian behavioral interactions were fairly cooperative (10) in 1950, and no interactions between China and Albania were recorded.

Thus, in 1950 none of the major conflicts which were to develop later in the Communist system was evident, and the bloc demonstrated a substantial degree of attitudinal co-orientation and behavioral cooperation in response to the West. In 1950 the Communist system was still tightly centered around the Soviet Union. Under Stalin the central authority of the Soviet Communist party as well as the total political power of the Soviet Union enforced ideological and institutional uniformity.[5] It is hardly surprising, therefore, that our data should indicate substantial unity among these eleven Communist party states in response to American involvement in Korea.

The behavioral indicators suggest that conflict/cooperation between the Communist system and NATO changed from 18.16 in 1950 to 13.34 in the first half of 1955 and to 13.49 in the second half, just slightly above the median level of conflict for all 19½ years. This reduced level of conflict was perceived by the Communist system, which evaluated the West as least hostile of the four periods (0.74) and much lower than in 1950 (1.48). On the evaluative dimension the West was perceived as only slightly negative (-0.06). Thus, on the average the Communist bloc perceived a substantially reduced threat from the West during this period.

As our hypothesis predicted, the Communist nations responded to this partial détente with increased differences in their perceptions of the West (0.50) compared with 1950 (0.32). Not only were the average differences for all pairs greater, but also the range between the extremes was even greater in 1955 (1.29) compared to 1950 (0.83). In 1955, the West was still evaluated in positive terms by the newly formed Democratic Republic of Vietnam (North Vietnam) (0.57), while Albania moved out to the negative extreme (-0.72). In response to the United States alone the difference between these two countries was substantial (2.47).

The Chinese Peoples' Republic also evaluated the West in relatively negative terms (-0.48) along with Rumania (-0.71) and Albania (-0.72). This contrasted rather noticeably with the response of the Soviet Union, which turned to a somewhat more positive view of the West (0.23). This meant that the differences between the Soviet Union and China increased substantially (0.71), greater than the average disagreement for the Communist system (0.50), and Soviet-Albanian differences also widened (0.95). These data thus suggest that Sino-Soviet disagreements over détente with the West appeared as early as the Geneva Conference of 1955, earlier than is noted in most of the literature. It also indicates that an even more extreme Albanian position at this time put Albania closer to China, in the attitudinal sphere at least, than had been the case earlier. In other words, some foundations for the later Sino-Albanian sub-alliance within the Communist bloc may have been laid as early as 1955. In spite of this attitudinal divergence, however, behavioral cooperation in the Sino-Soviet dyad (8) and the Albanian-Soviet dyad (7) remained high, indicating that this attitudinal divergence over relations with the West at Geneva had apparently not yet spilled over significantly in behavioral relations within these dyads.[6]

In short, in 1955 the early signs of conflict had appeared in the attitudinal responses of the Communist bloc to their western enemies. At this stage, however, the conflict appeared to be confined largely to the attitudinal realm and had not yet spilled over to affect interactive behaviors. This attitudinal "dissensus" was perhaps partially the result of a trend following the death of Stalin in 1953 toward greater institutional and ideological diversity in the Communist system.[7]

During the time intervening between 1955 and 1963 a major transition began to appear, both in the nature of East-West relations and in relations within the Communist system. In 1956 Khrushchev delivered his "de-Stalinization" speech to the Twentieth Congress of the Communist Party of the Soviet Union. At this time he questioned both the absolute validity of the Soviet Revolution as the sole model for Communist world-wide revolution, and he admitted the possibility of more than one road to socialism. Furthermore, he attacked the Stalinist "cult of personality" and thereby brought into question the absolute authority of the Soviet leader. This aroused among Communist leaders in many countries doubts about the leading role of the Soviet Union and raised questions even about the Soviet system of government.[8]

However, the interpretation by many of the Communist party states of the doctrine of "different roads to socialism" was quite different from that intended by the Soviet leaders. This doctrine had considerable appeal to Communist leaders like Imre Nagy of Hungary who were critical of Soviet orthodoxy. Thus, ironically, perhaps one result of the increased liberalization was the outbreak of the Hungarian Revolution in October 1956.

Soviet action to suppress these uprisings in Hungary and also in Poland appeared on the surface to be a reassertion of the unity of the Communist system under the brute force of Soviet power. Still a further irony, however, is the fact that this provided an additional impetus for the breakup of the unity of the Communist system. In the years immediately after 1956, Khrushchev attempted to replace the previously centralized discipline of the world Communist party with an ideological union of formally equal and independent parties revolving around Moscow. The belief that the ideological authority of the CPSU could maintain effective political unity proved to be illusory, and by 1958 major differences began to emerge between the Soviet Union and the Chinese Peoples' Republic. Different interpretations of Communist doctrine soon challenged Moscow's ideological authority.[9] Over the next five years the conflict expanded rapidly and became more explicit. At the same time political controls on the Eastern European satellites were gradually loosened, and many of the Warsaw Pact countries, especially Rumania and Poland, found new room to maneuver both within the system and in relations with the West.

By 1963, when the Partial Test Ban Treaty was signed, the Sino-Soviet conflict reached the point of open schism. On July 31, 1963, the Chinese issued a statement denouncing the Test Ban Treaty as a fraud and accusing the Soviet Union of "capitulation to U.S. imperialism." Part of the text of that statement reads as follows:

But now the Soviet government has made a 180-degree about-face, discarded the correct stand they once persisted in and accepted this re-production of the U.S.–British draft treaty, willingly allowing U.S. im-perialism to gain military superiority. Thus the interests of the people of the countries in the Socialist camp, including the people of China, have been sold out, and the interests of all peace-loving people of the world have been sold out.

The indisputable facts prove that the policy pursued by the Soviet government is one of allying with the forces of war to oppose the forces of peace, allying with imperialism to oppose Socialism, allying with the United States to oppose China, and allying with the reactionaries of all countries to oppose the people of the world.[10]

The Chinese apparently perceived the Test Ban Treaty as directed in part against them, since it would prevent the Chinese from testing to ob-tain nuclear weapons and thus preserve the American, British, and Soviet monopoly over nuclear weapons. Thus, in the absence of an external threat to pull in the opposite direction, the treaty undoubtedly contributed sub-stantially to the further deterioration of Sino-Soviet relations.

The Test Ban Treaty followed less than a year after the very serious in-ternational crisis over Cuba in the fall of 1962. During the second half of 1962 the level of East-West conflict increased to 13.71, and in the after-math of Cuba it reached 15.06, the highest level of conflict since the first half of 1953, the end of the Stalinist period. In the second half of 1963, however, this trend was dramatically reversed (9.39). Undoubtedly the signing of the Partial Nuclear Test Ban Treaty by the United States, the Soviet Union, and the United Kingdom largely contributed to this sudden increase in East-West cooperation.

Communist perceptions of the West in July 1963 reflected the am-biguity inherent in the sudden change. On the average they perceived the West as moderately hostile (1.19), more threatening than in 1955, which was probably a carry-over from the intense conflict of a few months earlier. However, the hostility score for the West was still less than in 1950 or 1965, indicating that the Communist countries on the average did per-ceive at least some signs of détente inherent in these events, in spite of the refusal of some members to adjust their perceptions accordingly. In-deed, a major source of dispute among them was over the issue of the ex-tent to which the United States was still a serious threat.

The result was that the mean differences among all eleven countries widened dramatically (0.91) in their orientations toward the West, causing the greatest differences for these four periods. Differences in perceptions of the United States, though not as great, were still high (0.70). The range between extremes was also greater (2.25) between North Vietnam, which had by this time become most negative in its evaluations of the West (-1.97), and East Germany, which averaged out to a positive evaluation (0.28). With the somewhat curious exception of Hungary (-1.81), the most negative evaluations were held by a subgroup of Communist states including, in order, North Vietnam (-1.97), Albania (-1.47), North Korea (-1.37), and the Chinese Peoples' Republic (-1.06). Thus a sub-bloc within the Communist system had begun to appear made up of the Asian countries plus Albania.

Finally, the Sino-Soviet conflict continued to widen (0.95), increasing the difference between rather negative Chinese evaluations (-1.06) and the rather moderate Soviet evaluation (-0.09). The Soviet-Albanian differences also widened to distances (1.38) even greater than in 1955.

The behavioral effects of these attitudinal divergences were not felt immediately. In the second half of 1963 the interactions within the Communist system were relatively cooperative (8.40), though, by the second half of 1964, this had declined to the lowest period of cooperation (11.64) for the entire 19½ years. Cooperation within the bloc then remained low through the end of 1967. In the Sino-Soviet dyad the behaviors became fairly conflictual (15) in 1963, and there were no reported interactions between Albania and the Soviet Union, perhaps as a result of the almost total break between them.

In short, in 1963 the combined effect of international détente and declining tightness of the bipolar international system had an impact on the cohesion of the Communist system. Although the Communist states perceived on the average a greater threat from the West in 1963 than in 1955, the added impact of change in the structure of the international system led to a reduction of attitudinal consensus within the Communist system to its lowest level in the four periods analyzed in this study. In addition, behavioral conflict increased in the Sino-Soviet dyad and spread throughout the entire system by the end of 1964. Once again the data tended to be consistent with the predictions of our hypotheses.

American bombing of North Vietnam in February 1965 brought a temporary end to the declining cohesion throughout the Communist system. At this time the index for conflict between the two blocs increased from 11.05 for the last six months of 1964, to 12.12 for the first half of 1965. While interactions were generally relatively cooperative, the war in Vietnam accounted for a major portion of the conflict at that time, offsetting a strong trend toward increasing cooperation. The war had particularly striking effects on the Communist states' perceptions of the West, as hostility rose significantly to the highest point for the four periods (1.76).

This increased hostility in the attitudes of members of the Communist system towards the West was also accompanied by a substantial increase in co-orientation. The average differences among all eleven Communist states narrowed (0.45), becoming less than in the two periods of détente and exceeded only by the consensus in 1950. The range for ten members of the system was also reduced (0.79), going from North Vietnam as most negative (-2.33) to Bulgaria (-1.54). The one clear deviant case was Hungary which was only moderately negative toward the West at this time (-0.84). In their reaction the Hungarians referred to the possibility of an exchange of visits between President Johnson and the Soviet leaders which had been proposed shortly before, only to be dropped by the other members of the bloc after the escalation of the Vietnam War. Even though the Hungarians observed that Johnson had severely damaged the chances for such a meeting with the leaders of the U.S.S.R. by attacking one of the Soviet Union's allies at the same time, they still appeared to hold out hope for such a meeting.[11]

This reduced difference in co-orientation among the eleven members of the Communist system was accompanied by a reduction of the Sino-Soviet conflict. The Soviet Union (-1.71) and the Chinese Peoples' Republic (-2.12) reduced the differences in their orientations toward the West (0.41) to slightly less than average for the fifty-five dyads (0.45) and well below 1963 (0.95). Soviet differences with Albania (-1.98) fell far below the previous two periods (0.27). Thus, even these long-standing conflicts may have been affected, if only temporarily, by these conflict events.

In spite of the reduction of these differences, the Asian sub-bloc plus Albania maintained the most negative evaluations of the West. North Vietnam was most negative (-2.33), followed by North Korea (-2.16), the CPR (-2.12), and Albania (-1.98). Therefore, this sub-bloc appeared to retain some unity as the most militant and anti-western coalition within the Communist system.

The behavioral indicators demonstrate that cooperation in the Communist system was relatively low throughout the mid-1960s. However, the period of escalation of the Vietnam War at least temporarily halted the trend toward increased conflict. In the last half of 1964, there was some net conflict within the Communist system (11.64). In the first six months of 1965, including the American aerial bombardment of North Vietnam, cooperation increased (11.09), followed by even more cooperation (10.04) during the second half of that year. This trend came to an end at that point, however, as conflict increased in the two halves of 1966 (10.61 and 11.74), the latter being the period of greatest conflict for all 19½ years within the Communist system.

Perhaps the major reason why the Vietnam conflict did not contribute to significant long-term increases in cohesion in the Communist system was that there were disagreements among the Communist nations about how to deal with the conflict and even competition between the Soviet Union and Communist China, both of which sought to maintain the dominant influence in North Vietnamese politics. Thus, while both countries aided North Vietnam in the war effort, they appeared to do so in part in competition with one another. The two countries represented different strategies for revolution. The Chinese actively backed wars of national liberation; the Soviets were more willing to give support to nationalist elements in the less developed countries whether or not they were Communist. Finally, the internal political situation in North Vietnam at that time represented a careful balance between pro-Soviet and pro-Chinese groups, and each nation sought to aid North Vietnam in such a way as to maintain the influence of their own respective supporters. The result of this competitive situation was that the external conflict had only a temporary effect on Sino-Soviet cohesion. Thus, during the escalation of the war in 1965, the conflict/cooperation score for the Soviets and Communist Chinese indicated a brief period of reduced conflict (12) compared to the more conflictual average in 1964 (14) and in the ensuing year, 1966 (18). Finally, the same pattern followed for Albanian-Soviet relations for the three years (12, 10, and 16, respectively).

Increased consensus among the Communist countries in response to American bombings of North Vietnam in 1965 appeared to have a short-range effect on the behavioral interactions among those countries. Cooperation within the bloc increased slightly in 1965, after these events, although the general trend toward increased conflict in the bloc which prevailed from 1962 to 1967 was resumed again in 1966. The combined effects of the two independent variables in this study were noticeable, even though they tended to work in the opposite direction. The general trend toward increasing conflict within the system as a result of the reduced tightness of polarity in the international system, as predicted by Corollary 2, prevailed throughout the overall period. Nevertheless, for the events in 1965 and especially in the attitudinal consensus produced by the events of February 7, the increased East-West conflict brought a temporary increase in cooperation and consensus among the members of the Communist system.

There are undoubtedly many other factors which have combined to affect the changes in cohesion in the Communist system during the postwar period, including personal conflicts between national leaders (e.g., between Nikita Khrushchev and Mao Tse-tung) and the existence of different stages of revolutionary processes (e.g., the different conditions of the revolutionary positions of the Soviet Union and the Chinese Peoples' Republic). Nevertheless, our data have also indicated that both the structure and the nature of interactions within the international system have been related to changes in the cohesion of the Communist system.

The Results for the North Atlantic Treaty Organization

The NATO Treaty was signed in Washington on August 4, 1949. It was an outgrowth of disillusionment on the part of the nations of Europe with the postwar hopes for peace. The Berlin blockade, combined with the Communist-aided insurrection in Greece and Turkey and the Communist *coup d'état* in Czechoslovakia in 1948, led to widespread fear in many nations of Western Europe of a Communist threat to their security. These fears placed the nations of Europe in substantial dependence on the United States for both economic and military security. This was particularly true of France which, before the war, had considered itself a major world power, but which had been destroyed in morale as well as physically devastated by the war. The NATO alliance bound the United States and most of the nations of Western Europe in a pact against Communist aggression in Europe. The heart of the treaty is contained in Article 5, which states: "Parties agree that an armed attack against one or more of them in Europe or North America shall be considered an attack against them all; and consequently, they agree that if such an armed attack occurs, each of them . . . will assist the Party or Parties so attacked by taking forthwith . . . such actions as it deems necessary, including the use of force." [12]

Although NATO was originally based on the defense of Europe and North America against a perceived threat of Communist aggression, the first direct military challenge to the western allies came in Asia when, on June 25, 1950, North Korean troops crossed the 38th parallel and entered South Korea. This led to an almost immediate American decision to send troops to aid South Korea in meeting this aggression. Thus, even though this aggression was not directed against the geographical areas protected by NATO, members of the alliance did make some response to this more distant threat in Asia.

The American reaction to this event emphasized the fear that the Communist attack upon Korea could be the beginning of a more general assault upon the West. President Truman expressed his concern about a possible "occupation of Formosa by Communist forces" which "would be a direct threat to the security of the Pacific area and to the United States forces performing their lawful function and necessary functions in that area." In addition, he proclaimed American support for the French position in Asia by stating: "I have similarly directed acceleration in the furnishing of military assistance to the forces of France and the associated states in Indo-

China and the dispatch of a military mission to provide close working relations with those forces." [13]

Even though Secretary of State Dean Acheson had declared South Korea to be outside the United States' defense perimeter only shortly before, the Americans perceived that North Korean aggression against South Korea might be a forerunner of Soviet aggression in Europe. Thus, President Truman also stated that "the attack upon Korea makes it plain beyond all doubt that communism has passed beyond the use of subversion to conquer independent nations, and now will use armed invasion and war." [14] Secretary of Defense Louis Johnson carried this point somewhat further when he argued that international communism was prepared to invade any free nation if it thought it could get away with it. He stated that the "real significance of the North Korean aggression is this evidence that, even at the resultant risk of starting a third world war, communism is willing to resort to armed aggression, when it believes it can win." [15] In the face of these interpretations of the Communist threat, it was not surprising that the United States placed renewed emphasis upon the cohesion and strength of NATO in response to the outbreak of the war in Korea, even to the extent of trying to obtain the force levels which had been prescribed by NATO to meet a potential Soviet attack.

This American view of the threat emanating from the Communist bloc over Korea was evidently shared by the eight NATO countries analyzed in this study, which perceived even greater hostility emanating from the Communist countries than the Communists perceived being projected by the West. As was noted previously, this was the period of highest conflict between the two blocs.

In spite of this high level of perceived threat, these NATO countries demonstrated a surprisingly low level of consensus in their evaluative attitudes towards the Communist bloc (Table 3). While all eight countries evaluated the Communist countries negatively on the evaluative dimension, they differed in the degree to which they did so. Indeed, the range between extremes was high (2.42) from the most negative, Denmark (-3.00), to the least, Italy (-0.58), with the United States (-1.98) falling in the middle. French and American differences were substantial (1.04), though less than the average for the entire group (1.21). The average differences were not nearly so great when the Soviet Union alone was the object of perception (0.68), though the results were based on only three countries, since five of the eight made no direct reference to the role of the Soviet Union in this event.

Cooperation, as measured by the behavioral index, was quite high among all fifteen members of NATO at this time. Nevertheless, in line with the attitudinal indicators, behavioral cooperation did decline from the first half of 1950 (9.77) to the second half of the year (10.00).[16] By 1951, this cooperation increased again (9.79). French-American relations in 1950 were fairly cooperative on the average (9).

In other words, the outbreak of the Korean War did not have the predicted effect on NATO in all respects. Although cooperation levels were generally high, they actually fell off slightly after the immediate outbreak of the war. Even more dramatically, attitudinal consensus levels were relatively low in the days immediately after June 25, 1950. Perhaps the ambiguous nature of the external threat best accounts for these results. Many Western European nations apparently perceived this threat not as directed against themselves, and they thus differed in their perceptions of its relevance to NATO. Furthermore, some nations perhaps feared that American commitments to the defense of South Korea might be at the expense of NATO, where the threat from the Berlin crisis remained salient. As American concerns for the Far East increased, many NATO members had little to fear in the way of retribution resulting from verbal disagreements among themselves, in contrast to the members of the Communist system at that time. Given the pluralistic structure of NATO, there was little to prevent the appearance of such diversity. In spite of this, however, cooperation in NATO remained fairly high through at least 1953.

By 1955 NATO had incorporated a rearmed West Germany into its membership. Perhaps the most significant changes in the external environment between 1950 and 1955 were the end of the Korean War and the death of Stalin, both occurring in 1953. Because many western leaders had apparently assumed that the Soviet dictator was himself personally responsible for a good deal of East-West hostility, they responded to his death with increased hopes for improved relations with the Soviet Union. These hopes reached their culmination at the conference of heads of state in Geneva in 1955. The three western leaders, President Dwight Eisenhower, Prime Minister Anthony Eden, and Premier Edgar Faure, represented their states in these meetings with the Soviet leaders.

The NATO decision-makers apparently perceived substantially reduced hostility from the Communist system at this time, and the hostility index (0.52) was the lowest for the four periods. This decline in hostility from 1950 was accounted for by decreases across all three dimensions of the semantic differential. At the time of this détente, when perceived hostility was relatively low, our hypothesis would predict relatively low cohesion in NATO, considering of course that this would be mitigated by the still relatively tight bipolar structure of the international system, as noted in Corollary 2.

The findings for NATO on the behavioral index were relatively consistent with this prediction. The cooperation dropped from the first half of 1955 (9.91), within the most cooperative 25 percent of periods, to the second half of the year (10.13), within the 25 percent most conflictual periods. Thus, conflict increased in NATO beginning from the time of the Geneva Conference in July 1955, and remained fairly high through the first half of 1959. Franco-American relations remained cooperative (9) through 1955.

The attitudinal indicators, however, did not change as predicted by our hypothesis. The mean difference for all twenty-eight dyads was 0.93, somewhat less than 1950 (1.21). Once again, the Soviet Union was perceived in a more diversified manner, with an average difference of 1.30, more in line with our hypothesis. The range between extremes in NATO perceptions of the Communist bloc remained high (2.36), though slightly less than 1950 (2.42). Six of the eight countries perceived the Communist bloc in relatively positive terms on the evaluative dimension, with Denmark (0.36) being the most positive, while the most negative perceptions of the enemy were held by Italy (-2.00).

In spite of the fairly wide range between extremes, several major NATO members exhibited a similar outlook; almost identical perceptions of the Communist bloc were held by the three western powers represented in the Geneva Summit Conference, the United States (0.25), France (0.13), and the United Kingdom (0.12). One of the reasons for the high unity at this time may have been the desire of the three major NATO allies to maintain a unified position at this time of negotiations with the Soviet leaders. The fact that three of the major powers were negotiating together at Geneva where all but one of the Communist countries were excluded may have partially accounted for the greater co-orientation among these NATO nations at this time. The three western countries came with similar proposals, as all emphasized the necessity for East-West agreement on arms control and the reunification of Germany. Thus, NATO seems to have been rather unified in perceiving a real détente in the summer of 1955, and there was apparently substantial agreement among the member nations about their position vis-à-vis the Communist system. This may explain the high degree of co-orientation within NATO in response to the 1955 Geneva Summit Conference.

This finding provides a clear exception to our hypothesis. It tends to suggest that external conflict may be a sufficient condition for alliance cohesion, but it is not a necessary condition. It is possible for an alliance to be cohesive at times of less external conflict, even though the generalization may still hold true in most cases that external conflict will tend to enhance cohesion. NATO's response to the 1955 Geneva Summit Conference indicates that an alliance can have some cohesion at times when the external threat is perceived to be low, especially in this case when it was possible for these nations to cooperate with their allies in seeking an international détente.

By 1963, however, a series of disputes had broken out within NATO.

In 1957 the Soviet Union launched the first earth satellite, adding credibility to their earlier claims that they had developed an intercontinental ballistic missile capable of delivering a nuclear warhead to the United States. This development rendered the North American continent directly vulnerable to a nuclear attack, causing America's allies to question the credibility of American commitments to risk nuclear war to protect themselves. At the same time in 1957, under the government of Premier Guy Mollet, the French began to develop their atomic bomb and plans for the *force de frappe*. De Gaulle's return to power in 1958 reinforced emphasis upon independence and grandeur for France. French resentment of the Anglo-American domination of NATO reached a peak following the meeting at Nassau between President Kennedy and Prime Minister Macmillan in December 1962. At that time the British acquiesced in American domination of the NATO nuclear deterrent by giving up their nuclear independence. The Americans decided to cancel production of a Skybolt missile system which had been promised to Great Britain. This was accompanied by Macmillan's acceptance of the American plan to create an integrated NATO deterrent, the Multilateral Force (MLF), which France had consistently opposed. De Gaulle indicated his opposition in early 1963 by vetoing the British request for membership in the European Economic Community and denouncing Britain as America's "Trojan horse." De Gaulle thus asserted French independence from NATO because of his opposition to the Anglo-Saxon domination of the alliance and in order to assert French military and political independence from the domination of the superpowers. He withdrew French forces from the integrated NATO commands in 1966, although France still remained formally as a member of the alliance and reaffirmed its pledge to come to the assistance of its allies if one were attacked in Europe or North America.

By 1963, therefore, De Gaulle's opposition to the Anglo-American "special relationship" within NATO had become quite pronounced. Although he still argued that "the fundamental factors of French-American relations are friendship and alliance," he also argued that American efforts to get France to integrate its defense into NATO were often taken "with a view to dissolving France in them, as if self renouncement were henceforth its sole possibility and even its only ambition, while the undertakings in the guise of integration were automatically taking American authority as a postulate." [17] French boycott of the Partial Test Ban Treaty increased tension and conflicting attitudes within NATO. Like the Chinese Communists, the French perceived that the Test Ban Treaty was designed to prevent the aspiring superpowers from obtaining nuclear weapons, the prime symbol of status in the nuclear age. They consequently insisted on their right to continue nuclear testing and refused to sign the treaty negotiated in Moscow. This conflict was thus at the center of renewed disagreements among the NATO members which had come to the fore by 1963.

It may be recalled that the events interaction data indicated that East-West relations changed dramatically from a rather conflictual relationship (15.06) in the first half of 1963 to increased cooperation (9.39) in the second half of the year after the signing of the Test Ban Treaty, resulting in the period of greatest East-West cooperation from 1948 through 1967. Furthermore, the Communist bloc continued to be perceived by the NATO countries in terms of relatively low hostility (0.69), slightly above 1955 (0.52). This was largely due to an increase in the perceived strength of the bloc, otherwise offsetting a shift from a slightly negative score on the evaluative dimension to a positive average (0.21) in 1963. The hypothesis as well as its corollaries thus would predict decreased cohesion in NATO due to both the reduction of tight polarity in the international system in 1963 and low perceived threat from the Communist bloc.

In 1963 both behavioral and attitudinal indicators of cohesion changed in the predicted direction. The average difference among the eight countries in perceptions of the Communist bloc increased to the highest for the four periods (1.84); similarly, for the Soviet Union alone differences were the greatest (1.49). In addition, the range between extremes widened (3.75) from Denmark's highly positive attitude toward the Communist system (2.00) to West Germany's very negative attitude (-1.75).

In spite of this general trend toward "dissensus" throughout NATO in 1963, the United States (-0.61) and France (-0.83) differed by a relatively small margin (0.22), far below average for the bloc (1.84). Even in their attitudes towards the Test Ban Treaty there was virtually no difference, since France perceived it positively (1.42) as did the United States (1.39). De Gaulle did not immediately attack the idea of the test ban as such, but he merely argued that France would not participate in it. He stated: "The fact that the Soviets and the Anglo-Saxons decided directly to halt their nuclear tests in space, the air and sea is itself satisfactory, and we share the joy that President Kennedy so eloquently expressed the day before yesterday on the subject of this event." But then he continued to explain why France refused to participate: "But we repeat that a mere agreement on tests between Soviets and Anglo-Saxons, already invested with immeasurable power, and who do not cease to strengthen it and thereby to confirm their respective hegemonies, a mere agreement will not prevent France also from equipping itself with the same kind of means, failing which, since others have these means, France's own security and its independence would never again belong to it." [18] De Gaulle's position might explain in part why the content analysis data indicated substantial agreement between himself and President Kennedy with respect to both the

Communist system and the Test Ban Treaty itself, in spite of his disagreement with the role played by the United States in this event. Although the United States and France exhibited a surprising degree of attitudinal co-orientation during this period, throughout these eight NATO nations a substantial degree of diversity of attitudes was found in response to the Test Ban Treaty, perhaps indicating substantially reduced cohesion.

The behavioral data also tended to reinforce these conclusions. Cooperation within the NATO alliance decreased from the last half of 1962 (9.93) to the two six-month periods of 1963 (10.11 and 10.13), both falling within the least cooperative quartile of periods for NATO. Similarly, on the French-American dyad cooperation declined from the last half of 1962 (9) to 1963 (10 and 11). In short, virtually all indicators pointed to reduced cohesion within NATO in 1963, when both a period of international détente and a looser bipolar structure of the international system were present simultaneously.

The war in Vietnam interrupted the détente which appeared to be developing since the successful resolution of the Cuban missile crisis in 1962. American involvement in the war increased substantially throughout this entire period. In August 1964, American aircraft for the first time bombed naval bases and oil depots in response to an alleged North Vietnamese torpedo attack on American vessels off the coast of Vietnam. This was followed by congressional passage of the Gulf of Tonkin resolution, authorizing further American involvement in Vietnam. The commencement of regular bombings of North Vietnam on February 7, 1965, signalled a significant escalation of this conflict between the United States, joined by several western powers, and North Vietnam, which was also receiving aid from other Communist states.

The escalation of the Vietnam War in early 1965 was accompanied by increased perceptions of threat emanating from the Communist bloc (1.36), second highest after the Korean War period. In response to this conflict, the attitudes of the eight NATO countries demonstrated greater unity than at any other period, with an average difference in their perceptions of the Communist bloc of 0.72. Also when perceiving the Soviet Union alone, they differed less than in the other three periods (0.66). The range between extremes in perceptions of the Communist bloc was reduced to 1.58 between the United States (-1.83) and France (-0.25). This represented a significant increase in Franco-American differences. French doubts about the American role in Vietnam probably were the result of American refusal to aid the French forces after their defeat at Dien Bien Phu in 1954, leading to their withdrawal from Indochina. After having encouraged the French to withdraw, the Americans had then assumed the role of the dominant western power in Southeast Asia, a role which was both resented and opposed by the French. Thus, by 1965, the French-American conflict had become fairly pronounced even though at this time of conflict between some NATO members and some Communist nations there was a fairly high degree of unity on the average among the other NATO members analyzed in this study.

In 1965, however, the increased cohesion in NATO appeared to have been confined largely to the attitudinal responses to the Vietnam War. The behavioral interactions only demonstrated slight increases in cooperation over the periods through 1964 and 1965, increasing slowly but constantly from the first half of 1964 (10.14) through the second half of 1965 (10.01). While the changes were all in the predicted direction, they did not appear to be great. In the French-American dyad the opposite trend appeared, changing from slight cooperation in the second half of 1964 (10) to slight conflict (12) for the first half of 1965.

In short, NATO's responses in 1965 followed the general pattern predicted by the hypotheses, although the primary impact of the conflict appeared to be on the attitudinal consensus of the allies with respect to Vietnam rather than on the long-term behavioral interactions among the members of NATO. Furthermore, the French-American dyad moved in the opposite direction, indicating the depth of that split by 1965.

In conclusion, our hypothesis and Corollary 2 were not confirmed as clearly for the NATO case as for the Communist system. Two of the four periods which we have focused on generally conformed to the predictions from our hypotheses, while the first two periods diverged from the predicted pattern. The NATO countries demonstrated a surprising degree of diversity in their perceptions of the Communist system in response to the outbreak of the Korean War, perhaps due to the ambiguity with which many European members of NATO perceived the Communist threat. Again in 1955, there was surprising agreement among the members of NATO, also contrary to the predictions of the hypothesis. This was apparently due to a substantial agreement on the part of some NATO allies, especially the three which participated in the Geneva Summit Conference, the United States, the United Kingdom, and France, about negotiating agreements and reducing tensions in relations with the Communist system. However, the responses of NATO to the Communist system at the time of the Partial Nuclear Test Ban Treaty and the escalation of the Vietnam War were predicted by our hypotheses. In addition, behavioral interactions generally conformed to the predictions of the hypotheses throughout all periods.

This suggests the conclusion that the structure of the international system and the nature of interactions between alliance systems are neither necessary nor sufficient conditions for alliance cohesion. Nevertheless, these international variables appear to be at least important facilitative conditions for alliance cohesion. This further suggests that unevenly distributed threats may detract from alliance cohesion, whereas consensus about alliance norms and objectives may contribute to cohesion, thus qualifying the overall generality of the hypotheses.

Comparison of NATO and the Communist System

While these hypotheses were examined for both NATO and the Communist system, some significant differences emerged between the responses of the two blocs to their interaction with one another. This contrast may be partially accounted for by differences in the structure of the two blocs. Although a distinction between the two alliances may be overdrawn, throughout much of the postwar period the structure of NATO has been more or less pluralistic, whereas the structure of the Communist system has been more centralized. This suggests that the structure of the Communist system has probably placed some restraints on its members which do not exist for members of NATO. Some of these differences were evident in our data.

For the Communist system our hypotheses were supported more strongly by the attitudinal rather than by the behavioral data. This suggests that the structure of the Communist system, especially in the early postwar period, probably placed significant restraints on the behavior of many members of the alliance. Significant behavioral deviations were prevented by Soviet military action, even as recently as in Czechoslovakia in 1968. However, strict control over attitudes is far more difficult, even in a centralized system, thereby permitting attitudes to vary more than behavior in response to external events such as détente and declining polarity in the international system.

For NATO our hypotheses were supported strongly by the behavioral data, whereas the attitudinal data diverged from the predicted patterns for the events occurring in the 1950s. This reflects the absence of some constraints on members of NATO, which permitted them to vary their behavior when external threat was reduced. In the attitudinal sphere it also reflects the greater adaptability of the more pluralistic alliance, which enabled its members to disagree about a conflict which was of no direct concern to some and also to find a source of consensus about negotiations, even in the presence of reduced external threat.

This suggests that more pluralistic alliances may be capable of adapting better to different external conditions than do more centralized alliances. This comparison will be developed further in Chapters Five and Six, which focus in detail on the nonconforming behavior of one member of each alliance—France and the Peoples' Republic of China.

Conclusions

There appears to be a relationship between the degree of conflict between alliance systems and the cohesion within them. This finding was generally, though not always, supported with respect to two components of alliance cohesion. An attitudinal component, the consensus among allies in their perceptions of the enemy, tended to be related to the level of threat which allies perceived to be emanating from the enemy. The greater the perceived threat, the greater the consensus in their attitudes; conversely, the less the perceived threat, the less the consensus. A behavioral component, the degree of cooperation or conflict among alliance members, was also directly related to the degree of conflict/cooperation between alliance systems. The greater the conflict that existed between alliances, the greater was the resultant cooperation within them. Conversely, decreased inter-alliance conflict was associated with reduced cooperation within alliances. However, conflict between alliances was neither a necessary nor a sufficient condition for alliance cohesion, but it did become a significant facilitative condition for cohesion. A corollary to this hypothesis which predicted that symmetrical changes in cohesion would occur over time on the part of competing alliances was not strongly confirmed. A second corollary, which predicted that alliance cohesion would tend to decline with reduced polarity in the structure of the international system, was demonstrated by reduced consensus among alliance members over time, controlling for the level of conflict. It was also supported by reduced cooperative behavior over time, especially in NATO, as the polarity of the international system became looser.

These findings were confirmed through an analysis of the attitudes and behaviors of the Communist system and NATO. In explaining changes in these two alliances, however, we have attempted to go beyond description of specific events. We have rather developed a model from which we have derived specific hypotheses, and a systematic research methodology was used to analyze these relationships. While the fact that these relationships were partly supported in two alliances as different as NATO and the Communist bloc gives us some reason to believe that they may be generally valid, considerable further testing will be necessary to verify this possibility. If this is accomplished, however, then this analysis would do more than help us to explain better those factors in the international system which affect the changing internal relations of NATO and the Communist system. It should help us better understand the dynamic processes of international politics which may affect the cohesion of alliances. In addition, this analysis has provided tentative confirmation of the cross-level generality of propositions which to date have been systematically tested only at the small group level. The apparent applicability of these propositions to the international level increases our confidence in their validity for many different social systems.

These results also have some tentative implications for American foreign policy. They tend to indicate that policies designed to improve East-West relations are not necessarily compatible with those designed to enhance the cohesion of NATO. Throughout the 1960s American presidents, including Kennedy, Johnson, and Nixon, all advocated measures designed to achieve these two objectives simultaneously. Yet our research suggests that efforts intended to improve relations with the Communist bloc, by reducing the level of inter-alliance conflict and thereby reducing the perceived level of threat, may actually contribute to the further disintegration of the NATO alliance. Conversely, policies designed to unify NATO may cause nations in the Communist bloc to perceive increased threat from the West. The likely consequence of this would be an increase in the level of East-West conflict and, if our hypothesis holds true, a corresponding increase in the cohesion of the Communist bloc. This could then lead to a vicious spiral of increasing conflict between alliances and an increasing cohesion within both alliances. Our finding that behavioral cooperation in NATO tends to be inversely related to the level of East-West cooperation suggests that these two goals are not likely to be maximized simultaneously. Even in the attitudinal sphere, in the two most recent periods alliance consensus was inversely related to the intensity of perceived Communist hostility.

It is true, however, that the settlement of some outstanding East-West disputes might have the reverse effect and contribute to the integration of NATO, at least in the short run. For example, disagreements between the United States and France appear to have been exacerbated by both the war in Southeast Asia and the conflict in the Middle East. It is at least plausible that a settlement of these conflicts might enable the United States and France to improve relations. Furthermore, the settlement of such conflicts would reduce the likelihood that domestic opposition to alignment with the United States in some NATO countries like Norway might lead to their defection from the alliance. The cases of East-West conflict to which this qualification applies, however, are not completely central to NATO concerns, and many NATO members do not perceive a significant threat to their security emanating from these events. Indeed, our theory suggested that threat which exerted different effects on different allies might be more likely to contribute to alliance disintegration rather than to cohesion. However, measures directed at improving American relations directly with the Soviet Union or at reaching a settlement of outstanding issues in Europe like demilitarization or the German problem are likely to enhance perceptions of détente in Europe. In so doing they are likely to lead to reduced cohesion in NATO. Even if there is attitudinal consensus among NATO members about the desirability of such détente, as was the case in response to the Geneva Summit Conference in 1955, there is no assurance that this consensus will be followed by long-run behavioral cooperation; it may be recalled that after the Geneva Conference of 1955, in spite of the attitudinal consensus exhibited by NATO members at the time, behavioral cooperation remained relatively low through 1959. Therefore, over the long-run East-West détente and increased NATO cohesion are not likely to be fully compatible goals.

We have also found that loosening polarity in the international system over time is associated with reduced cohesion in alliances. In NATO both behavioral cooperation and attitudinal consensus declined significantly throughout the postwar years. Ironically, efforts on the part of the United States to prevent the continuation of this trend into the future might have just the opposite effect, because they would probably be perceived by the NATO allies as an indication of an American desire to maintain dominance over the alliance. Most NATO members have long been suspicious of American "grand designs" for NATO cohesion, and such skepticism is likely to appear in response to future American proposals to unify NATO. This would probably encourage these nations to assert their independence in order to resist the perceived dominance by the United States, thereby reducing the cohesion of NATO even further.

On the other hand, some would argue that an alliance like NATO can find new sources of cohesion even in the absence of an external threat. This argument generally contends that the military integration created within NATO is likely to lead to increased cohesion over time as a result of a process of spill-over, in which cooperative habits learned in the military sector would be generalized to other sectors of NATO activity. The pluralistic structure of the NATO alliance might make it more resilient and better able to survive and develop new functions in periods of détente than could the more centralized Communist bloc. While this may be true to a degree, Beer's study of NATO has found that little such integrative spill-over has occurred.[19] A common ideology and culture may help preserve some minimal degree of unity within the North Atlantic bloc, but it alone is no guarantee that cohesion within NATO can be maintained in any meaningful sense over a long period of time in the absence of a significant external threat to most or all members of the alliance.

Given this situation, the future trend in NATO is likely to reflect reduced overall cohesion as bipolarity declines, so long as a major new Communist threat does not emerge in Europe. There may be constraints on the ability of American policy makers to reverse this trend. This is likely to produce a dilemma if they are forced to choose between acquiescing in this trend toward reduced NATO cohesion or searching for new sources of unity. The most likely source of overall unity would be an increase in tension and conflict between NATO and the Communist bloc. Yet this is likely to be a costly way to achieve increased cohesion within NATO. Since NATO was established primarily as a means of reducing the Communist threat and not as an end in itself, it would seem to be illogical to give highest priority to reasserting the unity of NATO, an unlikely outcome in any event, especially since it might have a detrimental effect on improving relations between the West and the Communist system. While this latter task may undoubtedly be difficult, any improvement in East-West relations would not only remove the conditions which made a cohesive NATO an essential objective of American foreign policy, but it would also reduce the likelihood of war between these two alliances.

Notes

1. Auto-correlation refers to a correlation between two variables which is accounted for by the correlation of each with a third variable, in this case with the passage of time. Thus, the fact that inter-alliance cooperation increases over time while NATO cooperation decreases over time, means that the two variables may be negatively related largely because they are each related in opposite directions to the time variable. However, time is not a behavioral process itself. While there may be some other time-related variable accounting for the statistical correlations, our theory nevertheless strongly suggests that the relationship between intra-alliance behavior and inter-alliance interaction is clearly plausible and theoretically sound. Nevertheless, we did remove trends from our data by computing the correlations between changes in each variable from one period to the next. The correlations were all weaker except for the six-month lagged relationship between inter-alliance relations and cohesion within the Communist system, for which we would not have anticipated a problem of auto-correlation anyway. This procedure does not provide a good test of our hypothesis, however; consequently, in the absence of some highly plausible third variable which could be accounting for our correlations, we are inclined to interpret our results as theoretically meaningful.

2. Further comparisons among the different types of data employed in this chapter may be found in P. Terrence Hopmann and Barry B. Hughes, "Events Data in the Measurement of Cohesion in International Political

Coalitions: A Validity Study," in Edward E. Azar and Joseph Ben Dak, eds., *International Interactions: Theory and Practice of Events Analysis,* Gordon and Breach, New York, forthcoming 1973.

3. Data on the conflict/cooperation scale range from 1 (maximum cooperation) to 30 (maximum conflict). For purposes of comparison, scores lower than 11.5 may be considered to be cooperative and those above 11.5 may be treated as relatively conflictual.

4. While many of the changes in the degree of cooperation/conflict may appear to be quite small considering that a 30-point scale was employed, the low standard deviations reported on the bottom of Table 5 make even relatively small changes in behavior scores rather significant. For example, the changes of only 1.80 points on the 30-point scale from the first half to the second half of 1950 for the Communist system represents a change of 1.67 times the standard deviation of 1.08.

5. Zbigniew K. Brzezinski, *The Soviet Bloc: Unity and Conflict,* Praeger, New York, 1961, especially Ch. 6.

6. The absence of behavioral indications of conflict within the Communist system in 1955 could have been explained by the failure of the western news sources to obtain and report information about carefully concealed or seemingly unimportant conflict events which may have occurred and which may have had an impact on attitudes.

7. Brzezinski, *op. cit.,* especially Ch. 8.

8. Richard Lowenthal, *World Communism: The Disintegration of a Secular Faith,* Oxford University Press, New York, 1964, p. 45.

9. *Ibid.,* p. 256.

10. Chinese statement on the Test Ban Treaty, July 31, 1963, in William E. Griffith, *The Sino-Soviet Rift,* M.I.T. Press, Cambridge, Mass., 1964, p. 327.

11. Radio Budapest, February 8, 1965.

12. Published in Roger Hilsman, "On NATO Strategy," in Arnold Wolfers, ed., *Alliance Policy in the Cold War,* Johns Hopkins Press, Baltimore, 1959, p. 196.

13. President Truman quoted in a statement by Warren Austin, U.S. Ambassador to the United Nations, *United Nations General Assembly Official Records,* June 27, 1950, p. 5.

14. *Ibid.,* p. 5.

15. U.S. Congress, Senate, Committee on Appropriations, *Hearings, Supplemental Appropriations for 1951,* 81st Congress, 2nd session, p. 272, cited in Robert E. Osgood, *NATO: The Entangling Alliance,* University of Chicago Press, Chicago, 1962, p. 69.

16. As was the case with the Communist system, small changes in NATO cooperation/conflict scores may still be significant due to the small standard deviation (0.43) for data analyzed on a six-month basis. Therefore, the increased conflict from the first to the second half of 1950, only 0.23 on a 30-point scale, is equivalent to a change of .53 standard deviations.

17. Charles De Gaulle, 8th Press Conference, July 29, 1963, *Ambassade de France, Service de Presse et d'Information*, New York.
18. *Ibid.*
19. Francis A. Beer, *Integration and Disintegration in NATO: Processes of Alliance Cohesion and Prospects for Atlantic Community*, Ohio State University Press, Columbus, Ohio, 1969.

CHAPTER FIVE

National Attributes, Bloc Structure, and Intra-Alliance Conflict

Introduction

Among the more spectacular developments in recent international relations has been the disintegration of unity within the two great alliances which emerged after World War II. France's withdrawal from NATO and the bitter public dialogue, punctuated by periodic border clashes, between Moscow and Peking since 1963 are only two indications that the era of international bipolarity is coming to an end. The cold war alliances may endure in some form for a number of years, but it seems unlikely that political relations within them can ever again take the form that they did during the 1950s. For example, discordant personalities and political styles among American, French, Soviet, and Chinese leaders have contributed to the disintegration of alliance unity. Yet if the consequences for Sino-Soviet relations of Nikita Khrushchev's political eclipse are an indication, it would appear unlikely that the eventual passing of Mao Tse-tung will restore Soviet hegemony over Communist nations to the degree that it existed during the first fifteen years after World War II. Nor did the replacement of Lyndon Johnson and Charles De Gaulle by Richard Nixon and Georges Pompidou appreciably change the trend of loosening cohesion within NATO.

In this and the next chapter we will examine French and Chinese policies in an effort to shed light on several of the issues introduced in Chapter One.

Our perspective and many of our concepts derive from a framework of "national-international linkages." [1] The discussions will explore some of the domestic and international factors that may account for similarities and differences in relations established by Paris and Peking with their allies.

The similarity of primary interest is that both nations have in effect withdrawn from the military commitments which they undertook within the first half decade following the end of World War II, even though France remains a nominal member of NATO and neither Moscow nor Peking has denounced their treaty of alliance signed on February 14, 1950. We shall also consider the very significant variations in French and Chinese foreign relations with members of NATO and the Communist system.

The next section investigates some aspects of internal political processes that may be related to alliance policy. Some similarities in present French and Chinese political processes will be described, and we will consider how these may give rise to foreign policies which deviate from alliance norms. From the many facets of the political processes which contribute to policy making, we have selected the socialization experiences of political elites and the stability of top leadership for examination.

Our consideration of internal political processes also explores some of the clear differences between French and Chinese politics that may be linked to the degree of their disassociation from the western alliance and Communist system respectively. The analysis stems from two observations. First, France and China have markedly different political systems. The former has many attributes of an open and pluralistic polity, whereas the latter is clearly an authoritarian system. Second, as indicated by the data to be presented in Chapter Six, the fissures between China and the Communist system are more extensive and severe than is the rupture between France and the western alliance. Our discussion considers whether there is any systematic link between these two points; that is, are there attributes of authoritarian polities which may give rise to a relatively complete break from an alliance? What characteristics of pluralistic nations may act to limit the disruption of relations with allies?

The analysis then turns to an external aspect of the problem—the *nature of the alliances* to which France and China belong. The western and Communist alliances differ in a number of important respects. In the final section of this chapter we will develop fourteen hypotheses linking these attributes to different patterns of conflict management within monolithic and pluralistic alliances. Chapter Six then presents data on many aspects of French and Chinese alliance relations with a view to shedding some light on two hypotheses which distinguish the consequences of intra-alliance conflict in monolithic alliances from those in pluralistic ones.

One point should be made explicit at the outset. Our primary purpose is not to identify the event or events that "caused" the Sino-Soviet conflict or the differences between Paris and Washington, nor do we seek to allocate blame in the disputes which may have led to French and Chinese disaffection with their alliances.[2] If Kremlinologists and their counterparts in the study of Chinese, French, or American policies cannot agree among themselves on such matters—an assessment that can be verified by a random selection of any half-dozen recent books on NATO or Sino-Soviet relations—surely the observations and data to be presented here will not resolve these issues. Although we cannot offer a definitive assessment of French and Chinese alliance policies, we are trying to suggest possible explanations that consider the attributes of both nations and alliances, and the linkages between them. Thus our speculations about French and Chinese alliance policies and our decisions regarding the types of data to be sought were governed by the definition of a linkage as "any *recurrent sequence of behavior* that originates in one system and is reacted to in another." [3]

Focusing on the linkages between national and international politics directs our attention to an almost limitless number of questions. This can be illustrated by considering a few of the questions one might ask about a single type of activity—Chinese purchases of wheat from western nations. A linkage analysis is initially concerned with the complex political processes by which a need for wheat was transformed first into a demand on the political system and then into a decision to negotiate a contract with wheat suppliers. Among the many interesting questions one might want to ask are the following: To what extent was the need generated by the disruptions associated with domestic programs such as the Great Leap Forward and the Cultural Revolution? Through what channels were demands for wheat communicated? What alternative means of meeting these demands were suggested, by whom, and within which institutions? What symbols were used to justify the decision to purchase wheat from "enemy" nations? Our analysis could consider not only the internal sources of the Chinese policy, but also its external consequences. For example, one might ask about the Canadian political system: What activities by interest groups preceded the sale of wheat to China? How did leaders, parties, and publics respond to the wheat sale? As the primary beneficiaries of the sale were farmers in the English-speaking provinces, did the decision have any impact on tensions between the English and French communities? What effect did the wheat sale have on the popularity of the ruling and opposition parties in Ottawa and in the provinces? [4] In short, a full investigation into the sources and consequences of national-international linkages raises a broad range of interesting questions, only a few of which can be considered in any detail here.

Political Processes and Nonconforming Alliance Policies

Of the many processes, institutions, actors, and attitudes which may be linked to foreign policy, we confine ourselves to the socialization of political elites, the stability of top leadership, and certain characteristics of open and closed polities. Even within these limited areas our discussion is necessarily speculative and illustrative rather than comprehensive and exact.

The Socialization of Political Elites.   French and Chinese leaders appear to have shared some striking similarities which may be related to deviation from their alliances. Mao Tse-tung and Charles De Gaulle were intellectuals, leaders of great personal stature, intensely nationalistic, and both were convinced that their vision of history gave them exceptional insight into the features of the politically relevant future. At least to some extent these characteristics appear to reflect some widely shared traits of their societies. A general attribute cited by virtually every student of French and Chinese politics is the nationalism, bordering on xenophobia, which permeates these nations. The Chinese philosophical tradition has long emphasized China's cultural superiority in contrast to the surrounding "barbarians" and has viewed China as the center of the world. French commentators have expressed similar views regarding France, the superiority of its culture, language, way of life, and its *mission civilisatrice*.[5] These sentiments have found their most eloquent contemporary expression in De Gaulle's pronouncements about France's international role, such as in a statement made at his twelfth press conference: "Indeed, the independence thus regained is enabling France to become, despite the ideologies and hegemonies of the colossi, for all the racial passions and prejudices, above and beyond the rivalries and ambitions of nations, a champion of cooperation, failing which the troubles, the interventions, the conflicts that lead to world war would go on spreading. Now France is, *par excellence,* qualified to act in this way." [6] Such feelings are often cited as a basic source of deviation from alliance norms: "The evidence suggests that where the [Chinese] communists move with the tide, i.e. nationalism, they are more successful than when they seek to move against it, i.e. 'the Russians are our brothers.' " [7]

Diffuse cultural factors are clearly not sufficient to explain French and Chinese foreign policy during the 1960s, because they also existed in the previous decade.[8] And although they may be viewed as background factors that have contributed to the political "education" of present leaders, providing at least latent support for foreign policies, they are not necessarily equally potent in both countries. Perhaps contributing to the differences between China and France is the fact that few top leaders in Peking, with the exception of Chou En-lai, have travelled extensively. For example, Lin Piao is reported never to have been outside China, and Mao Tse-tung, Liu Shao-chi and others have never been outside the bloc.[9] By way of contrast, French foreign policy leaders have travelled widely to virtually all parts of the world. Travel does not, of course, necessarily induce open-mindedness and flexibility in political behavior. But to the extent that travel is a relevant aspect of the socialization of political leaders, it is reasonable to suppose that it moderates any tendencies to view the world from a Manichean perspective.

For present purposes the most relevant socialization experiences of French and Chinese leaders are those related to international politics in general and alliance politics in particular. Historically France and China have been among the "great powers." But after experiencing considerable political instability during the inter-war years, both nations suffered invasion and catastrophic military defeats during the initial years of World War II, and only the military power of their allies enabled them to emerge victorious. During the war French and Chinese leaders often experienced disappointment and humiliation. Consider, for example, the key meetings of Allied leaders to which neither French nor Chinese representatives were invited, despite their nominal status as members of the "Big Five." Winston Churchill recalled that during the war, "The heaviest cross I had to bear was the Cross of Lorraine"; as De Gaulle's own memoirs have made clear, the General found that his relations with Allied Chiefs of State were equally frustrating.

Like statesmen in other nations who have successfully challenged their alliance leaders—for example, Tito in Yugoslavia or Hoxha in Albania—Mao and De Gaulle owed their positions to personal and national factors rather than to the intervention of their allies. The same has been true of their closest associates, including Georges Pompidou and Lin Piao, Mao's heir-apparent until late 1971. But even before achieving national leadership, they both experienced similar incidents with allies which may have convinced them of the virtues of self-reliance. Both developed something less than cordial relations with the leaders of their respective alliances. De Gaulle's frustrations in his dealings with Anglo-American leaders during World War II are well documented, as are Mao Tse-tung's disappointment with the halfhearted Soviet support for the revolution in China before and during World War II, and through a considerable period of the subsequent Chinese civil war. It is worth noting that these experiences were not limited to De Gaulle and Mao. Most of China's present leaders were with Mao during the revolutionary period,[10] and many prominent French political figures of the Fifth Republic were associated with De Gaulle's government-in-exile during World War II.

The political instability which had characterized China and France continued after the war, and only after the present regimes came to power in 1949 and 1958—after a civil war and near civil war—was internal stability restored. China and France were accorded some of the symbols of "Great Power" status but the realities of international politics during the cold war left little doubt that they were very junior partners in the alliances established by the Soviet Union and the United States. For economic reconstruction and national security both nations were heavily dependent upon Moscow and Washington. In many important respects France and China could be characterized as "penetrated" political systems [11] during this period. Although both were successful in resisting certain overt attempts by alliance leaders to force integration of their armed forces into those of the alliance—France rejected the European Defense Community in 1953 despite Dulles' threat of an "agonizing reappraisal," and China resisted Soviet overtures for some types of military integration in the late 1950s—the United States and the Soviet Union had an important influence on domestic and foreign policies in France and China.

From the point of view of French and Chinese leaders, the imbalance of costs over benefits deriving from their respective alliances must have become increasingly clear as a result of various international crises during the 1950s and early 1960s. As examples of the risks inherent in alliance membership they could point to the apparent Soviet and American willingness to drag their alliances close to the brink of nuclear war over Berlin and in other cold war disputes—or even over a few missiles on a small Caribbean island populated by neither Russians nor Americans. But if the potential risks of alliance membership were clear, the benefits must have appeared considerably more questionable. The Chinese were unable to count on Soviet support to regain offshore islands in the Taiwan straits, and they were publicly chided by Moscow for the frontier campaign against India in 1962. Promised Soviet support for China's nuclear weapons program was unilaterally broken off. Even Soviet economic aid was increasingly being diverted from China to nations in the "Third World" whose commitment to international revolution was suspect, and whose needs were not demonstrably greater than those of China.

Similarly, when interests defined as vital by the French were at stake—as in Indo-China and Algeria—they found that support from the alliance in general and from the United States in particular could scarcely be relied upon. Decisive French action to preserve control of the Suez Canal failed to elicit even a benevolent American neutrality, much less aid or sympathy. Indeed, during the height of the Suez crisis Vice-President Nixon and Secretary of State Dulles publicly lectured France on the obligations of international law, and in the United Nations the U.S. voted with the Soviets against France, Britain and Israel, while proclaiming American "independence" from the interests of "colonial" powers. Nor were the French more successful than the Chinese in gaining support for a nuclear weapons program, or even for genuine sharing of responsibility within NATO for decisions involving deployment or use of such weapons. Although General

De Gaulle was in temporary retirement during several of these episodes, it seems likely that they had considerable impact on his attitudes toward the western alliance.

Finally, whatever may have been the motives of American and Soviet leaders in signing the Nuclear Test Ban Treaty of 1963, Peking and Paris interpreted the treaty as a direct effort to retard their own nuclear weapons programs. Since that time China has regularly exploded nuclear weapons in the atmosphere, and the French suspended testing only temporarily in 1971. In short, as they defined their interests, by the early 1960s both Mao and De Gaulle had ample reason for dissatisfaction with their alliances and with the leadership provided by Moscow and Washington. If cold war crises have taught Soviet and American leaders that great caution is necessary to avoid a thermonuclear holocaust, the same events appear to have confirmed Chinese and French suspicions that their alliance commitments entailed far greater risks than benefits.

In part as a result of these and other experiences, both French and Chinese leaders have tended to define international alignments in a manner somewhat different from their bloc leaders, and these differences appear important for alliance relations. Repeated French calls for a Europe from "the Atlantic to the Urals" assume an end to the European sector of the cold war. Chinese conceptions of the international system have been less consistent. For a time during the 1960s leaders in Peking spoke of a group of middle-range powers providing a challenge to the two superpowers. Later this view was superseded by Lin Piao's thesis of a confrontation between the "cities of the world" and the "countryside of the world," which is similarly predicated upon major changes in international alignments.[12] In each of these definitions of the international system cold war alliances are transformed, for each view envisions a completely new role for Eastern Europe and the Soviet Union. It is not yet clear to what extent the end of the Cultural Revolution, the removal of Lin Piao, the Indo-Pak War, and the Nixon visit to China are a reflection of, or may result in, a new conception of the international system.

In summary, then, the alliance experiences of French and Chinese leaders appear analogous in a number of respects. The explanatory power of such anecdotal and unsystematic evidence may be quite limited, and certainly it provides no base from which to generalize to other dissatisfied alliance mavericks. It seems reasonable to suggest, however, that these episodes have helped to shape the political attitudes and predispositions of present French and Chinese elites. That is, might a generation of leaders who had not shared these experiences have been somewhat less prone to deviate from alliances which have been, in the main, products of American and Soviet policy?

The Stability of Top Leadership.   A second internal political characteristic which may be related to alliance policy is the stability of top leadership. The literature on alliance cohesion generally focuses on political attributes of the bloc leader. It is often asserted, for instance, that alliance cohesion depends upon stable leadership within the leading nation.[13] These propositions seem to have surface validity, but they do not appear adequate to explain recent disintegrative tendencies within the Communist system and the western alliance. Neither the United States nor the Soviet Union has experienced unusual elite instability during the past fifteen years. Individuals occupying top leadership positions have changed from time to time in both nations, but transitions from one set of leaders to another hardly appear to have arisen consistently from irrepressible demands for changes in foreign policy. Some writers have suggested that Nikita Khrushchev was ousted in 1964 owing to his espousal of a "hare-brained scheme" to launch a preemptive strike against Chinese nuclear installations but at best this appears to be pure conjecture.[14] A more plausible explanation is that the term "hare-brained scheme" referred to Khrushchev's agricultural policies. Lyndon Johnson's retirement may have been affected by public disaffection for his Vietnam policies, but other explanations may be equally valid. In the main the evidence appears to support Cohen's thesis [15] that Soviet and American leaders have effectively used the cold war through the mid-1960s to maintain political power, although by 1972 a reversal of this pattern may have been developing. President Nixon's visits to China and the Soviet Union appear to have been motivated at least in part by the premise that there was more electoral mileage in the politics of détente than in the politics of the cold war. Equally important, for our purposes, transitions in leadership have not had much impact on subsequent alliance policies. The leadership changes accompanying the demise of the Fourth Republic and the establishment of the Fifth Republic in France are perhaps the exception. Even the most sudden and unanticipated personnel changes—for example, the assassination of President Kennedy in 1963, the removal of Chairman Khrushchev a year later, the resignation of General De Gaulle in 1969, or the political and physical demise of Mao's one-time heir-apparent, Lin Piao—produced few basic changes in orientations toward allies. Thus it seems necessary to turn elsewhere in order to explain French and Chinese deviation from alliance commitments.

On the other hand, stable and effective leadership in nations other than the bloc leader may be a necessary, if not sufficient, condition for successful deviation from alliance norms. A casual survey of notable alliance mavericks—China, France, Rumania, Albania, or Yugoslavia since World War II, or Great Britain during the nineteenth century—appears to support this proposition. It may be that only leaders who enjoy some degree of structural protection against internal dissent, or who can afford to ignore it, are likely to undertake external policies which violate important bloc norms.[16] Unless leadership is stable and effective, the leading nation in the alliance may successfully appeal to and provide support for an alternative group of officials within the dissenting nation. While a study limited to two cases can only be suggestive, it is perhaps instructive to speculate about the consequences for alliance unity had the positions of Mao and De Gaulle been vulnerable to challenge by a strong opposition within China and France during the early 1960s. Might such circumstances have deterred Peking and Paris from challenging their alliance leaders? And if not, would the Soviets and Americans have been tempted to provide active support for a potentially more tractable group of leaders?

Instability of leadership characterized politics during the French Fourth Republic. Although personnel turnover was less spectacular than changes in governments, it was manifestly a source of difficulties in the formulation and execution of foreign policy. Not every American effort to guide French policy was a success; witness Dulles' spectacular failure to force France into the European Defense Community. Nevertheless, French political instability may have permitted greater American influence in French foreign policies at that time, whereas the absence of alternatives to De Gaulle and the Gaullist party during the Fifth Republic has left the United States with little choice but to accept French policies.

Similarly, few students of Chinese politics have failed to comment upon its stable leadership until recent years. Throughout its history most top positions in Peking have been filled by those who had been among Mao's leading lieutenants during the pre-1949 revolutionary period. With only a few exceptions—notably those of Kao Kang in 1954 and Peng Teh-huai in 1959—China had been free from periodic purges which seem to be a recurring feature of politics in other Communist nations.

This period of stability came to an end with the advent of the Cultural Revolution which brought with it purges reaching into the very highest echelons of Chinese leadership. Yet the events surrounding the Cultural Revolution do not necessarily nullify the proposition that stable leadership can be an important element in successful deviation from alliance norms. Whether one dates the breach between Moscow and Peking early (the late 1950s) or late (1962–63), the period of China's break with the alliance *was* one of elite stability. The fact that the deviation was maintained through the subsequent period of leadership instability suggests that by 1966 China's split with Moscow and many other Communist nations was probably already beyond repair. Moreover, despite post facto efforts to label purged officials such as ex-President Liu Shao-chi as "pro-Soviet," there is neither evidence that any top leaders in China have espoused the case for renewed deference to Moscow, nor that they could enhance their prospects for personal advancement by doing so. Soviet expressions of sympathy [17] (and material aid, according to unconfirmed reports) for anti-Mao factions within China also suggest that unstable leadership within the dissident nation will tempt the alliance leader to interfere in its internal political processes.

Stable leadership may be a necessary condition for an effective policy of deviation from bloc norms. Conversely, nonconforming alliance policies may serve to solidify the position of top leaders. This is, of course, a variant of the popular theory that antagonism toward foreign nations may prove the smoothest road for achieving or maintaining domestic political power. Cohen's suggestion that cold war competition has been instrumental in maintaining the American and Soviet "establishment" in power is a case in point. There is evidence that the symbols of intra-alliance competition have similarly been used by French and Chinese leaders.[18]

General De Gaulle effectively employed nationalistic and anti-alliance rhetoric in his successful political campaigns. And even results of the 1967 parliamentary elections, in which the Gaullist parliamentary majority was severely reduced, or the plebiscite which led to the General's resignation, do not appear to have reflected voter dissatisfaction with De Gaulle's foreign policies. In 1967, for example, supporters of Jean Lecanuet, the so-called "American candidate," suffered even worse losses than the Gaullists. Moreover, the largest gains were made by the Communists. This pattern suggests that issues other than French alliance policies were responsible for the election results.

A more dramatic version of the same political process appears to be taking place in China. It has often been suggested that the Cultural Revolution and its attendant political purges were triggered by Maoist efforts to cleanse Chinese society of all threats—manifest and latent, real and imagined—to revolutionary purity. To some extent this may be a general reaction against all foreign influences. But among the most salient and immediate threats to Maoist ideology and institutions are those of the Soviet "modern revisionists," who are not only geographically proximate, but who have also had the most opportunity for "subversion." The United States may be viewed by the Chinese as a threat to national security, but there is scarcely any danger that an emerging generation of Chinese leaders will emulate American social, political, ideological, or cultural norms. Among Chinese elites, few have ever visited the United States, and it would be surprising indeed if two decades of vitriolic anti-American sloganeering has not left most of them with indelible images of a social system without a single redeeming feature. Maoist leaders may feel less secure, however, that the Soviet variant of Marxism will not prove an attractive and viable model for future Chinese leaders. Thus portrayals of external enemies used to generate political activity on behalf of those in power in China are no longer confined to the western "imperialist" nations. The Soviet Union has perhaps surpassed the United States as the most bitterly criticized enemy of China. On October 1, 1972, the 23rd anniversary of the People's Republic, a joint editorial in three authoritative publications explicitly listed the Soviet Union as China's most dangerous enemy; at the same time it praised the "frank and beneficial talks" with President Nixon, noting that "the gate to friendly contacts between the people of the two countries is now open." [19]

As one observer has commented, "The rift with the Soviet Union has been critically important in maintaining the CCP suspicion of domestic heterodoxy and its determination to resist any political and economic concessions that might smack of 'revisionism.' " [20] Liu Shao-chi, Teng Hsiao-ping, Tao Chu and others who have fallen from Mao's grace have been attacked for following a pro-Soviet line. Whether they have in fact done so is far from evident; what is clear is that anti-Soviet symbols have become a dominant theme in Chinese political rhetoric. Major efforts to mobilize the population for extraordinary efforts have been justified in large part by invoking the threat to the north. Thus the competition and conflict within the alliance appear to be having at least as much impact on Chinese internal politics as competition between alliances.

Pluralistic and Authoritarian Polities. To this point we have suggested —anecdotally and impressionistically—some of the shared political attributes which may be linked to similar patterns of French and Chinese foreign policy toward their respective alliances and alliance leaders. We have treated these two political systems as members of a single class and we will present data to indicate that both have indeed deviated from important bloc norms. But there are dangers in attempting to carry the parallels too far. To do so would be to suggest: (1) that patterns of Chinese and French alliance policy are similar in all respects; (2) that manifest differences in the French and Chinese polities are politically less relevant than the similarities already discussed; and (3) that alliance policy is solely a reflection of internal political factors, and that striking differences in the structure and operation of the western alliance and the Communist system are irrelevant to French and Chinese policy. The remainder of this chapter will address itself to a critical examination of these three points by identifying some important dissimilarities in French and Chinese alliance policies and by attempting to link them to differences in national and alliance attributes.

Our initial observations indicate that French and Chinese alliance policies, while sharing a tendency toward deviation from norms of their respective alliances, diverge in the extent of their break with their alliances in general and with the alliance leaders in particular. That is:

French nonconforming behavior has remained confined to a few issue-areas, with little tendency for it to spill over into all issue-areas.

Chinese nonconforming behavior has tended to spill over into all issue-areas.

These assertions appear to have face validity in that the Sino-Soviet rift and Moscow's ability to mobilize other Communist nations in a polemical battle against Peking seems to exceed by a considerable margin the disruption within the western alliance. However, they do not indicate the reasons for the differences. In an attempt to do so we will turn first to attributes of the French and Chinese political systems in an effort to illustrate the linkages between some basic dissimilarities in internal political processes and the alliance policies to which they give rise.

By virtually any method of classifying political systems the differences between France and China are considerably more obvious than the similarities. It has been suggested, for instance, that a "pre-theory" of comparative foreign policy might be developed by classifying political systems on three dimensions: *open polity–closed polity,* economically *developed-underdeveloped,* and *large-small.*[21] On the first two attributes France and China are sufficiently different in that there is no difficulty in determining which is the more open or the more developed economically, and they differ, if somewhat less spectacularly, with respect to size. This discussion will focus on the first of these attributes—the political dimension.

The hypotheses can be restated in terms which link the nature of the political system to differences in alliance policy.

Nonconforming alliance policies of an open polity tend to remain confined to a few issue-areas; that is, there is little tendency for disputes to spill over into all issue-areas.

Nonconforming alliance policies of a closed polity tend to spill over into all issue-areas.

These hypotheses derive from the view that in a pluralistic system foreign policy elites operate under significant constraints against sudden and complete changes in policy. These include multiple internal and external channels of communication, relative freedom for divergent interests to make political demands, and a limited ability of top leaders to mobilize all politically relevant groups and institutions in support of their policies.

One significant barrier against a complete French break from its alliance exists in the many national and international organizations—governmental, semigovernmental and private—through which French elites can communicate with their counterparts in allied nations. Even if communication between top leaders is not particularly good, as was the case between Paris and Washington during much of General De Gaulle's tenure, other formal and informal channels of communication remain. Such organizations tend to generate multiple interests and loyalties which cut across national boundaries, as well as across issues. The existence of these ties, which are likely to survive alliance disunity in one issue area, have been used to explain the relatively moderate rupture in Franco-American relations.

> In both countries, the political 'establishment' contains a large cadre of men deeply involved in the development of NATO and European unity, and in the application of American aid to the recovery of France; this has created a special bond of understanding and shared interest. In each country there were prominent individuals pleading for reciprocal restraint and cooperation. To the United States, individuals such as Jean Monnet or Robert Schumann were an important source of reassurance that the basic ties were not being severed. To the French leader, the voices of General Norstad, Ambassador Gavin, and Governor Rockefeller meant that his conceptions had important American interpreters; and this too was vital in maintaining a relationship of continuing discussion.[22]

Equally important, a pluralistic polity is generally characterized by at least a moderate degree of functional autonomy. Public officials who owe their positions in part to technical expertise, rather than merely to political loyalties, are likely to be more numerous and influential in policy making. Individuals, groups and institutions responsible for policy in various issue-areas may represent quite different values, loyalties, and interests. They are likely to serve as barriers against central control of policy in all issue-areas and therefore may act as a moderating force against radical policy changes. That technical experts in an open polity may develop interests and loyalties which resist complete control by top political leaders is illustrated in a study of agricultural politics in the European Economic Community. "The relative power and prestige of 'technical ministers,' such as agriculture, have typically been enhanced . . . generating further interest on their part in maintaining the system [EEC]. Ministers of foreign affairs who have tried to maintain control of community matters by preserving the distinction between foreign policy and domestic policy have, in general, been fighting a losing battle." [23]

Other potential internal constraints operating against a complete rupture of French alliance policy can be illustrated by some recent opinion surveys. French political elites approved of the trend toward increasingly nationalistic policies in a world which is becoming more multipolar. But they also indicated a preference for maintaining strong links to the United States. They agreed that French security is largely dependent on the United States, and they seemed confident that American commitments to European security will be honored. Public opinion data revealed a similar ambivalence to Gaullist foreign policies. A majority opposed alignment with the United States; at the same time most respondents indicated that France's interests are closely tied to the United States and public attitudes toward the United States have become more favorable during the period of the Fifth Republic. A poll taken in March 1970, for example, revealed that only 11 percent of the population was "unhappy" or "very unhappy" with Franco-American relations. Another poll by the French Opinion Survey Organization revealed that most Frenchmen, even Communist voters, regard the United States as their country's best friend and ally. A similar pattern of attitudes has existed toward Great Britain and its possible entry into the Common Market. Despite De Gaulle's emphasis on an independent nuclear force, there was limited support for this program both among elites and the public. Finally, while elites, masses, and newspapers indicated reservations about NATO, these doubts have not spilled over into other areas of international cooperation such as trade and cultural activities.[24]

No doubt one reason for these findings is that neither French nor American leaders have made any real effort to mobilize public opinion against the other nation. In any case, it is far from evident that they would have been successful had they tried. In a relatively open political system such public views are likely to act as at least partial constraints against revolutionary and thoroughgoing changes in policy, even when a leader as commanding as De Gaulle or as popular as Eisenhower heads the nation.

Hence, whether policy formulation is considered vertically (hierarchical levels of responsibility for policy) or horizontally (responsibility for policy in different issue-areas), in a pluralistic polity there are likely to be sufficient cross-cutting interests and loyalties to preclude a complete break from preexisting policies. Equally important, there appears to be no compulsion to define nations with which one disagrees as total enemies.

A similar line of reasoning suggests that the linkages between political processes in an authoritarian polity and its international environments will differ from those of pluralistic political systems. On the one hand, the "party line" on foreign policy in an authoritarian political system tends to define acceptable policy in all issue-areas. Within nations in the Communist system, the sources of these guidelines include the all-encompassing world view of Marxist-Leninist thought, or at least whatever version of the catechism that currently finds favor in Moscow or Peking. Compounding the problem is the fact that Marxist theory blurs, if not eliminates, the distinction between politics and ethics; an adversary is not merely an adversary, he becomes the incarnation of evil. Thus once it is determined that the erstwhile alliance partner is among the "enemies," as Chinese and Soviet leaders now appear to categorize each other, this designation is expected to guide policy makers in all issue-areas. This point is amply illustrated by polemics originating in Moscow and Peking. In perhaps the bitterest attack on China to date, a twenty-four-column *Pravda* editorial charged that, "The people in Peking emulate the ringleaders of the Nazi Reich." But it was not sufficient merely to level political broadsides; even Chinese cultural policies came under fire: "Not a single work of fiction was published in the last four years, not a single feature film was made and museums and libraries are closed." [25] Chinese replies have been equally sweeping. On the fiftieth anniversary of the October Revolution, the USSR was condemned for failings ranging from betrayal of the revolution to poor medical services for the masses and cultural decadence.[26] Even the long-dead Russian theatrical producer, Stanislavsky, has been singled out for attack.[27]

Authoritarian polities, moreover, tend to lack institutionalized barriers against radical changes in policy—of which nonconforming alliance behavior is an example—in all issue-areas. Minimal channels of communications with allies, a relative absence of elites and groups representing multiple interests and possessing multiple loyalties, and centralization of policy formulation functions reduce the probabilities that alliance disunity in one issue-area can be contained within limited spheres of alliance activity.

Because an authoritarian polity such as China possesses limited channels of communication with allies, a rupture at the top leadership level has more severe consequences for alliance policy than would be the case for a pluralistic nation. Once the Sino-Soviet conflict had engulfed top levels of Chinese and Russian leadership, there were no effective channels at lower echelons through which the ties could be maintained and perhaps repaired; informal or nongovernmental ones simply did not exist. This is emphasized by the following:

> Because of the monolithic structure of the Soviet and Chinese systems, any such informal and indirect ties would have automatically threatened the stability of their respective leaderships. Formal communication exhausted all communication, with no safety valve of the indirect approach and no commonly shared experience in constructive understandings as a cushion. The Soviet and Chinese leaders met only on several formal occasions; there was simply no "Sino-Soviet Establishment" to

plead the cause of unity and to moderate the increasingly immoderate language of the debate.[28]

This interpretation does not necessarily contradict the more specific reasons often given for the rift between Peking and Moscow, for example, explanations which locate a major source of conflict in personality differences between Mao, Khrushchev and others.[29] It is precisely because few external channels of communication exist in authoritarian polities that personality differences between top Chinese and Soviet leaders take on great political importance. Such differences also existed between Presidents Eisenhower, Kennedy, and Johnson on the one hand, and De Gaulle on the other, but their political consequences were less far-reaching. Stated more generally, idiosyncratic factors such as personality are likely to have a more significant impact on formulation of foreign policy in a closed political system.[30]

Authoritarian political systems also lack effective internal barriers against a spill-over of alliance disputes from one issue-area to all of them. Leaders responsible for policy in all issue-areas are likely to embrace similar attitudes and policies toward the alliance and its members. Moreover, Mao has effectively ensured that all of his subordinates have been brought into the battle of polemics against Moscow.[31] Hence one internal consequence of the dispute with the Soviet Union has been that officials responsible for policy in *all* issue-areas have been drawn into an anti-Soviet position. This has in turn contributed to an increasingly intransigent Chinese policy toward Moscow.

The absence of effective constraints appears not only in the top level of leadership but also at all levels in the bureaucracy, where political loyalty tends to take precedence over competence, especially during periods of crisis. Moreover, the nature of Chinese bureaucracy tends to preclude the development of cliques which represent interests other than those of the political leadership. The kinds of extranational bureaucratic loyalties which have developed in France are unlikely to be found in China, for, "The balance of power is clearly in the hands of the higher authorities, and the systematic breaking up of possible cliques by sending in outsiders, and transferring out insiders in a rudimentary clique prevents true cliques from developing." [32]

Other evidence also suggests that, during the period in which the Sino-Soviet break developed, an increasing concentration of decision making authority and a concomitant standardization of policy in all issue-areas took place. Senior party leaders were sent from Peking to assignments in regional bureaus, reversing an earlier tendency to promote the most capable regional leaders to Peking; ambassadorial appointments were increasingly drawn from party operatives rather than from experienced foreign service officers; and in the central control commission closer links were established between top leaders in Peking and the provinces.[33] Whatever the reasons for these changes, they reduced potential constraints on a mobilization of internal support against the Soviet Union in all issue-areas.

Finally, it is sometimes said that freedom from broadly-based domestic constraints permits China to pursue an aggressive policy against the West.[34] But such freedom may be even *more* important to mobilize a vast population against a nation once hailed as the vanguard of the international socialist movement.

In their analysis of western and Communist alliance management, Brzezinski and Huntington conclude that "factors peculiar to the American and Soviet political systems" were "decisive" in containment of the Franco-American dispute and in escalation of the Sino-Soviet split.[35] The point we have been developing here is a complementary, not a contradictory one. That is, political factors in France and China—some of which have been described in this discussion—have also contributed to different patterns of deviation from alliance norms. That is, basic differences in the French and Chinese political processes appear systematically linked to different patterns of relationships with their allies.

Alliance Structure and Nonconforming Alliance Policies

In the preceding sections we speculated about some of the ways in which internal political processes might be linked to patterns of nonconforming alliance policies. At this point we shift our focus to consider how characteristics of the alliances themselves may be linked to differences in coalition politics.

Observers who have considered problems of alliance cohesion and disintegration by comparing the Communist system with the western alliance have differed rather sharply in their analyses and predictions. Liska and Morgenthau tend to judge developments within the two alliances as rather similar in character, whereas Dinerstein and Kissinger emphasize differences between the blocs, viewing schisms within the Communist system as far more serious.[36] Explanations of deviation from alliance norms also take many forms. Among the more plausible are those which point to a decreased level of inter-bloc conflict, the nature of bloc leadership, or the diffusion of military technology.[37] Others have attempted to explain a somewhat different aspect of the problem—the *form* that nonconforming behavior takes—with propositions linking the nature of the alliance to patterns of nonconforming behavior. Each of these propositions is testable, but we will limit ourselves to an assessment of hypotheses relating attributes of alliances and forms of deviation from alliance norms. The following discussion specifies some differences between monolithic and pluralistic alliances, from which fourteen propositions that predict differences in *forms* of nonconforming behavior by numbers of monolithic and pluralistic alliances are derived.

A pluralistic alliance is marked by fragmented authority and recognition that member-nations may legitimately maintain diverse social systems and ideologies. Conversely, in a monolithic alliance decision making authority is centralized—it is usually exercised by its leading member nation—and conformity is demanded in most areas of public policy, not excluding what are usually considered purely internal questions. These definitions are intended to describe "ideal types" which no alliance is likely to match in every detail. Our propositions will be tested with data on French and Chinese relations with their allies. We do not imply, however, that the Communist system is absolutely monolithic, nor that the western alliance is pluralistic in all respects. We hold only that the latter is the closer of the two to the pluralistic end of the continuum, and that the distinction between the two is sufficiently evident to permit their use as examples of alliances that differ in structure.[38] It should also be stated that, being unable to reject competing explanations of the same behavior on the basis of two cases, we can only undertake the most preliminary test of the propositions.

Monolithic Alliances.   Solemn words about sovereignty and equality in treaties of alliance notwithstanding, we assume that in a monolithic bloc the ability to influence goals, strategy, and tactics will be unequally distributed and highly concentrated. In practice such an alliance will be marked by a rigidly hierarchical organization with the relationships between the leading nation and the others clearly defined. These qualities will be reflected in the formulation of all key policies. Thus,

DEFINITION 1.   *A monolithic bloc possesses a greater degree of centralization of decision making authority than a pluralistic alliance.*

Monolithic blocs are characterized by a common outlook and orientation, often imposed by the bloc leaders, to each other and to the external environment. This outlook is "total" in the sense that it enters into all aspects of bloc and polity activities. This seems especially true of the Communist system, which has been described as "a functionally diffuse grouping in which cooperation is not tied to one specific goal, but potentially embraces all spheres of international activity." [39] Put somewhat differently, among Communist nations everything is political, including trade, culture, and the like; no area of activity is permitted to remain autonomous from political relationships. The "Brezhnev Doctrine," under which the Soviet Union reserves the right to use Warsaw Pact forces to intervene in the internal affairs of any Communist nation in order to "preserve socialism," illustrates both the wide scope of alliance activities and the concentration of effective authority.

DEFINITION 2. *A monolithic bloc has a wider sectorial scope, operating in many issue-areas, than a pluralistic alliance.*

A bloc that operates in many issue-areas has more potential sources of conflict than one with more limited functions. As Modelski has noted,

> the Communist system creates a type of difficulty which is not very apt to reach the governmental level in non-Communist countries but which does so in the Communist system because of the complete state control over economic and other fields of life. Hence within the system the likelihood is greater of disputes over prices set in trade agreements, over the quality of goods delivered, over quantity of foreign aid, over the behavior of Soviet civilians, troops, and specialists, over special privileges granted to one state, etc.[40]

Two solutions to the problem of maintaining cohesion suggest themselves: a reduction in heterogeneity among alliance members or a reduction in bloc membership.[41] The invasion and repression of Hungary in 1956 and Czechoslovakia in 1968 illustrate the first method; expulsion of Yugoslavia from the Cominform and exclusion of Albania from Warsaw Pact meetings are examples of the second. From the perspective of the bloc leader the former approach may seem preferable, except when there are geographical or other constraints against direct repression, as was the case with both Yugoslavia and Albania. Thus,

PROPOSITION 1. *The wider the sectorial scope of an alliance, the greater the necessity for consensus.*

The existence of status differences, the large number of issue-areas within which the alliance operates and the requirement for consensus in a monolithic alliance imply that the leading nation will tend to become dominant in all issue-areas. For instance, within the more pluralistic western alliance the United States is not dominant with respect to cultural relations, as all members tend to relate to each other as equals in this area as well as many others, whereas within the Communist system the Soviet Union dominated all issue-areas, including cultural relations. Thus,

PROPOSITION 2. *The more monolithic the alliance, the more likely it is that the alliance leader is dominant in all issue-areas.*

An alliance leader intent on maintaining both its dominant position and bloc cohesion is likely to use coercive means to repress strains on any major issue.[42] To bargain with subordinates implies some lessening of differences in status. Within the more pluralistic western alliance a tradition of compromise and adjustment has contributed to containment of disputes. Perhaps equally important has been the general lack of compulsion to force each issue to complete resolution. Recent Franco-American relations illustrate the latter point; each side appears more or less resigned to the other's policies, and both have carefully tended to ignore the issues which divide them. Within the Communist system, on the other hand, the pragmatic style of conflict resolution is quite alien. When opposing views on substantive issues are couched in doctrinal terms, each dispute in effect becomes two—one substantive and one ideological—and demands buttressed by claims of ideological purity and charges of doctrinal heresy do not easily lend themselves to compromise. Thus,

PROPOSITION 3.   *The higher the necessity for consensus in all issue-areas, and the more explicit the status differences within the alliance, the more likely it is that the alliance leader will use repression rather than bargaining to resolve strains.*

The observation that nonconforming behavior is less likely to occur in more hierarchical and structurally centralized alliances, because they are capable of acting with greater energy with respect to intra-bloc and inter-bloc issues, is a recurring one in the alliance literature.[43] Moreover, status differences associated with a monolithic alliance are likely to be based in substantial part on the leader's superior coercive capabilities, further suggesting that successful deviation by subordinate members of the alliance is unlikely. Thus,

PROPOSITION 4.   *The more monolithic the alliance, the lower the probability that nonconforming behavior will be successful.*

According to Proposition 2, the leading nation within a monolithic alliance is likely to maintain a hegemonic position in all issue-areas. Within such an alliance, deviation from bloc norms in any issue-area is likely to be construed as a challenge to the leader in all of them. On the other hand, a nation within a pluralistic alliance, not faced with a leader supreme in all areas of activity, may more readily be able to deviate from alliance norms in some issue-areas without doing so "across the board." If an American president expresses a preference for California over French wines, or a French movie receives a bad review in London, the diplomatic consequences are likely to be less than shattering. But let an "approved" Soviet novel be denounced in Peking, or let an exuberant crowd in Prague celebrate a Czech victory over a Soviet ice hockey team, and it will immediately take on serious political overtones. Thus,

PROPOSITION 5. *The more monolithic the alliance, the more likely is successful nonconforming behavior in any issue-area to be treated as a challenge to the leader's dominance.*

Successful defiance of the alliance norms is improbable in a monolithic bloc. But such behavior by subordinate nations in any issue-area is unlikely to be tolerated by the bloc leader. Hence any deviation from alliance norms is likely to spur the leader into renewed action in all issue-areas to maintain a dominant position. And, characteristically, the means are likely to be coercive; as Brzezinski notes with respect to the Communist system, "The suppression of diversity and the forceful imposition of unity almost inevitably result in excessive reliance on force." [44] Thus,

PROPOSITION 6. *In a monolithic alliance, unsuccessful efforts to repress nonconforming behavior in one issue-area will impel the bloc leader toward increased efforts to maintain its position and alliance consensus by reasserting its dominance in other issue-areas.*

One of the interesting questions posed by students of integration is that of "role differentiation" versus "spill-over" theories.[45] According to the former theory, cooperation between political units in one issue-area neither depends upon, nor enhances the prospects for, collaboration in other types of activities. Spill-over theory, on the other hand, asserts that agreement for concerted action in one issue-area induces the partners to make further agreements in other enterprises; for example, proponents of foreign trade or cultural exchange programs often assert that they will result in closer political relations between the participating nations. As suggested by the somewhat contradictory conclusions in the integration literature, the superiority of either theory, or the conditions under which each is more valid, remains to be demonstrated conclusively.

Little attention has been paid to the reverse process—the extent to which *nonconforming* or *disintegrative* behavior in one issue-area is likely to affect alliance relations in others—although several observers have suggested the likelihood of a general erosion of unity with the Communist system: ". . . the cohesion of the Communist alliance system, once pressed into a rigid mold, will suffer much greater disintegration than the always loose non-Communist system." [46] Proposition 7 (and 7a below) can be viewed as a way of suggesting that role differentiation and spill-over theories may also be applied to disintegrative processes, and that the latter may be more valid in monolithic alliances, whereas the former theory is more applicable to pluralistic ones. Thus,

PROPOSITION 7   *In a monolithic alliance, if nonconforming behavior should be successful in one issue-area, there is a high probability that such behavior will spill over into other issue-areas (that is, the efforts of the bloc leader to contain differences are likely to fail).*

Pluralistic Alliances.   The propositions identifying the characteristics of pluralistic alliances, and the line of reasoning we offer in support of them, are essentially the converse of those describing monolithic alliances.

DEFINITION 1A.   *Decision making authority in a pluralistic alliance is less centralized than in a monolithic one.*

DEFINITION 2A.   *A pluralistic alliance has a narrower sectorial scope, operating in fewer issue-areas, than a monolithic alliance.*

PROPOSITION 1A.   *The narrower the sectorial scope of an alliance, the less is the necessity for consensus.*

PROPOSITION 2A.   *The more pluralistic an alliance, the less likely it is that the alliance leader is dominant in all issue-areas.*

PROPOSITION 3A.   *The less the necessity for consensus in all issue-areas, and the less explicit the status differences within an alliance, the more likely it is that the leader will bargain to resolve strains rather than attempt to repress them.*

PROPOSITION 4A.   *The more pluralistic the alliance, the higher the probability that nonconforming behavior will be successful.*

PROPOSITION 5A.   *In a more pluralistic alliance, successful nonconforming behavior is likely to be treated as a challenge to the bloc leader in only limited issue-areas. (This follows from Proposition 2A which states that the bloc leader is unlikely to be dominant in all issue-areas.)*

PROPOSITION 6A.   *In a more pluralistic alliance, unsuccessful efforts to forestall nonconforming behavior are less likely to result in attempts by the bloc leader to assert dominance in other issue-areas.*

PROPOSITION 7A.   *In a more pluralistic alliance, if nonconforming behavior within a specific issue-area is successful, there is a low probability that such behavior will spill over into other issue-areas.*

The relevance of these propositions to the study of Chinese and French nonconforming behavior depends upon the assumption that the definitions spelled out above are applicable to the Communist system and the western alliance; namely, that the Communist system is intended to operate across a wider spectrum of issue-areas than is the western alliance, and that the former is more hierarchically organized than the latter. If these assumptions are valid we would expect, according to Proposition 7, to find China at odds with its alliance partners—and especially the Soviet Union—in nearly all issue-areas. On the other hand, French relations with its allies should remain relatively intact in several issue-areas if Proposition 7A is valid. The intervening propositions (1–6 and 1A–6A linking the definitions with predictions about differences in alliance relationships are capable of being tested empirically. We shall not do so here, however. The data presented in the next chapter are intended only to shed light on the differences between Chinese and French policies as predicted by Propositions 7 and 7A.

Conclusion

This chapter has explored some of the linkages between the attributes of nations which deviate from alliances and the nature of the alliances themselves. We have described some of the similarities and differences in French and Chinese political processes, and speculated about their consequences for alliance policy. We also considered some of the differences between monolithic and pluralistic alliances, and suggested how these might be linked to the fact that France's relations with the western alliance have been less severely disrupted than those of China with the Communist system. In the next chapter we shall present data on French and Chinese alliance relations in order to test Propositions 7 and 7a.

Notes

1. James N. Rosenau, "Toward the Study of National-International Linkages," in Rosenau, ed., *Linkage Politics: Essays on the Convergence of National and International Systems,* Free Press, New York, 1969. We have also profited from reading his "Pre-Theories and Theories of Foreign Policy," in R. Barry Farrell, ed., *Approaches to Comparative and International Politics,* Northwestern University Press, Evanston, 1966. We are aware of the distinction sometimes made between "blocs" and "alliances." We will use the terms interchangeably only for literary reasons.
2. Some would maintain that it is the United States and the Soviet Union, rather than France and China, which have deviated from bloc norms. We shall not address ourselves to this question. To do so would be to stray from our purpose of examining the impact of national and alliance attributes on intra-alliance friction, and place us back in the position of weighing the merits of claims and counter-claims made in current controversies within the two alliances.

3. Rosenau, "Toward the Study of National-International Linkages," *op. cit.,* p. 45 (italics added).
4. Such a list of questions could be endless. Spinning out all determinants or consequences of any foreign policy undertaking would be limited only with the advent of a developed theory of "linkages" which predicted specific consequences as a result of polity or environmental outputs. Were such a theory available, it would be necessary to examine only those consequences predicted by the theory in order to evaluate it. Yet these few questions indicate that even if we leave to the historian the task of reconstructing unique events in all their complexity, identifying and describing theoretically important national-international linkages will require the collective energies of a substantial proportion of those who consider themselves students of comparative or international politics. This is not said in criticism of the enterprise or to discourage what seems to us a clearly desirable course of events.
5. Brzezinski and Huntington have noted that ". . . the two restless allies considered themselves to be the real repositories of the essential values of the Western and communist camps respectively. The struggle of the West, as the French saw it, was not to safeguard American civilization, but primarily to defend the European tradition—and who could be a better interpreter of that than France? To the Chinese, the cause of communism was not to make the Soviet Union a member of the 'international establishment'—a cause they suspected Khrushchev of pursuing—but to assist in the spread of the revolution, particularly among the post-colonial masses of the underdeveloped nations. For these struggling masses, what could serve as a more appropriate model than the Chinese revolution?" Zbigniew Brzezinski and Samuel P. Huntington, *Political Power: USA/USSR,* The Viking Press, New York, 1964, p. 390.
6. Ambassade de France, Service de Presse et d'Information, "President De Gaulle Holds Twelfth Press Conference," Speeches and Press Conferences No. 228, Sept. 9, 1965, p. 8.
7. Robert A. Scalapino, "The Foreign Policy of the People's Republic of China," in Joseph E. Black and Kenneth W. Thompson, eds., *Foreign Policies in a World of Change,* Harper & Row, New York, 1963, p. 563.
8. See, for example, Benjamin I. Schwarz, "The Maoist Image of World Order," *Journal of International Affairs,* 21, 1967, who demonstrates some of the dangers of assuming that Chinese decision-makers merely reflect uniform cultural attributes.
9. Donald Klein, "Peking's Leaders: A Study in Isolation," *China Quarterly,* 7, 1961. Lack of foreign experience is also reflected in the membership of the CCP Central Committee. Of 126 members for whom data were available, only 41 have been abroad, 35 of them to the USSR. None has ever visited the United States. Jurgen Domes, "The Ninth CCP Central Committee in Statistical Perspective," *Current Scene,* 9, 1971, p. 9.
10. Over 80 percent of the Ninth Central Committee membership joined the CCP prior to the Long March in 1935. Domes, *op. cit.,* p. 10.

11. This term is borrowed from Rosenau, "Pre-Theories and Theories of Foreign Policy," *op. cit.,* pp. 65 ff.

12. Michael B. Yahuda, "Chinese Foreign Policy After 1963: The Maoist Phases," *China Quarterly,* 36, 1968, pp. 93–113.

13. George Liska, *Nations in Alliance: The Limits of Interdependence,* Johns Hopkins Press, Baltimore, 1962, p. 93. On the other hand, Jacob and Teune suggest that governmental ineffectiveness, which presumably indicates the absence of stable and effective leadership, may provide added incentives for seeking larger units of community. Philip E. Jacob and Henry Teune, "The Integrative Process: Guidelines for Analysis of the Bases of Political Community," in Philip E. Jacob and James V. Toscano, eds., *The Integration of Political Communities,* J. B. Lippincott Co., Philadelphia, 1964.

14. The argument that Khrushchev was ousted because of his plans for a preemptive strike against China is developed in Harold C. Hinton, *Communist China and World Politics,* Houghton Mifflin, Boston, 1966, Ch. 17. A strong case against Hinton's thesis appears in Walter C. Clemens, Jr., "Chinese Nuclear Tests: Trends and Portents," *China Quarterly,* 32, 1967.

15. Bernard Cohen, "National-International Linkages: Superpolities," in James N. Rosenau, ed., *Linkage Politics: Essays on the Convergence of National and International Systems,* Free Press, New York, 1969.

16. This interpretation is at variance with that of Peter S. H. Tang, who asserts that the relative absence of internal competition for political leadership in China and the Soviet Union supports cooperation, rather than conflict between them. Tang, *Communist China Today,* 2d ed., Research Institute on the Sino-Soviet Bloc, Washington, 1961, p. 488.

17. See, for example, Kosygin's press conference in London, February 10, 1967.

18. This has not been confined to France and China. For example, the fast-rising "Waffle" faction of the New Democratic Party in Canada offers an almost pure brand of anti-American and anti-NATO rhetoric. The Waffleites never fail to find evil Yankee capitalism at the root of every national and international problem, be it the plight of Canadian Indians or the absence of peace in any part of the world.

19. *Los Angeles Times,* October 2, 1972, p. 1. A content analysis of the authoritative *Jen-min Jih-pao* [*Peoples' Daily*] for the period 1967–1969 revealed a rising concern for Soviet external policy and declining attention to American foreign policy. Daniel Tretiak, "Changes in Chinese Attention to Southeast Asia, 1967–1969: Their Relevance for the Future of the Area," *Current Scene,* 7, 1969, p. 11. See also John J. Taylor, "The Maoist Revolutionary Model in Asia," *Current Scene,* 9, 1971, p. 15.

20. James R. Townsend, "Internal Politics Since 1956," *Bulletin of the Atomic Scientists,* 22, 1966, p. 65.

21. Rosenau, "Pre-Theories and Theories of Foreign Policy," *op. cit.* For quantitative evidence of the vast differences between France and China on these three dimensions, see Jack E. Vincent, "Generating Some Empiri-

cally Based Indices for International Alliance and Regional Systems Operating in the Early 1960's," *International Studies Quarterly,* 15, 1971.

22. Brzezinski and Huntington, *op. cit.,* pp. 404–405. For a more general discussion of the advantages enjoyed by open polities in formulating foreign policy, see Kenneth N. Waltz, *Foreign Policy and Democratic Politics,* Little, Brown and Co., Boston, 1967, esp. Ch. 11.

23. Leon N. Lindberg, "Decision Making and Integration in the European Community," *International Organization,* 19, 1965, p. 74.

24. The data in this paragraph were derived from Karl W. Deutsch, "Integration and Arms Control in the European Political Environment: A Summary Report," *American Political Science Review,* 60, 1966; W. W. Kulski, *De Gaulle and the World: The Foreign Policy of the Fifth French Republic,* Syracuse University Press, Syracuse, 1966; Michel Gordey, "The French People and De Gaulle," *Foreign Affairs,* 62, 1964; Ambassade de France, Service de Presse et d'Information, Press Release No. 1363, April, 1970; and "U.S. called best friend in poll of Frenchmen," *Christian Science Monitor,* January 7, 1972, p. 3.

25. *Pravda,* May 18, 1970, reprinted in the *New York Times,* May 19, 1970, p. 14.

26. *China Quarterly,* 33, 1968, pp. 172–174.

27. The Editor, "1969 Through Peking's Eyes: A Survey of Chinese Media," *Current Scene,* 8, 1970, p. 6; Shanghai Revolutionary Mass Criticism Writing Group, *On Stanislavsky's System,* 1970.

28. Brzezinski and Huntington, *op. cit.,* p. 405.

29. David Floyd, *Mao Against Khrushchev: A Short History of the Sino-Soviet Conflict,* Praeger, New York, 1964, p. 77; Scalapino, *op. cit.,* p. 568.

30. Cf. Rosenau, "Pre-Theories and Theories of Foreign Policy," *op. cit.,* pp. 90–91.

31. Donald W. Klein, "Succession and the Elite in Peking," *Journal of International Affairs,* 18, 1964, p. 8.

32. Ezra Vogel, "Politicized Bureaucracy: Communist China," paper read at American Political Science Association meeting, 1966, p. 8. Useful discussions of the Chinese Foreign Ministry appear in Donald W. Klein, "The Management of Foreign Affairs in Communist China," in John M. H. Lindbeck, ed., *China: Management of a Revolutionary Society,* University of Washington Press, Seattle, 1971; and Melvin Gurtov, "The Foreign Ministry and Foreign Affairs during the Cultural Revolution," *China Quarterly,* 40, 1969.

33. Donald Klein, "Chinese Communist Leadership: Some Problems of Control, Mobility and Policy Making," paper read at American Political Science Association meeting, 1966, pp. 3–4.

34. Tang, *op. cit.,* p. 488.

35. Brzezinski and Huntington, *op. cit.,* p. 407.

36. George Liska, *op. cit.,* pp. 12–13; Hans J. Morgenthau, "Alliances in Theory and Practice," in Arnold Wolfers, ed., *Alliance Policy in the Cold War,* Johns Hopkins Press, Baltimore, 1959, p. 185; Herbert S. Dinerstein,

"The Transformation of Alliance Systems," *American Political Science Review*, 59, 1965, p. 593; Henry A. Kissinger, *The Troubled Partnership*, McGraw-Hill, New York, 1965.

37. Liska, *op. cit.*, pp. 89–90; Morton A. Kaplan, *System and Process in International Politics*, John Wiley & Sons, Inc., New York, 1957, pp. 62–63, 79–80; Kissinger, *op. cit.*, p. 9; William H. Riker, "Politics in the Age of Maneuver," in Morton Berkowitz and P. G. Bock, eds., *American National Security: A Reader in Research and Policy*, The Free Press, New York, 1962, p. 182; R. W. Tucker, *Stability and the Nth Country Problem*, Institute for Defense Analyses, Washington, D.C., 1962, p. 13; George Modelski, *The Communist International System*, Center for International Studies, Princeton, 1960; A. L. Burns, "Military Technology and International Politics," *Yearbook of World Affairs*, Stevens and Sons, Ltd., London, 1961, p. 188; R. N. Rosecrance, *Problems of Nuclear Proliferation*, Security Studies Paper No. 7, U.C.L.A., 1966, p. 26 ff.; and Richard A. Brody, "Some Systemic Effects of the Spread of Nuclear Weapons Technology: A Study Through Simulation of a Multi-nuclear Future," *Journal of Conflict Resolution*, 7, 1963.

38. For a further discussion of this point, see Chapter One, footnotes 28 and 29.

39. Modelski, *op. cit.*, p. 7. See also Zbigniew K. Brzezinski, *The Soviet Bloc: Unity and Conflict*, Harvard University Press, Cambridge, 1960, p. 395.

40. Modelski, *op. cit.*, p. 63.

41. Amitai Etzioni, "The Dialectics of Supranational Unification," *American Political Science Review*, 56, 1962, p. 931.

42. Liska, *op. cit.*, p. 73; Brzezinski, *op. cit.*, pp. 394–395; and Bruce M. Russett, "Toward a Model of Competitive International Politics," *Journal of Politics*, 25, 1963, p. 227.

43. Roger D. Masters, "A Multi-Bloc Model of the International System," *American Political Science Review*, 55, 1961, p. 795; Kaplan, *op. cit.*, pp. 40–41, 75–76; Richard C. Snyder, *Deterrence, Weapons Systems and Decision-Making*, U.S. Naval Ordnance Test Station, China Lake, Calif., 1961, p. 70.

44. Brzezinski, *op. cit.*, pp. 394–395.

45. Karl W. Deutsch, "Transaction Flows as Indicators of Political Cohesion," in Philip E. Jacob and James V. Toscano, eds., *The Integration of Political Communities*, J. B. Lippincott Co., Philadelphia, 1964, p. 95. The concept of "spill-over" is derived from Ernst B. Haas, *The Uniting of Europe*, Stanford University Press, Stanford, 1958.

46. Dinerstein, *op. cit.*, p. 601; Brzezinski, *op. cit.*, p. 394 ff.; Kissinger, *op. cit.*, p. 251.

CHAPTER SIX

Bloc Structure and Intra-Alliance Conflict: France and China as Alliance Mavericks

Nations which are members of an alliance establish characteristic patterns of relations with other nations, alliances, regional groupings, and international organizations. A bloc member in good standing thus adheres to certain predictable patterns of behavior with other members of the alliance, the leading nations in the bloc, nations within the opposing alliance and nonaligned states. In these terms deviation from bloc norms is the establishment of qualitatively and quantitatively different patterns of interaction with various international environments.

The data on France and China to be presented here do not exhaust all relevant aspects of their alliance relations, but they are assumed to index at least some important dimensions of relations among alliance members. Data on actions, elite attitudes, international trade, foreign aid, and treaties and agreements are presented in an effort to assess the hypotheses that intra-bloc frictions will have different consequences in pluralistic and monolithic alliances.[1]

The categories into which our data are coded are derived largely from the previously cited national-international linkages framework. *International environments* are defined according to political (*intra-bloc, inter-bloc, non-bloc*) and geographical (*contiguous, regional*) criteria. The test of bloc membership is a treaty commitment—either multilateral or bilateral —of a military/security nature. Thus membership in such organizations as NATO, SEATO, CENTO or the Warsaw Pact defines bloc assignment, as does a bilateral agreement linking such nations as Spain, Japan, Taiwan, or Cuba to one alliance or the other. Nations without such agreements were coded into the non-bloc category. The *contiguous* environment is defined as those nations with which a polity shares a common frontier. Thus the contiguous environment for France includes Belgium, Luxembourg,

West Germany, Switzerland, Italy, Spain, and Andorra. As used here the *regional* environments of France and China are based primarily upon geographical and cultural factors. East and Southeast Asia are included in China's regional environment, while continental Europe and the British Isles are included in France's regional environment.[2]

Because nations often undertake a wide variety of activities within the framework of an alliance—military cooperation, foreign aid, technical assistance, trade agreements and the like—an approach which permits a separate analysis of linkages in each issue-area is particularly relevant for our purposes. We will consider activities in five issue-areas: *security* (military aid, bases, weapons, military actions, etc.), *territory* (boundary definitions, colonies, etc.), *status* (diplomatic recognition, consular and diplomatic relations, status of representatives, membership in organizations, etc.), *human resources* (cultural activities, education or training programs, travel, etc.), and *nonhuman resources* (trade, foreign aid, transportation, exchange rates, and many other activities relating to the acquisition and deployment of nonmilitary goods).

Action Data

Chinese and French actions from 1950 through 1969 were coded to provide a broad index of changes toward nations in various international environments. All French and Chinese activities, physical or verbal, which crossed their respective national boundaries were coded from three sources.[3]

In coding these data, each action was given an identification number indicating the source, year, month, and day of the action. The target nation was recorded as well as any third party mentioned in the action. Each action was coded for one of the issue-areas identified previously. The "other" category includes actions which encompassed more than one issue-area.

The final classification used was type of action. The original coding of types of actions included twenty-four categories, for example: defend, propose, accuse, demand, threaten, sign agreement, send aid, confer, seize property, troop mobilization, attack, etc. For present purposes these were collapsed into two categories—positive and negative actions.

There are several potential sources of systematic error in these data. First, our sources may have employed biased selection procedures and we have no control over such error.[4] It is almost certain, for instance, that the data understate the degree of conflict between China and the Soviet Union. Peking has charged that between October 15, 1964 (the date of the first Chinese nuclear explosion) and March 15, 1969, the USSR provoked

TABLE 1. Chinese Actions Toward Nations in Various
International Environments: 1950–1969

Environment of Target Nation	1950	1951	1952	1953	1954	1955	1956	1957	1958
Inter-bloc:									
Positive	14	108	114	86	40	76	67	31	54
Negative	105	89	83	28	203	229	117	85	324
% Positive	11.7	54.8	57.8	75.4	16.4	24.9	36.4	26.7	14.2
Intra-bloc:									
Positive	20	14	14	29	26	11	25	35	13
Negative	3	1	2	0	0	0	4	1	8
% Positive	87.0	93.3	87.5	100.0	100.0	100.0	86.2	97.2	61.9
Non-bloc:									
Positive	5	5	11	5	16	0	49	15	26
Negative	3	1	2	1	0	0	5	1	5
% Positive	62.5	83.3	84.6	83.3	100.0	0.0	90.7	93.8	83.9
General: *									
Positive	11	8	4	6	19	15	9	5	7
Negative	19	1	2	3	7	2	3	4	1
% Positive	36.6	88.9	66.7	66.7	73.1	88.2	75.0	55.6	87.5
Total:									
Positive	50	135	143	126	101	102	150	86	100
Negative	130	92	89	32	210	231	129	91	338
% Positive	27.8	59.4	61.6	79.7	32.5	30.6	53.8	48.6	22.8
USSR:									
Positive	16	12	10	24	16	10	18	15	6
Negative	1	0	2	0	0	0	1	0	0
% Positive	94.1	100.0	83.3	100.0	100.0	100.0	94.7	100.0	100.0
Contiguous:									
Positive	24	18	25	31	31	11	45	26	13
Negative	6	0	8	1	0	0	4	0	1
% Positive	80.0	100.0	75.8	96.9	100.0	100.0	91.8	100.0	92.9
Regional:									
Positive	11	11	19	17	35	4	57	26	36
Negative	21	11	18	2	105	117	62	52	162
% Positive	34.4	50.0	51.4	89.5	25.0	3.3	47.9	33.3	18.2

* Target nation unspecified, or target nation in more than one environment.

TABLE 1. *Continued*

1959	1960	1961	1962	1963	1964	1965	1966	1967	1968	1969
16	19	24	14	20	30	33	21	12	33	29
97	107	88	57	55	107	45	104	84	46	37
14.1	15.0	21.4	19.7	26.7	21.9	42.3	16.8	12.5	41.8	43.9
31	43	60	40	19	55	34	48	19	29	50
7	6	8	25	29	45	35	93	75	45	81
81.6	87.8	88.2	61.5	39.6	55.0	49.3	34.0	20.2	39.2	38.1
26	44	31	28	55	66	82	13	11	18	24
21	10	6	64	18	13	35	29	43	4	2
55.3	81.4	83.3	30.4	75.3	83.5	70.1	31.0	20.4	81.8	92.3
9	16	21	10	11	17	5	11	4	5	2
14	8	15	1	6	11	16	8	5	5	10
39.2	66.7	58.3	90.1	64.7	60.7	23.8	57.9	44.4	50.0	16.7
82	122	136	92	105	168	154	93	46	85	105
139	131	117	147	108	176	131	234	207	100	130
37.1	48.2	53.8	38.5	49.3	48.8	54.0	28.4	18.2	45.9	44.7
15	14	18	11	6	25	8	12	1	2	19
1	3	5	13	25	38	28	87	61	31	73
93.7	82.4	78.3	45.8	19.4	39.7	22.2	12.1	1.6	6.0	20.7
34	47	40	37	30	45	40	42	12	24	42
22	9	10	76	42	51	29	97	99	39	87
60.7	83.9	80.0	32.7	41.7	46.9	58.0	30.2	10.8	38.1	32.6
33	43	38	35	43	51	84	45	17	24	41
78	41	17	83	32	24	18	35	54	10	15
29.7	51.2	69.1	29.7	57.3	68.0	82.4	56.2	23.9	70.6	73.2

4189 frontier incidents. They further stated that an additional 1600 provocations took place during the preceding four years.[5] Even allowing a generous discount for hyperbole and revolutionary zeal, it seems clear that the *New York Times* failed to report many genuine incidents and that, as a consequence, they are not included in our data.

There are also two potential types of errors in cross-referencing the *Times Index*. If an action was not properly cross-referenced, it would be missing from our data. But we did search for all actions which were cross-referenced more than once, and duplicate cards removed. The final source of error is coder error in identifying or classifying data into appropriate categories. These operations required relatively little judgment once the categories had been defined. Although we cannot estimate the level of error attributable to coding, and while some error no doubt exists in our data, we assume that at least major trends in Chinese and French policy are accurately portrayed.

Some striking features emerge from the summary of Chinese actions in Table 1. Until the early 1960s there was an apparent consistency in Chinese actions toward various groups of nations. Primarily owing to a single type of recurring activity—the armistice negotiations directed at ending the Korean War—Chinese actions toward nations in the western alliance appear quite positive during 1951–1953. But except for the period of the armistice negotiations and the period immediately preceding the Cultural Revolution, actions toward western nations have been overwhelmingly negative. Consistency also marked actions toward members of the Communist system and non-bloc nations, but signs of serious deterioration with the former appeared by 1963. With the onset of the Cultural Revolution in 1966, Chinese policy toward virtually all nations, including nonaligned ones, took a serious turn for the worse. We shall return to this point in discussing some other indicators of Chinese foreign policy.

For present purposes Chinese relations with other Communist nations are of most interest.[6] Table 2 reveals the extent of Peking's disaffection since 1963 with its erstwhile allies. Equally important from the standpoint of our hypothesis, it is evident that no facet of Chinese relations with her allies has remained free from conflict—every issue-area has been affected.

A more precise picture emerges when the data are examined by country. Clearly there has been a dramatic change in every aspect of Peking's policy toward Moscow. Although these figures do not shed light on the origins of the Sino-Soviet conflict, they do provide stark testimony to the inability—or unwillingness—of either side to contain it. The second group of nations in Table 2 includes Albania, North Vietnam, North Korea, and Cuba, Communist states which have either taken a pro-Peking stance or have avoided making a complete commitment to Moscow in its policy toward China. Chinese actions toward these countries have generally remained cordial, a point to which we shall return later. Rumania is treated separately here because it provides interesting insights into coalition politics. Until the early 1960s there was little evidence of Chinese interest in Rumania. But increasingly Bucharest has also dissented against a Moscow-centric conception of the alliance, although it has done so in a relatively low-keyed manner. Our data indicate that this point of mutual interest between Bucharest and Peking has not gone unrecognized. Finally, Chinese relations with the remaining Communist countries—those in East Europe other than Albania and Rumania, plus Mongolia—have deteriorated, following the pattern of Sino-Soviet differences.

In summary, then, these data are generally quite consistent with the hypothesis that within a monolithic alliance disputes will tend to spill over into all issue-areas rather than remain confined to the original source of conflict. They also reveal something about the alignments that have taken place within the Communist bloc as both Moscow and Peking have attempted to mobilize as many members as possible against the other.

The French action data are also generally consistent with our hypotheses. Since 1960 there has been a moderate decline in friendly relations with members of the western alliance in general and with the United States in particular (Table 3). But friction between France and its allies has not approached in intensity the rupture between China and many Communist countries. On balance, France continues to maintain cordial relations with other western nations, even with those that have disagreed with Paris on Vietnam, Biafra, NATO, Quebec, and other issues.

The Chinese and French data also reveal one other difference. Worsening relations between Peking and most members of the Communist system have not been accompanied by significantly less Chinese hostility toward the West, although the opening of contacts since 1969 with most leading western nations, including the United States, may be an indicator of or may result in a less acrimonious stance toward them. By 1964, on the other hand, French actions were characterized by friendly overtures toward Communist countries, including China. Even the invasion of Czechoslovakia, which called into serious question many Gaullist assumptions about Soviet policy and European security, marked only a brief respite in French efforts toward a détente with Moscow. President Pompidou's visit to Moscow and the Franco-Russian Treaty of 1970 represent major steps in this diplomatic campaign.

When French actions toward its allies are analyzed according to issue-area, the most striking finding is the absence of significant changes between the Fourth and Fifth Republics. As might be expected given the differences on NATO, there has been some deterioration of cordiality in the se-

TABLE 2.   Chinese Actions Toward Communist Nations

Issue-Area	All Members of the Communist System		USSR	
	1950–1962	1963–1969	1950–1962	1963–1969
Security:				
Positive	98	84	49	9
Negative	30	183	17	164
% Positive	76.6	31.4	74.2	5.2
Territory:				
Positive	6	7	5	5
Negative	2	22	0	21
% Positive	75.0	24.1	100.0	19.2
Human Resources:				
Positive	13	15	6	5
Negative	2	21	1	18
% Positive	86.7	71.4	85.7	21.7
Non-human Resources:				
Positive	47	26	22	9
Negative	0	21	0	18
% Positive	100.0	55.3	100.0	33.3
Status:				
Positive	97	87	37	28
Negative	11	57	2	46
% Positive	89.8	60.4	94.9	37.8
Other:				
Positive	100	35	66	17
Negative	20	99	6	76
% Positive	83.3	26.1	91.7	18.3
TOTAL:				
Positive	361	254	185	73
Negative	65	403	26	343
% Positive	84.7	38.7	87.7	17.5

curity issue-area, but in most respects French ties to other allies (including the United States) appear to have remained stable (Table 4). Certainly the French experience has been distinctly different from that of China in at least three respects: the degree of disagreement about security matters has been far less severe; there is no evidence that existing sources of friction have spilled over into other issues; and any discord between Paris and Washington has tended to remain geographically contained because

Albania, Cuba, North Korea and North Vietnam		Rumania		All Other Communist Nations	
1950–1962	1963–1969	1950–1962	1963–1969	1950–1962	1963–1969
29	64	0	2	20	9
1	8	0	0	12	11
96.7	88.9	0.0	100.0	62.5	45.0
0	1	0	0	1	1
1	0	0	0	1	1
0.0	100.0	0.0	0.0	50.0	50.0
6	7	0	1	1	2
0	0	0	0	1	3
100.0	100.0	0.0	100.0	50.0	40.0
18	14	0	2	7	1
0	0	0	0	0	3
100.0	100.0	0.0	100.0	100.0	25.0
30	34	1	17	29	8
0	2	0	0	9	9
100.0	94.4	100.0	100.0	76.3	47.1
18	11	0	2	16	5
0	3	0	2	14	18
100.0	78.6	0.0	50.0	53.3	21.7
101	131	1	24	74	26
2	13	0	2	37	45
98.0	91.0	100.0	92.3	66.7	36.6

neither country's leaders have felt any compulsion to force other allies into choosing sides, as has happened within the Communist bloc.

Elite Attitudes

A crude index of elite attitudes relevant to alliance relations was obtained through content analysis of Chinese and French documents. The content

TABLE 3. French Actions Toward Nations in Various International Environments: 1950–1969

Environment of Target Nation	1950	1951	1952	1953	1954	1955	1956	1957	1958
Inter-bloc:									
Positive	15	31	22	28	23	35	21	4	21
Negative	24	36	15	8	29	29	11	9	19
% Positive	38.5	46.3	59.5	77.8	44.2	54.7	65.6	30.8	52.5
Intra-bloc:									
Positive	245	205	209	177	165	146	143	65	98
Negative	80	27	39	29	16	41	20	14	7
% Positive	75.4	88.4	84.3	85.9	91.2	78.1	87.7	82.3	93.3
Non-bloc:									
Positive	6	12	13	16	22	58	50	28	47
Negative	6	11	27	12	3	8	35	19	31
% Positive	50.0	52.2	32.5	57.1	88.0	87.9	58.8	59.6	60.3
General: *									
Positive	21	26	20	25	31	36	39	20	22
Negative	7	5	24	8	4	17	23	10	12
% Positive	75.0	83.9	45.5	75.8	88.6	67.9	62.9	66.7	64.7
TOTAL:									
Positive	287	274	264	246	241	275	253	117	188
Negative	117	79	105	57	52	95	89	52	69
% Positive	71.0	77.6	71.5	81.2	82.3	74.3	74.0	69.2	73.2
United States:									
Positive	42	51	34	39	32	19	31	30	28
Negative	11	11	15	6	1	15	8	5	1
% Positive	79.2	82.3	69.4	86.7	97.0	55.9	79.5	85.7	96.6
Contiguous:									
Positive	36	14	20	15	22	25	15	9	10
Negative	16	4	7	5	6	6	3	0	2
% Positive	69.2	77.8	74.1	75.0	78.6	80.6	83.3	100.0	83.3
Regional:									
Positive	99	98	91	91	79	74	71	26	45
Negative	44	42	23	17	33	38	17	10	20
% Positive	69.2	70.0	79.8	84.3	70.5	66.1	80.7	72.2	69.2

* Target nation unspecified, or target nation in more than one environment.

TABLE 3. *Continued*

1959	1960	1961	1962	1963	1964	1965	1966	1967	1968	1969
14	10	4	6	1	18	92	18	18	21	13
6	18	23	10	6	4	38	0	5	13	3
70.0	35.7	14.8	37.5	14.3	81.8	70.8	100.0	78.3	61.8	81.3
100	77	74	66	80	85	150	64	54	76	62
16	8	11	18	22	35	79	42	37	37	24
86.2	90.6	87.1	78.6	78.4	70.8	65.5	60.4	59.3	67.3	72.1
34	32	42	23	19	33	78	16	22	25	16
11	18	20	2	4	1	28	2	10	3	10
75.6	64.0	67.7	92.0	82.6	97.1	73.6	88.9	68.7	89.3	61.5
36	13	16	8	11	28	55	16	17	24	28
14	14	22	6	12	12	62	2	14	17	4
72.0	48.1	42.1	57.1	47.8	70.0	47.0	88.9	54.8	58.5	87.5
184	132	136	103	111	164	375	114	111	146	119
47	58	76	36	44	52	207	46	66	70	41
79.7	69.5	64.2	74.1	71.6	75.9	64.4	71.3	62.7	67.6	74.4
23	16	24	22	13	18	45	19	10	17	25
7	2	6	10	8	10	24	7	14	12	7
76.7	88.9	80.0	68.8	61.9	64.3	65.2	73.1	41.7	58.6	78.1
20	13	8	15	17	17	36	10	12	10	13
1	1	0	0	0	7	2	3	3	7	3
95.2	92.9	100.0	100.0	100.0	70.8	94.7	76.9	80.0	58.8	81.2
48	37	24	38	43	46	137	35	38	51	33
10	16	25	15	11	16	63	5	14	25	17
82.8	69.8	49.0	71.7	79.6	74.2	68.5	87.5	73.1	67.1	66.0

Bloc Structure and Intra-Alliance Conflict

TABLE 4. French Actions Toward Nations in the Western Alliance

Issue-Area	All Members of the Western Alliance 1950–1957	1958–1969	United States 1950–1957	1958–1969	United Kingdom 1950–1957	1958–196
Security:						
Positive	720	444	184	137	57	32
Negative	176	209	54	82	8	6
% Positive	80.4	68.0	77.3	62.6	87.7	84.2
Territory:						
Positive	17	5	3	1	1	0
Negative	4	0	1	0	1	0
% Positive	81.0	100.0	75.0	100.0	50.0	0.0
Human Resources:						
Positive	28	20	6	1	2	2
Negative	7	4	2	0	0	0
% Positive	80.0	83.3	75.0	100.0	100.0	100.0
Non-human Res.:						
Positive	164	114	31	25	14	15
Negative	17	35	5	11	3	6
% Positive	90.6	76.5	86.1	69.4	82.4	71.4
Status:						
Positive	296	275	26	79	21	21
Negative	44	42	6	6	4	7
% Positive	87.1	86.8	81.2	92.9	84.0	75.0
Other:						
Positive	131	130	28	17	14	11
Negative	18	44	4	7	2	3
% Positive	87.9	74.7	79.4	70.8	87.5	78.6
TOTAL:						
Positive	1356	988	278	260	109	81
Negative	266	334	72	106	18	22
% Positive	83.6	74.7	79.4	71.0	85.8	78.6

analysis data may be considered both as elite responses to activities in-
itiated in international environments and as elite predispositions to undertake certain policies toward these environments. But we can identify only
in the most general sense the events which gave rise to these attitudes or
their consequences for policy formulation.

A random sample of 525 Chinese editorials (twenty-five per year) published in the authoritative newspaper *Jen-min Jih-pao* (Peoples' Daily) and

Common Market Nations		Other NATO Members		All Other Allies	
1950–1957	1958–1969	1950–1957	1958–1969	1950–1957	1958–1969
32	49	2	28	445	198
13	14	1	9	100	98
71.1	77.8	66.7	75.7	81.7	67.6
4	3	0	0	9	1
1	0	0	0	1	0
80.0	100.0	0.0	0.0	90.0	100.0
6	2	1	6	13	9
2	2	0	1	3	1
75.0	50.0	100.0	85.7	81.3	90.0
25	23	2	16	92	35
2	9	0	4	7	5
92.6	71.9	100.0	80.0	92.9	87.5
55	73	16	28	178	74
14	7	2	10	18	12
79.7	91.3	88.9	73.7	90.8	86.0
16	33	2	6	71	63
6	7	0	1	6	26
72.7	82.5	100.0	85.7	92.2	70.8
138	183	23	84	808	380
38	39	3	25	135	142
78.4	82.4	88.5	77.0	85.7	72.8

the biweekly magazine *People's China* was selected for analysis. The French documents consisted of the speeches, press conferences, and similar statements made by the President, Premier, and Foreign Minister. All 270 French documents located in a half-dozen sources,[7] rather than a sample of them, were coded. After pretesting a number of content categories, only a few of which are reported here, coders were instructed to determine whether these categories appeared as a "major theme" within each docu-

TABLE 5. **Themes Relating to the Communist System and the Western Alliance in Chinese Editorials**

Theme and Issue-Area	1950–1962 (325 Documents)		1963–1970 (200 Documents)	
	No. and % of Documents in Which Themes Appear			
	N	%	N	%
Praise of USSR				
Security	38	11.7	0	0.0
Territory	0	0.0	0	0.0
Human Resources	2	0.6	0	0.0
Non-human Resources	34	10.5	0	0.0
Status	5	1.5	0	0.0
Other	36	11.1	0	0.0
Criticism of USSR				
Security	0	0.0	36	18.0
Territory	0	0.0	10	5.0
Human Resources	0	0.0	6	3.0
Non-human Resources	0	0.0	10	5.0
Status	1	0.3	13	6.5
Other	0	0.0	68	34.0
Praise "Socialist Camp"				
Security	23	7.1	1	0.5
Territory	0	0.0	0	0.0
Human Resources	0	0.0	0	0.0
Non-human Resources	11	3.4	1	0.5
Status	14	4.3	2	1.0
Other	25	7.7	2	1.0
Criticism of "Socialist Camp"				
Security	0	0.0	1	0.5
Territory	0	0.0	1	0.5
Human Resources	1	0.3	0	0.0
Non-human Resources	0	0.0	0	0.0
Status	1	0.3	3	1.5
Other	1	0.3	4	2.0

TABLE 5. *Continued*

Theme and Issue-Area	1950–1962 (325 Documents)		1963–1970 (200 Documents)	
	No. and % of Documents in Which Themes Appear			
	N	%	N	%
Criticism of US				
Security	167	51.2	121	60.5
Territory	20	6.2	16	8.0
Human Resources	5	1.5	13	6.5
Non-human Resources	13	4.0	15	7.5
Status	10	3.1	12	6.0
Other	41	12.6	85	42.5
Criticism of Western Alliance				
Security	41	12.6	5	2.5
Territory	1	0.3	0	0.0
Human Resources	1	0.3	0	0.0
Non-human Resources	6	1.8	1	0.5
Status	2	0.6	2	1.0
Other	11	3.4	7	3.5
Criticism of Any Western Nation (Except US)				
Security	48	14.8	32	16.0
Territory	11	3.4	4	2.0
Human Resources	7	2.2	6	3.0
Non-human Resources	1	0.3	4	2.0
Status	8	2.5	6	3.0
Other	30	9.2	24	12.0
Praise Western Alliance or Any Western Nation				
Security	4	1.2	1	0.5
Territory	1	0.3	0	0.0
Human Resources	1	0.3	0	0.0
Non-human Resources	1	0.3	1	0.5
Status	2	0.6	0	0.0
Other	8	2.5	4	2.0

TABLE 6. Themes Relating to the Western Alliance and the Communist System in French Documents

Theme and Issue-Area	1945–1957 (103 Documents) N	%	1958–1970 (167 Documents) N	%
	No. and % of Documents in Which Themes Appear			
Praise of US				
Security	15	14.6	12	7.2
Territory	3	2.9	0	0.0
Human Resources	2	1.9	2	1.2
Non-human Resources	11	10.7	6	3.6
Status	4	3.9	0	0.0
Other	4	3.9	17	10.2
Criticism of US				
Security	2	1.9	26	15.6
Territory	0	0.0	1	0.6
Human Resources	0	0.0	2	1.2
Non-Human Resources	0	0.0	9	5.4
Status	0	0.0	2	1.2
Other	1	1.0	9	5.4
Praise Western Alliance				
Security	14	13.6	32	19.1
Territory	1	1.0	0	0.0
Human Resources	1	1.0	1	0.6
Non-human Resources	2	1.9	2	1.2
Status	4	3.9	2	1.2
Other	4	3.9	10	6.0
Criticism of Western Alliance				
Security	1	1.0	19	11.4
Territory	0	0.0	0	0.0
Human Resources	0	0.0	0	0.0
Non-human Resources	1	1.0	1	0.6
Status	0	0.0	8	4.8
Other	0	0.0	8	4.8

TABLE 6. *Continued*

Theme and Issue-Area	1945–1957 (103 Documents)		1958–1970 (167 Documents)	
	No. and % of Documents in Which Themes Appear			
	N	%	N	%
Criticism of USSR				
Security	14	13.6	29	17.4
Territory	10	9.7	13	7.8
Human Resources	2	1.9	3	1.8
Non-human Resources	1	1.0	5	3.0
Status	3	2.9	3	1.8
Other	2	1.9	10	6.0
Criticism of Soviet Bloc				
Security	3	2.9	4	2.4
Territory	4	3.9	2	1.2
Human Resources	1	1.0	3	1.8
Non-human Resources	0	0.0	2	1.2
Status	1	1.0	2	1.2
Other	0	0.0	2	1.2
Criticism of any Communist Nation (Except USSR)				
Security	0	0.0	3	1.8
Territory	1	1.0	3	1.8
Human Resources	0	0.0	2	1.2
Non-human Resources	0	0.0	3	1.8
Status	0	0.0	0	0.0
Other	0	0.0	0	0.0
Praise Soviet Bloc or Any Communist Nation				
Security	6	5.8	3	1.8
Territory	3	2.9	0	0.0
Human Resources	2	1.9	8	4.8
Non-human Resources	2	1.9	3	1.8
Status	2	1.9	3	1.8
Other	0	0.0	11	6.6

ment. If they did, coders recorded them as present and identified the is-sue-area being discussed. The scoring method thus indicates the number of documents within which a content category appears as a major theme; it does *not* take into account the frequency with which a given theme might appear in a single document.[8]

Results of the content analysis are summarized in Tables 5 and 6. French data are divided into two periods corresponding to the Fourth and Fifth Republics. There was no such obvious division point for the Chinese data. The periods 1950–1962 and 1963–1969 are arbitrary ones, sug-gested in part by events during 1962–1968—the Cuban missile crisis, the Sino-Indian border conflict, and the Nuclear Test Ban Treaty—and in part by the data themselves.

Comparison of Chinese and French attitudes reveals both similarities and differences. Both view the opposing alliance, its leader, and other member nations critically. But unlike the Chinese view of the western alli-ance, the attitudes of French elites toward the USSR and its allies have never been unambiguously negative. This ambivalence is supported by a recent opinion survey in which 99 percent of French elite respondents ex-pected relations with countries in Eastern Europe to become more cor-dial.[9] Sharper differences emerge with respect to attitudes about the intra-bloc environment. Chinese and French elites have been considerably more critical of their alliances and bloc leaders during the more recent periods. But if their attitudes are analyzed according to issue-areas the Chinese ap-pear consistently critical of the Soviet Union in *all* issue-areas. If the USSR possesses any redeeming features, it is not apparent from the Chinese documents. Even the abundant praise voiced by Peking toward the Communist system as a whole through the early 1960s has virtually ceased. On the other hand, French attitudes about the western alliance and its leading member have become more critical with respect to security and status, but have not changed significantly in other issue-areas. Again the previously cited survey reveals similar public and elite attitudes: French skepticism toward supranational organizations seems focused largely on NATO. Thus these data are at least consistent with the proposition that disagreements among allies are more likely to spill over across issue-areas within the more monolithic bloc.

International Trade and Foreign Aid

Elites and political analysts of many ideological persuasions have looked upon international trade as an integrating force. During the decades prior to World War I it was fashionable to argue that while competition for in-ternational markets might exacerbate international conflict in the short run, over the long run trade ties would make war unthinkable. At the more limited level of the region or alliance, functionalist and neo-functionalist theorists have suggested that the effects of economic cooperation would spread into other issue-areas, and at least one of them assigns the highest spill-over potential to economic cooperation because its effects are felt by all sectors of society.[10] Similarly, Nikita Khrushchev predicted in 1959 that, "the further development of the socialist countries will in all probability proceed along the lines of consolidation of the single-world socialist economic system. The economic barriers which divided our countries under capitalism will fall one after another. The common economic basis of world socialism will grow stronger, eventually making the questions of borders a pointless one." [11]

Whether or not these predictions overstate the political significance of economic factors, trade data should provide one important quantitative index of alliance relations. In other studies trade has been found to be a good "lead indicator" of political relations among nations.[12] If the hypotheses of a higher spill-over effect resulting from nonconforming behavior in the more monolithic bloc are valid, we should find that Chinese intra-bloc trade patterns have been more extensively disrupted than those of France.

Perhaps more clearly than any other indicator, foreign trade data (Table 7) reveal how sharply Chinese relations with the Soviet Union and other Communist nations have changed in recent years.[13] During the first decade of its existence more than two-thirds of China's trade was with partners within the Communist system. As late as 1960 there appeared to be little reason to believe that China's economy was not becoming increasingly dependent upon bloc members, especially the Soviet Union, which consistently accounted for nearly half of China's total trade turnover. Since then China's trade relations with Communist nations have deteriorated dramatically. Some of the increase in trade with western nations may be attributed to factors other than intra-alliance strife. For example, it is unlikely that China's emergency grain requirements in recent years could have been met within the Communist system, as the Soviet Union has also been forced to purchase wheat periodically on the world market. Other considerations which have no doubt made trade with western capitalist nations appear attractive include lower prices, higher quality, and faster delivery time. Nevertheless, changes in the distribution of China's trade and the decline in the total value of goods exchanged with alliance partners cannot be accounted for merely by the emergency in Chinese agriculture.

That differences within the Communist system have spilled over into trade relations is further confirmed when Sino-Soviet trade data are examined. The decline both in Russia's proportion of total Chinese trade and in

TABLE 7. Distribution of Chinese Trade in International Environments

	1952	1953	1954	1955	1956	1957	1958	1959	1960
Total Imports									
(US $ millions)	890	1107	1260	1321	1465	1391	1865	2011	1912
Intra-bloc %	79.4	82.6	82.5	78.3	72.4	63.8	60.4	67.8	66.7
Inter-bloc %	12.7	8.0	9.5	11.6	16.6	19.9	29.3	21.4	23.0
Non-bloc %	7.9	9.4	8.0	10.1	11.0	16.3	10.3	10.8	10.3
From Bloc									
Leader (USSR)%	62.2	63.0	65.6	56.6	50.0	39.1	34.0	47.4	42.7
Regional %	14.9	8.5	11.3	14.0	15.8	17.3	13.4	10.7	11.2
Contiguous %	64.8	63.8	63.5	63.4	56.2	44.9	38.9	51.9	48.4
	1952	1953	1954	1955	1956	1957	1958	1959	1960
Total Exports									
(US $ millions)	871	1093	1119	1345	1612	1615	1911	2211	2010
Intra-bloc %	66.8	65.9	72.8	69.1	66.4	67.1	66.5	71.7	65.3
Inter-bloc %	26.3	26.6	21.4	25.2	24.2	24.5	24.0	19.2	24.7
Non-bloc %	6.8	7.5	5.8	5.7	9.4	8.4	9.5	9.1	10.0
To Bloc									
Leader (USSR)%	47.8	45.7	51.7	47.8	47.4	45.7	46.1	49.8	42.2
Regional %	25.1	23.3	21.1	23.6	25.6	26.6	25.3	21.5	25.5
Contiguous %	64.6	57.9	63.4	60.4	61.5	61.2	61.0	63.8	59.2

* 1968–1971 data are not detailed enough to permit analysis of trade with regional and contiguous partners.
** 1969–1971 data are not detailed enough to distinguish between inter-bloc and non-bloc partners.

the absolute value of goods exchanged has been even sharper than that with the Communist bloc as a whole, thereby supporting the conclusion that the Sino-Soviet rift has severely disrupted economic relations. After reaching a peak in 1959 of $2 billion in goods exchanged, there has been a spectacular decline in Sino-Soviet trade. By 1969 the USSR accounted for less than 2 percent of Peking's total trade turnover of just less than $4 billion. In 1970 trade between the two nations fell to less than $45 million, roughly 1 percent of China's total. Thus the Soviet Union ranked in importance with the Netherlands and Sweden as a Chinese trade partner; it was far behind countries such as Australia and Canada, neither of which has even 10 percent of Russia's population. Conversely, in 1969 Soviet-American trade was worth roughly four times the value of the goods exchanged between China and the USSR. A one-year trade pact was signed

1961	1962	1963	1964	1965	1966	1967	1968	1969	1970	1971
1414	1139	1228	1475	1770	2035	1945	1820	1825	2165	2247
54.2	48.3	40.6	27.8	27.1	24.8	17.4	18.7	17.8	15.0	20.4
34.0	38.9	45.5	55.1	56.1	60.0	67.7	69.0 }	82.2 **	85.0 **	79.6 **
11.8	12.8	13.9	17.1	16.8	15.2	14.9	12.3 }			
26.0	20.5	14.8	9.2	10.8	8.6	2.6	2.6	1.6	1.1	3.5
19.0	24.4	27.3	27.5	28.8	31.0	27.4	*	*	*	*
39.0	35.3	30.9	17.3	18.2	14.8	8.6	*	*	*	*

1961	1962	1963	1964	1965	1966	1967	1968	1969	1970	1971
1571	1597	1605	1780	2085	2170	1915	1890	2060	2060	2364
67.6	59.4	53.4	39.9	32.6	27.4	24.0	24.4	22.9	25.0	24.9
27.3	29.2	35.2	42.1	45.8	47.3	50.6	49.0 }	77.1 **	75.0 **	75.1 **
10.1	11.4	11.4	18.0	21.6	25.3	25.4	26.6 }			
35.0	32.3	25.7	17.6	11.8	6.6	3.0	2.5	1.4	1.1	3.2
32.1	36.2	42.5	52.7	49.8	56.7	52.0	*	*	*	*
58.1	57.5	53.3	48.9	41.6	37.7	33.6	*	*	*	*

in November 1970 and renewed in 1971, but even after the projected increases Sino-Soviet trade will be of minor importance to both nations.

Evidence that the Sino-Soviet rift has also spilled over into Peking's relations with other Communist nations may also be found in the trade figures. As late as 1961–1963, between one-quarter and one-third of China's trade was with Communist nations *other than* the USSR. By 1969, this figure had dropped to less than 20 percent. Moreover, although political considerations seem to be a minor factor in trade with the West, they appear to play a significant role in economic relations with other Communist countries. For example, while trade with Communist countries as a whole was falling precipitously, that with Rumania rose sharply, increasing by one-third during 1970 alone.[14]

Nonaligned nations appear to have played a relatively minor role in Chinese trade, at least in economic terms. Despite China's professed interest in the Afro-Asian and other emerging nations, at no time has trade with these partners reached 25 percent of the total turnover, and it has usually remained at about half that level. Moreover, the 1968 figures indicate a rather clear decline from the previous year's trade with non-bloc nations; in fact, China appears to have imported fewer goods from these nations in 1968 than in any year since 1963 despite an increase in the total value of imports during the intervening years.

Until the massive internal upheavals associated with the Cultural Revolution, the value of China's international trade was increasing steadily despite the disruption of its economic relations within the Communist system because trade with the West has expanded uninterruptedly since 1960. Even disregarding large purchases of grain from Canada, Argentina, and Australia, trade with leading members of the western alliance has increased markedly. Among the more influential western nations, only the United States has not increased its trade with Peking during the past few years. China's most active trade partners in recent years have included Australia, Great Britain, West Germany, Canada, Italy, France, and Japan (Table 8). The latter is China's top trade partner, but it should also be pointed out that Japan's trade with Taiwan (population 14 million) exceeds that with Mainland China (population 750–800 million).[15]

Further insight into ties between China and the Communist system in the nonhuman resources issue-area may be derived by examining foreign aid data. It is difficult to determine precisely how much aid China has received from other Communist nations. Part of the problem is defining what constitutes "foreign aid." Some sources use the term only for outright grants, others include credits and loans, and at least in a few cases, some parts of foreign trade are included in the calculation of "aid."[16] Despite these discrepancies all sources agree on this point: China has been the recipient of little, if any, aid during the past decade and a half. Eckstein's data, which are consistent with the trends if not with the exact amounts in other sources, indicate that China received something under U.S. $1.5 billion aid from the Soviet Union through the first half of the 1950s and that since 1957 such aid has "virtually ended."[17] Assistance from other bloc members, never at a level comparable to Soviet aid, also appears to have ceased.

Whether Soviet aid even during the early years of the Peking regime was considered adequate by Chinese leaders—at least one observer suggests that Stalin's niggardliness in negotiating the February 1950 aid agreement was the initial source of Mao's disaffection with the Soviets— there is little reason to doubt that withdrawal of economic and technical aid has been a major irritant in relations between Moscow and Peking.[18] According to one of many similar Chinese statements,

In July 1960, the Soviet authorities . . . suddenly and unilaterally decided on a complete withdrawal of the 1390 experts who were in China

TABLE 8.   China's Leading Trade Partners
(Total Turnover)

Rank	1953	1957	1961	1965	1970
1	USSR	USSR	USSR	Japan	Japan
2	Hong Kong	Hong Kong	Hong Kong	Hong Kong	Hong Kong
3	E. Germany	E. Germany	Canada	USSR	W. Germany
4	Ceylon	Czechoslo-vakia	United Kingdom	Cuba	Australia
5	Hungary	Japan	Australia	Australia	United Kingdom
6	W. Germany	W. Germany	E. Germany	United Kingdom	Canada
7	Poland	Poland	Japan	W. Germany	France
8	United Kingdom	Malaysia/Singapore	Czechoslo-vakia	Canada	Singapore
9	Switzer-land	United Kingdom	W. Germany	France	Italy
10	Malaysia/Singapore	Egypt	Malaysia/Singapore	Italy	Malaysia
Top Ten Partners Which Are:					
Communist Nations	4	4	3	2	0
NATO Members	2	2	3	5	5

to help in our work, they tore up 343 contracts for experts and the supplements to these contracts and abolished 257 items for scientific and technical cooperation and since then, they have reduced in large numbers the supplies of complete sets of equipment and key sections of various other equipment. This has caused our construction to suffer huge losses, thereby upsetting our original plan for the development of our national economy and greatly aggravating our difficulties.[19]

Such statements are clear evidence of a linkage between Soviet actions and significant consequences within China. Unfortunately, beyond the rather trivial observation that these Soviet actions have contributed to a change in elite attitudes toward Moscow (see Table 5), we cannot trace out the specific consequences on political processes in China. Among the interesting

TABLE 9. Chinese Foreign Aid

		1953	1954	1955	1956	1957	1958
Total Aid (US $ mil.)		344.0	15.0	204.0	105.9	89.8	120.6
Recipients							
Intra-bloc	%	100.0	100.0	100.0	46.7	60.1	68.0
Inter-bloc	%	0.0	0.0	0.0	0.0	0.0	0.0
Non-bloc	%	0.0	0.0	0.0	53.3	39.9	37.0
Regional	%	100.0	0.0	98.0	86.6	39.9	86.2
Contiguous	%	100.0	0.0	98.0	49.7	0.0	68.2

questions which might be asked are the following: Have patterns of re-cruitment into the Chinese Communist Party changed to place heavier em-phasis on technically trained personnel? What bureaucratic changes re-sulted from the withdrawal of Soviet aid? What institutions and elites (party, military, bureaucracy, etc.) gained or lost influence as a result of this development in Sino-Soviet relations? Unfortunately these and many other intriguing questions are easier to ask than to answer.

Whereas there is some disagreement on what constituted Soviet aid to China, there seems to be more consensus on the calculation of Chinese grants to other nations, the first of which was made in 1953.[20] The data in Table 9 are consistent with trends in trade relations—an increasing pro-portion of aid has been going to nations outside the Communist system since 1956. By itself, increased Chinese attention to non-bloc nations is not proof of deviation from bloc norms. Indeed, this could be interpreted as Chinese emulation of a pattern established earlier by the Soviet Union. But there are a number of indications that Chinese aid, both within and outside the Communist system, has been granted in direct competition with Moscow. For example, Floyd asserts that,

> Competition between Russians and Chinese for the friendship of non-Communist countries, especially those which had freshly acquired inde-pendence, was apparent elsewhere. In May Chou En-lai visited Outer Mongolia . . . to conclude a treaty of friendship and mutual aid and to extend a loan of 200 million roubles. It is perhaps not without signifi-cance that in August 1960 Khrushchev's critic, Vyacheslav Molotov, was withdrawn from the Soviet embassy in Ulan Bator. The extension of a $35 million loan by Russia to the new state of Guinea in Africa was followed by one of $25 million from the Chinese. Khrushchev's ef-fort to make a firm friend of Fidel Castro in Cuba by extending eco-nomic and military aid were [sic] followed by a Chinese undertaking to

1959	1960	1961	1962	1963	1964	1965–9	1970	1971
150.2	296.5	456.0	16.3	88.1	287.9	837.0	1034.0	567.0
79.2	74.2	61.8	0.0	0.0	0.03	64.5	31.4	17.6
0.0	0.0	0.0	0.0	0.0	20.8	5.9	19.3	7.8
20.8	25.8	38.2	100.0	100.0	79.1	29.6	49.2	74.6
86.6	68.3	64.0	89.0	0.0	22.3	56.8	26.3	33.3
66.6	59.4	55.0	24.5	0.0	0.03	49.6	25.1	27.7

trade with Cuba and lend her $21 million. Even in the Middle East, an area of predominantly Russian interest, the Chinese were competing for influence, for example, in Iraq.[21]

Moreover, nearly all aid within the Communist system has been granted to Albania, Rumania, North Vietnam, and North Korea, nations which have tended, at least until very recently, to be moderately sympathetic to Peking's position in its continuing conflict with the Soviet Union.

In summary, the pattern of Chinese foreign aid, like that of foreign trade, indicates increasing attention outside the Communist system. But whereas patterns of trade appear to be based in part on considerations of economic necessity—since the disruptions of the Sino-Soviet trade relations, only nations of the West are in a position to provide for China's requirements for grain and capital goods—aid has been supplied to nations which appear most likely to support China's policies not only vis-à-vis the United States, but also the Soviet Union and India.[22]

The pattern which emerges from French foreign trade data (Table 10) is markedly different from that of China, and these differences are consistent with the proposition that discord within a pluralistic alliance can be contained without poisoning all types of relations among bloc partners.

However serious French disagreements with the United States and other NATO allies have been, it is evident that they have scarcely affected trade with members of the alliance.[23] The value of intra-alliance trade has expanded virtually every year since World War II, and even the proportion of total trade within the alliance has risen consistently. The sharpest increases have been within the contiguous environment, which is nearly identical with the Common Market. French trade with NATO countries has also risen dramatically; even for NATO partners outside the Common Market the proportion of imports and exports has

TABLE 10.   Distribution of French Trade in International Environments

		1947	1948	1949	1950	1951	1952	1953	1954	1955	1956
Total Imports											
(bil. new francs)		4.0	6.7	9.3	10.7	16.1	15.9	13.8	15.2	16.7	19.8
Intra-bloc	%	60.0	49.9	51.6	50.6	50.3	47.7	46.8	46.6	48.8	52.8
Inter-bloc	%	0.5	0.8	0.6	0.4	0.2	0.5	0.5	2.2	1.6	1.9
Non-bloc	%	39.5	49.2	47.8	49.0	49.5	51.8	52.7	51.2	49.6	45.3
From Bloc											
Leader (US)	%	30.2	17.6	17.6	12.3	11.3	10.0	9.8	8.8	9.6	12.1
Regional	%	21.2	23.0	25.6	27.8	27.8	29.3	28.6	32.2	30.6	37.1
Contiguous	%	11.6	12.8	14.4	17.2	15.8	16.8	17.0	17.5	19.9	20.8

		1947	1948	1949	1950	1951	1952	1953	1954	1955	1956
Total Exports											
(bil. new francs)		2.2	4.3	7.8	10.8	14.8	14.2	13.2	15.0	17.4	16.2
Intra-bloc	%	38.3	36.9	39.4	45.0	41.2	35.2	41.2	40.9	47.7	46.1
Inter-bloc	%	1.1	0.8	0.8	0.4	0.2	0.3	0.5	1.5	2.3	2.1
Non-bloc	%	60.6	62.3	59.8	54.6	58.6	64.5	58.3	57.6	50.0	51.8
To Bloc											
Leader (US)	%	2.7	3.6	2.0	4.1	5.9	3.9	4.8	3.6	4.2	4.8
Regional	%	40.0	38.8	37.5	42.5	37.0	37.0	36.3	43.4	47.8	48.2
Contiguous	%	21.5	19.1	16.3	22.0	19.2	22.6	22.4	26.4	27.8	30.3

remained steady, and the absolute value of goods exchanged has increased significantly. This is true even of the decade ending in 1969, *the period of maximum political friction between France and her NATO allies.*

Partner	% Imports: 1959	1969	% Exports: 1959	1969	% Change, 1959–1969, in Value of Goods: Imports	Exports
All NATO Nations	42.1	65.5	44.1	61.5	+460	+290
Common Market Nations	26.7	50.0	27.1	47.5	+570	+390
All Other NATO Nations	15.4	15.5	17.0	14.0	+260	+130

The same conclusion emerges from an examination of trade with the United States. Although it has remained a relatively constant proportion

1957	1958	1959	1960	1961	1962	1963	1964	1965	1966	1967	1968	1969
22.7	26.6	25.2	31.0	33.0	37.1	43.1	49.7	51.1	58.7	61.2	69.2	90.0
53.8	49.1	52.8	58.0	59.3	61.1	63.8	67.1	67.3	75.0	68.7	69.5	71.1
1.9	2.6	3.3	2.7	2.5	2.6	2.8	3.1	3.4	3.8	3.7	3.2	3.3
44.3	48.3	43.9	39.3	38.2	36.3	33.4	29.8	29.3	21.2	27.6	27.3	25.6
13.3	10.0	8.4	12.5	11.0	10.3	10.3	11.3	10.5	10.1	9.8	9.4	8.4
35.6	37.2	41.6	42.9	46.7	49.5	52.8	54.3	55.5	58.2	60.2	63.4	66.3
21.4	22.7	26.3	28.7	31.0	33.5	35.3	36.0	37.4	39.9	42.0	44.9	48.1

1957	1958	1959	1960	1961	1962	1963	1964	1965	1966	1967	1968	1969
18.9	21.5	27.7	33.9	35.7	36.4	39.9	44.4	49.6	53.8	56.2	62.8	77.8
45.9	44.1	50.8	51.6	50.0	59.3	60.2	61.9	64.6	66.8	66.3	64.8	68.1
2.0	2.3	4.1	4.0	3.6	4.1	3.7	3.9	4.3	5.1	5.9	5.7	4.5
52.1	53.6	45.1	44.4	46.4	36.6	36.1	34.2	31.2	28.1	27.8	29.5	27.4
4.7	5.9	8.4	3.8	5.8	5.8	5.2	5.2	5.9	6.0	5.8	6.0	5.4
45.8	41.3	46.0	50.4	49.5	60.6	62.0	63.9	65.5	66.6	66.3	66.4	69.2
29.0	23.6	29.7	32.7	31.3	41.4	43.6	44.2	45.4	46.6	45.0	45.3	48.8

of total trade turnover, the actual value of goods exchanged has increased consistently. Since the beginning of the Fifth Republic in 1958, the total trade turnover has increased from 3.9 to 11.8 billion francs, or slightly over 200 percent. Thus, Franco-American trade has increased at a faster rate than the Gross National Product of either nation.

Finally, trade with Communist nations increased during the 1960s, but it continues to represent a very minor part of both French imports and exports.

The internal sources and consequences of international trade are considerably easier to assess for France than for China. Opinion surveys indicate that French mass and elite attitudes about NATO are unfavorable, but opinions toward economic and cultural organizations remain favorable. For example, French respondents favored the Common Market over NATO by a ten-to-one margin.[24] Other studies have shown a significant effect on political socialization, interest articulation and aggregation, and decision making in France as a result of trade activities in Europe. Some of these consequences are described in a study of agricultural policies in the European Economic Community.

> In a real sense public discussion of agricultural policy is carried on in terms of a single political arena covering the six countries. Increasingly there is a common set of issues, of institutions, of personalities, and these are known to all the actors in the system and to the attentive public. New patterns of interactions and communication are involved, as well as new political styles. Agricultural committees of these national parliaments which try to maintain some control and oversight of agricultural policy are forced to spend the bulk of their time on issues raised by the Community. The attention of interest groups is similarly directed beyond the national system to the Community system. These phenomena tend to contribute to an increased incidence of a self-conscious sense of "European identity." [25]

In summary, whether measured in the value of goods exchanged, in the proportion of intra-bloc trade, or in trade with the alliance leader, Chinese and French patterns of international trade have changed as predicted by our hypotheses. And while information on political processes is at best sketchy, it seems reasonable to assume that altered patterns of international trade have had a significant impact on political processes in France and China.

Treaties and Agreements

Treaties and agreements have traditionally served as an index of a nation's relations with other nations and have thus been of interest to students of alliances. Whatever deviations from traditional diplomatic methods have characterized the foreign policies of Communist nations, they appear not to have extended to the use of treaties and agreements. The sheer volume of Chinese treaties suggests a heavy reliance on formal agreements to make explicit relations in virtually every issue-area.[26] A quantitative analysis of treaties and agreements, such as that described here, inevitably ignores important questions, the answers to which depend upon qualitative aspects of the treaty. Thus while the present data—based on an analysis of 2084 Chinese and 1254 French treaties—reveal some interesting patterns they are most useful when combined with other data.

Until 1963 treaties with members of the western alliance accounted for a very small proportion of all Chinese agreements (Table 11).[27] Although there has been marked increase in agreements with western nations during the past several years, nearly all of them (fifty-nine of eighty-four since 1963) have been confined to the nonhuman resources issue-area, as might be expected given the deterioration of Chinese economic relations within the Communist bloc and the marked increase in Chinese trade with western nations. Thus Peking's treaty relations with members of the western alliance have remained rather narrowly confined to trade matters; there has been little evidence of closer cooperation on other issues. Typically, the first tangible results of renewed Sino-American contacts concerned trade—the sale of Boeing aircraft and wheat to China in 1972.

In recent years nonaligned nations have supplanted members of the Communist system as China's leading treaty partners. Again the reasons are not wholly indicative of deviation from bloc norms. With the greatly expanded number of new nations, Chinese treaty relations with such nations would have shown some increase even in the absence of serious disagreement among Communist nations. On the other hand, Sino-Soviet competition among the new nations has probably contributed to the frequency of Chinese trade, aid, and cultural agreements with non-bloc members.

The treaties most relevant to an analysis of alliance cohesion are those with other members of the alliance. Despite the limitations inherent in a quantitative analysis, some revealing patterns emerge from the data. During the first decade of its existence an overwhelming proportion of China's agreements were signed with other Communist nations. During the 1960s, however, more treaties have been signed with nations outside the bloc than within it. A more interesting picture emerges when each of China's intra-bloc treaty partners is revealed (Table 12). The Soviet Union was China's primary treaty partner during the first decade of the PRC's existence, but this has changed dramatically during the 1960s. Since 1965 only Mongolia, Czechoslovakia, Hungary, East Germany, and Yugoslavia—the last at best a nominal member of the Communist system—have signed fewer agreements with China than has the Soviet Union; it is noteworthy that Czechoslovakia, Hungary, and Yugoslavia have also been considered among the more "liberal" Communist nations. With the notable exception of Albania and Rumania, all of the Eastern European nations have also fallen from their former positions as favored treaty partners in Peking. On the other hand, Albania, Rumania, North Korea, and North Vietnam have joined Cuba as the nations with which most Chinese agreements are signed.

These data are consistent with propositions that China is attempting to form a bloc within the Communist system consisting of the less developed but ideologically "purer" nations.[28] This is apparent if we compare the frequency of Chinese treaties with various partners during an early period (1949–1952) and a later period (1966–1971) with the GNP per capita of

TABLE 11. Chinese Treaties in Various International Environments, All Issue-Areas

		1949	1950	1951	1952	1953	1954	1955	1956	1957	1958
TOTAL		8	44	30	70	69	99	112	127	116	125
Intra-bloc		6	29	25	38	49	76	72	74	77	82
	%	75.0	65.9	83.3	54.3	71.0	76.8	64.3	58.3	66.4	65.6
Non-bloc		2	7	5	10	6	19	32	42	29	31
	%	25.0	15.9	16.7	14.3	8.7	19.2	28.6	33.1	25.0	24.8
Inter-bloc		0	7	0	16	6	3	8	10	8	11
	%	—	15.9	—	22.9	8.7	3.0	7.1	7.9	6.9	8.8
Other		0	1	0	6	8	1	0	1	2	1
	%	—	2.3	—	8.6	11.6	1.0	—	0.8	1.7	0.8
With bloc leader (USSR)		1	22	7	10	7	16	10	15	15	10
	%	12.5	50.0	23.3	14.3	10.1	16.2	8.9	11.8	12.9	8.0
Regional		7	6	5	19	15	42	48	50	42	50
	%	87.5	13.6	16.7	27.1	21.7	42.4	42.9	39.4	36.2	40.0
Contiguous		8	25	11	18	16	55	45	46	37	47
	%	100.0	56.8	36.7	25.7	23.2	55.6	40.2	36.2	31.9	37.6

the treaty partner. During the earlier period there was a very high rank-order correlation ($r_- = .75$) between the number of treaties signed by China and the wealth of the other signatory. The six wealthiest Communist nations (Soviet Union, Czechoslovakia, East Germany, Poland, Hungary, and Rumania) were among the most frequent treaty partners. Of the poorest nations (Mongolia, North Vietnam, North Korea, Albania, and Yugoslavia), only North Korea ranked near the top in the number of treaties signed with Peking. The relationship between the frequency of agreements signed and the wealth of the partner is markedly different for the most recent period ($r_s = -.59$). The Soviet Union and some of the relatively prosperous nations of Eastern Europe have been replaced by such nations as Cuba, North Vietnam, North Korea, and Albania as China's leading treaty partners. In addition to their low level of economic development, these four nations also share one other attribute in that they are the four members of the Communist system farthest removed geographically from the heartland of the Soviet Union.

Finally, an examination of the Chinese treaties according to issue-areas reveals that the decline in the number of intra-bloc agreements has tended

1959	1960	1961	1962	1963	1964	1965	1966	1967	1968	1969	1970	1971
111	127	150	124	144	164	160	107	51	43	12	20	71
87	75	83	78	71	79	60	49	21	13	3	11	28
78.4	59.1	55.3	62.9	49.3	48.2	37.5	45.8	41.2	30.3	25.0	55.0	39.4
23	52	63	37	54	75	78	47	25	27	9	5	33
20.7	40.9	42.0	29.8	37.5	45.7	48.8	43.9	49.0	62.8	75.0	25.0	46.5
1	0	4	7	19	10	22	11	5	3	0	4	10
0.9	—	2.7	5.6	13.2	6.1	13.8	10.3	9.8	6.9	—	20.0	14.1
0	0	0	2	0	0	0	0	0	0	0	0	0
—	—	—	1.6	—	—	—	—	—	—	—	—	—
15	7	16	9	6	3	5	4	1	0	0	1	1
13.5	5.5	10.7	7.3	4.2	1.8	3.1	3.7	2.0	—	—	5.0	1.4
33	54	54	46	48	55	64	41	16	16	4	7	17
29.7	42.5	36.0	37.1	33.3	33.5	40.0	38.3	31.4	37.2	33.3	35.0	23.9
41	29	59	40	31	42	35	31	11	12	2	8	15
36.9	22.8	39.3	32.3	21.5	25.6	21.9	29.0	21.6	27.9	16.7	40.0	21.1

to affect all issue-areas (Table 13). This is most evident in the case of treaties with the Soviet Union. Since 1962 the proportion of Chinese agreements with the Soviet Union has decreased in every issue-area. Indeed, in 1969 Peking and Moscow did not even sign a trade protocol.

Although the treaty figures for the most recent years may be incomplete, they do indicate the extent to which China withdrew from external relations during 1967–1969. By 1967 the number of Chinese agreements had fallen to the lowest levels since the height of the Korean War, and the figure fell again during each of the following two years, reaching a nadir in 1969. This period coincided with the Cultural Revolution, a primary target of which was the Ministry of Foreign Affairs. It also followed a series of calamitous defeats for Chinese diplomacy: Peking's influence in Indonesia was all but destroyed by the civil war of 1965; the second "Bandung Conference," scheduled for Algiers, was cancelled; in 1965 and 1966 four African nations—Burundi, Central African Republic, Dahomey and Ghana—expelled Chinese diplomats for subversive activities and severed relations with Peking.[29] During this period all ambassadors but one (stationed in Cairo) were recalled and minor officials were left as chiefs of

TABLE 12. Bilateral Chinese Intra-bloc Treaties and Agreements, All-Issue Areas

	1949–1952			1953–1955			1956–1958		
	N	%	Rank	N	%	Rank	N	%	Rank
U.S.S.R.	40	40.8	1	33	16.8	1	40	17.2	1
Poland	13	13.3	2	15	7.6	7.5	20	8.6	4
Czechoslovakia	11	11.2	3	15	7.6	7.5	15	6.4	8.5
E. Germany	8	8.2	4	25	12.7	2	15	6.4	8.5
N. Korea	7	7.1	5	16	8.1	5	31	13.3	2
Hungary	6	6.1	6	15	7.6	7.5	18	7.7	5.5
Bulgaria	5	5.1	7	13	6.6	10	15	6.4	8.5
Rumania	4	4.1	8	17	8.7	4	13	5.6	11
N. Vietnam	3	3.1	9	23	11.7	3	22	9.4	3
Mongolia	1	1.0	10	15	7.6	7.5	15	6.4	8.5
Yugoslavia	0	—	11.5	0	—	12	18	7.7	5.5
Albania	0	—	11.5	10	5.1	11	11	4.7	12
Cuba	—	—	—	—	—	—	—	—	—
TOTAL	98	100.0		197	100.1*		233	99.8*	

* Does not equal 100.0 because of rounding error.

mission. Coinciding with the withdrawal from active diplomacy was a campaign of vilification aimed at virtually all governments, not excluding such erstwhile friends as North Korea, and glorification of the supposedly Maoist "masses" everywhere.[30] Only in 1970 did China fully emerge from its self-imposed isolation with a full-fledged campaign of opening contacts with the West, including the United States. The resumption of relations with the Soviet Union at the ambassadorial level in November 1970 marked the end of a four-year hiatus, but relations between Peking and Moscow have generally remained frigid. With the outbreak of civil disorder in Poland toward the end of 1970, *Jen-min Jih-pao* and other Chinese sources verbally flayed Wladyslaw Gomulka and his successor, Edward Gierek, as members of a "counter-revolutionary revisionist clique"[31] that was subservient to the USSR. Moscow, in turn, has expressed a willingness to return to normal relations, but only if the Chinese capitulate on ideological differences: "Our readiness to develop relations on the basis of uniting against the imperialists does not signify any concessions of principle whatsoever in ideological discussions."[32] The Indo-Pak War in 1971 and the Nixon visit to China the following year did little to improve relations between Moscow and Peking.

The French treaty data are summarized in Table 14.[33] The distribution

1959–1962			1963–1965			1966–1971		
N	%	Rank	N	%	Rank	N	%	Rank
47	14.6	1	14	6.7	8	7	5.6	7
23	7.1	8	12	5.7	10	8	6.4	5.5
24	7.4	6.5	14	6.7	8	3	2.4	12.5
24	7.4	6.5	14	6.7	8	6	4.8	8.5
29	9.0	4	23	11.0	3	16	12.8	3
21	6.5	10	10	4.8	12	5	4.0	10.5
14	4.3	12	11	5.2	11	6	4.8	8.5
18	5.6	11	18	8.6	5	14	11.2	4
39	12.1	2	27	12.9	1	26	20.8	1
25	7.7	5	16	7.6	6	5	4.0	10.5
4	1.2	13	3	1.4	13	3	2.4	12.5
33	10.2	3	26	12.4	2	18	14.4	2
22	6.8	9	22	10.5	4	8	6.4	5.5
323	99.9*		210	100.2*		125	100.0	

of the 546 bilateral and 708 multipartite treaties is similar in some respects with that of China and differs in a number of others. There has been a general decline in intra-bloc treaties and in those agreements limited to contiguous partners during the years of the Fifth Republic. However, this change is somewhat misleading because *all* "multiple bloc" treaties include at least one other member of the western alliance and many include contiguous nations. Concomitantly there has been a significant rise in the proportion of treaties with partners in the opposing alliance and a somewhat less marked increase in agreements with nonaligned nations and in treaties with signatories in more than a single bloc. The proportion of regional and organizational treaties remained stable between the two periods.

When French agreements are further analyzed according to treaty partner and issue-area (Table 15), the pattern which emerges differs from that of China in one important respect. Like China, France concluded a substantial proportion of its agreements with the bloc leader. But whereas there has recently been a sharp decline in the number of Sino-Soviet treaties, this has not occurred within the western alliance. Rather, during the Fifth Republic the number of French agreements with the United States has shown an increase in proportion to those with other partners, and in

TABLE 13. Chinese Treaties and Agreements by Issue-Areas 1949–1962

		USSR	N. Vietnam	N. Korea	E. Germany	Poland	Czech.	Hungary	Mongolia	Albania	Rumania	Bulgaria	Cuba	Yugo.	All Others
Security (N=33)		7	0	1	2	0	1	1	1	0	0	0	0	0	20
	%	21.2	—	3.0	6.1	—	3.0	3.0	3.0	—	—	—	—	—	60.6
Territory (N=21)		3	0	1	0	0	0	0	2	0	0	0	0	0	15
	%	14.3	—	4.8	—	—	—	—	9.5	—	—	—	—	—	71.4
Human Resources (N=350)		47	19	22	27	30	31	28	16	17	23	24	9	10	47
	%	13.4	5.4	6.3	7.7	8.6	8.9	8.0	4.6	4.9	6.6	6.9	2.6	2.9	13.4
Non-human Res. (N=837)		97	68	59	42	41	32	31	37	37	29	23	13	12	316
	%	11.6	8.1	7.0	5.0	4.9	3.8	3.7	4.4	4.4	3.5	2.7	1.6	1.4	37.8
Status (N=67)		3	0	0	1	0	1	0	0	0	0	0	0	0	62
	%	4.5	—	—	1.5	—	1.5	—	—	—	—	—	—	—	92.5
Other (N=4)		3	0	0	0	0	0	0	0	0	0	0	0	0	1
	%	75.0	—	—	—	—	—	—	—	—	—	—	—	—	25.0
TOTAL (N=1312)		160	87	83	72	71	65	60	56	54	52	47	22	22	461
	%	12.2	6.6	6.3	5.5	5.4	5.0	4.6	4.3	4.1	4.0	3.6	1.7	1.7	35.1

TABLE 13. *Continued*

1963–1971

	USSR	N. Vietnam	N. Korea	E. Germany	Poland	Czech.	Hungary	Mongolia	Albania	Rumania	Bulgaria	Cuba	Yugo.	All Others
Security (N=13)	0	4	1	0	0	0	0	0	0	0	0	0	0	8
%	—	30.8	7.7	—	—	—	—	—	—	—	—	—	—	61.5
Territory (N=12)	0	0	0	0	0	0	0	3	0	0	0	0	0	9
%	—	—	—	—	—	—	—	25.0	—	—	—	—	—	75.0
Human Resources (N=230)	9	21	18	11	12	9	7	9	14	15	10	12	0	83
%	3.9	9.1	7.8	4.8	5.2	3.9	3.0	3.9	6.1	6.5	4.3	5.2	—	36.1
Non-human Res. (N=468)	12	28	20	8	8	8	8	9	30	17	7	18	6	289
%	2.6	6.0	4.3	1.7	1.7	1.7	1.7	1.9	6.4	3.6	1.5	3.8	1.3	61.9
Status (N=40)	0	0	0	0	0	0	0	0	0	0	0	0	0	40
%	—	—	—	—	—	—	—	—	—	—	—	—	—	100.0
Other (N=5)	0	0	0	1	0	0	0	0	0	0	0	0	0	4
%	—	—	—	20.0	—	—	—	—	—	—	—	—	—	80.0
TOTAL (N=768)	21	53	39	20	20	17	15	21	44	32	17	30	6	433
%	2.7	6.9	5.1	2.6	2.6	2.2	2.0	2.7	5.7	4.2	2.2	3.9	0.8	56.4

**TABLE 14.   French Treaties in Various International
Environments, All Issue-Areas**

		1945	1946	1947	1948	1949	1950	1951	1952	1953	1954
TOTAL		26	60	69	77	60	63	68	69	73	98
Intra-bloc		10	46	39	45	34	39	40	28	34	38
	%	38.5	76.7	56.5	58.4	56.7	61.9	58.8	40.6	46.6	38.8
Inter-bloc		3	2	2	3	0	0	0	0	3	3
	%	11.5	3.3	2.9	3.9	—	—	—	—	4.1	3.1
Non-bloc		0	2	5	2	5	2	2	7	3	6
	%	—	3.3	7.2	2.6	8.3	3.2	2.9	10.1	4.1	6.1
Organizational		0	2	13	17	9	3	11	7	6	20
	%	—	3.3	18.8	22.1	15.0	4.8	16.2	10.1	8.2	20.4
Multiple blocs*		13	8	10	10	12	19	15	27	27	31
	%	50.0	13.3	14.5	13.0	20.0	30.2	22.1	39.1	37.0	31.6
With bloc leader** (U.S.)		3	17	10	18	3	7	4	6	2	2
	%	11.5	28.3	14.5	23.4	5.0	11.1	5.9	8.7	2.7	2.0
Contiguous		2	5	9	10	9	10	2	5	10	6
	%	7.7	8.3	13.0	13.0	15.0	15.9	2.9	7.2	13.7	6.1
Regional		9	26	26	27	28	30	16	26	42	27
	%	34.6	43.3	37.7	35.1	46.7	47.6	23.5	37.7	57.5	27.6

* Multipartite treaties and general international agreements with partners in more than one international environment.
** Bilateral treaties only.

no issue-area has there been a significant decline in agreements between Paris and Washington.

These results should be interpreted with considerable caution, in part because the French treaty data for the most recent years are almost certainly incomplete, in part because the frequency with which treaties are signed may not prove an adequate index of relations between states. Despite obvious limitations in the data, differences in the patterns of Chinese and French intra-bloc treaties are consistent with the proposition that in the more pluralistic alliance, nonconforming behavior in one issue-area is less likely to spill over into all of them.

Conclusion

Data on French and Chinese actions, elite attitudes, trade, foreign aid, and treaties were consistent with the hypotheses developed in the previous

1955	1956	1957	1958	1959	1960	1961	1962	1963	1964	1965	1966– 1967
85	67	70	59	71	48	36	47	26	35	25	24
26	29	29	23	24	14	19	10	10	14	10	6
30.6	43.3	41.4	39.0	33.8	29.2	52.8	21.3	38.5	40.0	40.0	25.0
0	2	6	5	8	8	0	1	0	0	2	2
—	3.0	8.6	8.5	11.3	16.7	—	2.1	—	—	8.0	8.3
3	4	1	4	5	2	4	6	5	1	3	0
3.5	6.0	1.4	6.8	7.0	4.2	11.1	12.8	19.2	2.9	12.0	—
41	6	10	9	10	9	3	8	3	5	5	10
48.2	9.0	14.3	15.3	14.1	18.8	8.3	17.0	11.5	14.3	20.0	41.7
15	26	24	18	24	15	10	22	8	15	5	6
17.6	38.8	34.3	30.5	33.8	31.3	27.8	46.8	30.8	42.9	20.0	25.0
5	9	3	8	7	8	9	4	3	1	1	2
5.9	13.4	4.3	13.6	9.9	16.7	25.0	8.5	11.5	2.9	5.0	8.3
3	7	11	7	4	3	5	8	0	6	1	6
3.5	10.4	15.7	11.9	5.6	6.3	13.9	17.0	—	17.1	5.0	25.0
15	31	46	27	37	15	13	16	3	7	5	4
17.6	46.3	65.7	45.8	52.1	31.3	36.1	34.0	11.5	20.0	20.0	16.7

chapter. But there are some significant limitations in this analysis which must at least be noted. In examining the intra-alliance conflicts we have been able to develop indices on many of the recurring international activities which France and China have undertaken and to which they have responded, but admittedly gross categories have been used to report the findings. For example, trade figures were not further broken down according to commodities, and treaties were classified only according to issue-area, without further consideration of the precise terms of the agreement. A more serious limitation is that we have been able to consider only some facets of the complex interaction of actors, institutions, attitudes, and processes from which foreign policies emerge and which may be directly or indirectly affected by events in various international environments. Our data reveal trends on some aspects of Chinese or French foreign policy quite precisely, but many interesting questions remain unexplored, in part because trying to answer them would have taken us far from our central concern with alliances, in part because even anecdotal information on Chinese decision making is scarce. It is easy to ask questions about how Chinese actors, institutions, attitudes, and political processes contribute to

TABLE 15. French Treaties and Agreements by Issue-Area

Issue-Area		United States	Common Market Nations	"Outer Seven" Nations*	Other Allies	Multi-Partite Treaties	All Other Treaties
		1945–1957 Treaty Partner					
		Intra-bloc					
Security							
(N = 25)		3	0	3	1	8	10
	%	12.0	—	12.0	4.0	32.0	40.0
Territory							
(N = 32)		2	13	3	2	3	9
	%	6.3	40.6	9.4	6.3	9.4	28.1
Human Resources							
(N = 241)		14	44	23	7	12	141
	%	5.8	18.3	9.5	2.9	5.0	58.5
Non-human Resources							
(N = 467)		70	38	37	59	48	215
	%	15.0	8.1	7.9	12.6	10.3	46.0
Status							
(N = 115)		0	1	2	3	37	72
	%	—	0.9	1.7	2.6	32.2	62.6
Other							
(N = 5)		0	0	3	1	0	1
	%	—	—	60.0	20.0	—	20.0
Total							
(N = 885)		89	96	71	73	108	448
	%	10.1	10.8	8.0	8.2	12.2	50.6

* Excludes treaties with non-bloc Switzerland, Austria and Sweden (17 treaties 1945–57; 6 treaties 1958–67).

foreign policy decisions or how they are affected by the policies of other nations, but it is often impossible, even for specialists in Chinese politics, to answer them.

Finally, even though the data appear consistent with our hypotheses about the consequences of domestic and alliance characteristics on patterns of deviation from alliances, we have in fact only taken the most preliminary steps toward exploring these linkages. We have found that France, the more pluralistic nation and a member of the more pluralistic alliance, has disrupted its relations with allies in a limited manner. There have been open disagreements between Paris, London, Bonn, Ottawa, Washington, and other western capitals on a number of major issues: NATO, nuclear

Issue-Area		United States	Common Market Nations	"Outer Seven" Nations*	Other Allies	Multi-Partite Treaties	All Other Treaties
			1958–1967 Treaty Partner				
			Intra-bloc				
Security							
(N = 12)		4	0	0	1	2	5
	%	33.3	—	—	8.3	16.7	41.7
Territory							
(N = 13)		6	2	0	0	0	5
	%	46.1	15.4	—	—	—	38.5
Human Resources							
(N = 97)		4	9	12	2	13	57
	%	4.1	9.3	12.4	2.1	13.4	58.8
Non-human Resources							
(N = 197)		28	7	8	11	13	130
	%	14.2	3.6	4.1	5.6	6.6	66.0
Status							
(N = 46)		1	0	0	1	5	39
	%	2.2	—	—	2.2	10.9	84.8
Other							
(N = 4)		0	0	1	0	0	3
	%	—	—	25.0	—	—	75.0
Total							
(N = 369)		43	18	21	15	33	239
	%	11.7	4.9	5.7	4.1	8.9	64.8

sharing, the Test Ban Treaty, Vietnam, Biafra, the Middle East, and Quebec. But never has there been a suggestion that these issues could not be dealt with by normal diplomacy. Nor has political disagreement resulted in the attenuation of trade, cultural, or other types of relationships.

China, an authoritarian polity within the more monolithic alliance has, for all practical purposes, ceased to be an ally of the USSR. If claims from both sides are to be believed, the dramatic battles on the China-USSR frontier in 1969 are far from isolated incidents. And, as is clear from the evidence adduced in this chapter, few if any sectors of Sino-Soviet relations have escaped the consequences of the conflict. Moreover, virtually all Communist nations have been pressured into choosing sides in the controversy, with the consequence that Peking's relations with many East European nations have deteriorated markedly. But an important question which remains to be explored is the relative potency of domestic and international factors on policy decisions. That is, do we attribute the pattern of French and Chinese policies to their internal political processes, to the characteristics of alliances they joined, or to some combination of both?

Although the generality of the present findings can only be determined through study of other alliances, they provide at least preliminary empirical support for our hypotheses. They are also consistent with a suggestion made in the introductory chapter—that there is limited theoretical mileage to be gained from efforts to spell out propositions purported to be valid for all alliances, irrespective of the nature of the alliance or its constituent nations. To reiterate the point made earlier, our understanding of international alliances is less likely to be advanced by efforts to demonstrate the universal verity of a single theory than by investigations that attempt to specify the conditions under which competing explanations are valid.

Notes

1. The importance of such data as indicators of Chinese foreign policy is not universally accepted. Karl Wittfogel, for example, asserts that, "In the course of this intricate process the leading Communist countries may have grave differences of opinion on details of economic cooperation and domestic and foreign policy. But any analyst who, because of such secondary differences, disregards the primary ties between Moscow and Peking, appraises the Communist power system with the standards of a Babbitt or a Colonel Blimp." Wittfogel, "A Stronger Oriental Despotism," *China Quarterly*, 1, 1960, p. 34. At the risk of being guilty of Babbitry, we assume that our data do in fact shed some light on developments in Sino-Soviet relations.

2. Determination of the regional environments for France and China involved some arbitrary decisions, one of which was to consider the Soviet Union as a European rather than an Asian nation, and therefore within the French but not the Chinese regional environment. One reason for this decision was that it would be useful to have one environmental category that cuts across cold war alignments. Perhaps French and Chinese leaders would define regions similarly. De Gaulle talked of a Europe from "the Urals to the Atlantic," and Chinese leaders have sought to exclude the Soviet Union from the "Afro-Asian" world.

3. *New York Times Index*, 1950–1969; Charles McClelland *et al.*, *The Communist Chinese Performance in Crisis and Non-crisis: Quantitative Studies of the Taiwan Straits Confrontation, 1950–1964*, Naval Ordnance Test Station, China Lake, Calif., 1965; and William H. Vatcher, *Panmunjom*,

Praeger, New York, 1958. The McClelland and Vatcher sources were chronologies and it was necessary only to record each action as it appeared. The *New York Times Index* employs a system of cross-referencing which necessitated the following approach. The main section for each country contained cross-references indicating international actions by both countries. These cross-references were to geographical, issue, and organizational items. With one exception, we coded all actions appearing in these sources. We abandoned efforts to report every military engagement in Korea, or in Indo-China, Algeria, and other former French dependencies. The problem of determining what level of engagement (e.g., squad, company, battalion) should be included was not readily solvable. Moreover, such activities were often described as "reported" military encounters and verifying them would have proved a virtually impossible task.

4. For excellent discussions of the problems associated with using a single source such as the *New York Times Index* or *Deadline Data*, see Edward E. Azar *et al.*, "The Problem of Source Coverage in the Use of Events Data," *International Studies Quarterly*, 16, 1972; and Charles F. Doran, Robert E. Pendley, and George E. Antunes, "A Test of Cross-National Event Reliability," *International Studies Quarterly*, 17, 1973.

5. Quoted in *The Sun*, Vancouver, May 30, 1969.

6. Chinese verbal attacks against Yugoslavia account for the results in 1958 during which only 62 percent of Chinese actions toward members of the Communist system were positive.

7. Texts were derived mostly from: *United States Foreign Broadcast Information Service, United Nations General Assembly Official Record, Vital Speeches of the Day*, and the many publications of the French Service de Presse et d'Information, including the *Speeches and Press Conferences* series, and *French Affairs*.

8. This method of scoring is similar to that used by Harold D. Lasswell, Daniel Lerner, and Ithiel deSola Pool in their RADIR studies of editorials appearing in elite newspapers. See their *The Comparative Study of Symbols*, Stanford University Press, Stanford, 1952.

9. Karl W. Deutsch, "Integration and Arms Control in the European Political Environment: A Summary Report," *American Political Science Review*, 60, 1966, p. 361. See also Morton Gorden and Daniel Lerner, "The Setting for European Arms Control: Political and Strategic Choices of European Elites," *Journal of Conflict Resolution*, 9, 1965.

10. Amitai Etzioni, "The Dialectics of Supranational Unification," *American Political Science Review*, 56, 1962, pp. 931–932. Cf. Karl W. Deutsch *et al.*, *Political Community and the North Atlantic Area*, Princeton University Press, Princeton, 1957, p. 197; and Henry Kissinger, *The Troubled Partnership*, McGraw-Hill, New York, 1965, p. 39.

11. Quoted in Zbigniew K. Brzezinski, *The Soviet Bloc: Unity and Conflict*, Harvard University Press, Cambridge, 1960, p. 402.

12. R. V. Burks, "The Rumanian National Deviation: An Accounting," cited in Barry Hughes and Thomas Volgy, "Distance in Foreign Policy Behav-

ior: A Comparative Study of Eastern Europe," *Midwest Political Science Review,* 14, 1970.

13. Chinese trade data have been gathered from Alexander Eckstein, *Communist China's Economic Growth and Foreign Trade,* McGraw-Hill, New York, 1966; U.S. Mutual Defense Assistance Control Act Administrator, *Reports to Congress,* annual; Pauline Lewin, *The Foreign Trade of Communist China,* Praeger, New York, 1964; *Far East Economic Review, Yearbook,* 1969, pp. 147–149; The Editor, "China's Foreign Trade in 1968," *Current Scene,* 7, 1969; The Editor, "China's Foreign Trade in 1969," *Current Scene,* 8, 1970; The Editor, "China's Foreign Trade in 1970," *Current Scene,* 9, 1971; and The Editor, "China's Foreign Trade in 1971," *Current Scene,* 10, 1972, pp. 1–17.

Some controversy surrounds determination of the exact value of goods exchanged within the Communist system. See, in addition to the above, Kang Chao, "Pitfalls in the Use of China's Foreign Trade Statistics," *China Quarterly,* 19, 1964; and Feng-hwa Mah, "The Terms of Sino-Soviet Trade," *China Quarterly,* 17, 1964. But such discrepancies should not affect our results, which are concerned with comparisons across time, rather than with the absolute level of trade in any given year.

14. "PRC Trade and Diplomatic Relations," *Current Scene,* 9, 1971; "China and Eastern Europe," *Current Scene,* 9, 1971.

15. In 1971 Sino-Japanese trade reached a figure of $900 million, an increase of 9.4 percent over 1970. *Christian Science Monitor,* February 28, 1972, p. 8.

16. This becomes evident if one compares the figures in Choh-ming Li, "China's Industrial Development," *China Quarterly,* 17, 1964, pp. 3–38; Eckstein, *op. cit.;* David Floyd, *Mao Against Khrushchev: A Short History of the Sino-Soviet Conflict,* Praeger, New York, 1964; Kang Chao, *op. cit.;* Boris Meissner, "The People's Commune: A Manifestation of Sino-Soviet Differences," in Kurt London, ed., *Unity and Contradiction: Major Aspects of Sino-Soviet Relations,* Praeger, New York, 1962; and Leonard Shapiro, "The Chinese Ally from the Soviet Point of View," in Kurt London, ed., *op. cit.*

17. Eckstein, *op. cit.,* pp. 181–182.

18. Floyd, *op. cit.,* p. 12.

19. Editorial in *People's Daily,* Dec. 4, 1963, quoted in Choh-Ming Li, *op. cit.,* p. 32.

20. Table 9 was constructed from data in Eckstein, *op. cit.;* Lewin, *op. cit.;* Maurice D. Simon, "Communist System Interaction with the Developing States, 1954–62; A Preliminary Analysis," Stanford Studies of the Communist System, mimeo, 1965; and Leo Tansky, "China's Foreign Aid: The Record," *Current Scene,* 10, 1972, pp. 1–11. It should be noted that the figures in Table 9 refer to *grants,* not to actual *deliveries,* which may be considerably smaller in many cases, or which may be spread out over a number of years. For example, of $950 million pledged to African nations during 1954–1966, only $200 million was delivered. Alex Blake, "Peking's

African Adventure," *Current Scene*, 5, 1967, p. 7. Cf. Eckstein, *op. cit.*, p. 162; and A. M. Halpern, "China in the Postwar World," *China Quarterly*, 21, 1965, p. 54.

21. Quoted in Floyd, *op. cit.*, p. 81. See also W.A.C. Adie, "China, Russia, and the Third World," *China Quarterly*, 11, 1962.

22. The first aid to a member of the western alliance, a grant of $60 million to Pakistan, was announced in 1964. In 1970 Pakistan received another $200 million in aid, but it is not known whether any aid agreements were signed during the Indo-Pak War.

23. Table 10 was constructed from data in *The Yearbook of International Trade* through 1965, and from figures made available by the French Embassy, Washington, D.C. for 1966–1969.

24. Deutsch, "Integration and Arms Control in the European Political Environment," *op. cit.*, p. 360.

25. Lindberg, *op. cit.*, p. 75.

26. "In Stalin's lifetime the impression was widespread that the remaining forms of state sovereignty and international procedure, the diplomatic and consular arrangements, the patterns of international legal rights and obligations . . . were 'survivals' of the bourgeois era, destined soon to be replaced by more progressive superstructures. More recent years have seen the negotiation and completion of formal instruments in a variety of less important fields which earlier would not have been thought worth troubling about." Modelski, *op. cit.*, pp. 29–30.

27. Chinese treaties were located in the following sources: Robert Slusser and Jan F. Triska, *A Calendar of Soviet Treaties, 1917–1957*, Stanford University Press, Stanford, 1959; George Ginsbergs, "A Calendar of Soviet Treaties," *Ost Europa Recht*, annual; *China Mainland Review*, 1, 1965, pp. 1–3; *Peking Review*, 1958–1971; American Consulate General, Hong Kong, "Agreements between Communist China and Foreign Countries," *Current Background*, No. 545, 1959, and No. 651, 1961; American Consulate General, Hong Kong, *Survey of the Chinese Mainland Press*, Index; five volumes in a series published by the Institut für Asienkunde, *Die Verträge der Volksrepublik China mit anderen Staaten*, Alfred Metzner Verlag, Frankfurt, 1957; *Verträge der Volksrepublik China mit anderen Staaten: Süd-under Ostasien*, Alfred Metzner Verlag, Frankfurt, 1962; *Verträge der Volksrepublik China mit anderen Staaten: Die Länder des Vorderen Orients und Afrikas*, Alfred Metzner Verlag, Frankfurt, 1963; *Verträge der Volksrepublik China mit anderen Staaten: Die nichtkommunistischen Länder Europes under die Länder Amerika (einschliesslich Kubas)*, Alfred Metzner Verlag, Frankfurt, 1965; *Verträge der Volksrepublik China mit anderen Staaten: Nachträge zu Band XII/1 bis XII/3*, Otto Harrassowitz, Wiesbaden, 1968; Douglas M. Johnston and Hungdah Chiu, *Agreements of The People's Republic of China, 1949–1967: A Calendar*, Harvard University Press, Cambridge, 1968; *United Nations Treaty Series*, Vols. 1–626; and *Current Scene*, 1970–72. Tables 11–15 include treaties, agreements, and protocols, but exclude joint statements, commu-

niqués, minutes of meetings, and agreements with unofficial organizations in other countries, which are sometimes included in treaty collections.

28. Brzezinski, *op. cit.,* pp. 405–406; Jan F. Triska *et al.,* "The World Communist System," Studies of the Communist System, Stanford, no date, p. 5.

29. Blake, *op. cit.*

30. Daniel Tretiak, "The Chinese Cultural Revolution & Foreign Policy," *Current Scene,* 8, 1970. See also Robert A. Scalapino, "The Cultural Revolution and Chinese Foreign Policy," *Current Scene,* 6, 1968.

31. Quoted in Tillman Durdin, "Peking Supports Polish Dissidents," *New York Times,* Dec. 23, 1970.

32. Pravda, quoted in the *New York Times,* Jan. 7, 1971, p. 3.

33. French treaties were located in the *United Nations Treaty Series,* Vols. 1–626; Slusser and Triska, *op. cit.;* and Ginsbergs, *op. cit.* Owing to the time lag in publication of the *Treaty Series,* the French data are almost certainly less complete than those for China, especially for the late 1960s. Although an excellent source, the UN *Treaty Series* also presents several other problems, one of which is the very irregular time gap between ratification of a treaty and its appearance in UNTS. For instance, French ratification of a supplement to the Warsaw Convention, enacted on January 24, 1964, appeared in Volume 500 of the *Treaty Series.* But seven French treaties with Ireland, signed between 1947 and 1951, were not published until Volumes 553, 557, and 558.

CHAPTER SEVEN

Conclusion

Approaches to the Study of Alliances

At various points throughout this book we have expressed some doubts that any one of the existing theories of international alliances can lay claim to universal validity. On the premise that claims on behalf of any single theory may be either premature or misdirected, the studies in the preceding chapters have employed an eclectic research strategy that was not informed by a single theory, confined to one level of analysis, nor tied to a single set of data and indicators. As acknowledged earlier, this variety is not an unmixed blessing, but it does provide us with the opportunity to assess, at least in part, a number of approaches to the study of alliances. It is to this task that we shall now turn.

An overview of the findings in the preceding chapters provides an initial clue that general theories of alliance may actually have only limited validity. The analysis in Chapter Two examined some 130 alliances formed during the span of more than a century. The independent variables that were selected—ideology, political stability, geographical dispersion, size, goals, and international conflict—are among the most prominent in the alliance literature. Yet none of them was consistently associated with the nature and performance of the alliances formed during the period between the end of the Napoleonic Wars and the outbreak of World War II. The most striking result is the consistency of *low* correlations. In contrast, Chapters Three and Four compared only two alliances (NATO and the Communist system) for a period of two decades (1948–1967). Under these circumstances many potential intervening variables would be likely to remain relatively constant. For this smaller sample and more restricted time period there was a relatively close correspondence between theory and data. Finally, the hypotheses in Chapters Five and Six stressed *differences* rather than similarities in French and Chinese relationships within their respective alliances. The data provided strong support for the proposition that the outcome of intra-bloc disputes depends in part on the nature of the alliance. Thus, each of these studies seems to point to the need for defining the limits of general explanations.

The presence of many low correlations in the survey of alliances formed during 1815–1939 is not surprising, however, because the data were selected to test *competing* theories of alliance formation and performance. It is scarcely likely that all correlations would be high, nor would such a result have been very informative. The next question, then, is whether we can discern a pattern in the results that would tend to support propositions drawn from one theory in preference to those drawn from another. We can use our findings to undertake a very preliminary and crude assessment of three approaches to alliances: "affiliation theories," "balance of power theories," and "minimum winning coalition theories."

Affiliation theories stipulate that alliances are often the political reflection of common culture, values, institutions, and the like. Without denying that international "marriages of convenience" may take place, they suggest that the bonds of alliance often arise from considerations other than utilitarian calculations of power. If this reasoning is valid, we would expect to find that ideologically homogeneous alliances were characterized by a higher level of commitment, fewer premature terminations, a higher renewal rate, and a longer life span. The data in Chapter Two provide only minimal support for these propositions. During 1815–1939 there was a moderate tendency for nations that shared an ideological viewpoint to undertake more binding commitments, but there was no support for the prediction that such alliances would enjoy greater longevity; if anything, they were less likely than heterogeneous alliances to be renewed or to endure for a long time.

We may use one further source of evidence as an indirect test of affiliation theories. Nations within the same region are presumably somewhat more likely to share a common culture and values than are those in widely separated continents. To the extent that this premise is valid, affiliation theories would predict that geographically distant nations are less prone to undertake commitments of the highest class (military pacts), and that dispersed alliances are less likely to endure or to be renewed. The data, however, provide little support for the belief that distance is an important consideration in the nature of alliances or their performance, even though most of the period under study *preceded* the introduction of the airplane, communication satellites, and other inventions that have reduced the relationship between distance and time. Admittedly, this is an indirect and very imperfect test of affiliation theories, but it is consistent with the generally negative findings that emerged from the data on ideological homogeneity.

In summary, then, at least for the century and a quarter ending with the

Nazi invasion of Poland in 1939, theories that predict international alignments on the basis of ideological or institutional similarities appear to be
of limited validity. Perhaps this result should not surprise us. Most of the
period under study was, after all, the "classical era" of balance of power
politics. Although there are many variants of power theories, they all
agree that alignments based on sentiment serve the interests of neither the
nation nor of the international community.

We might therefore expect that the data for 1815–1939 should support
predictions derived from power theories. Were this the case, we would expect to find that politically stable nations, being the more desirable allies
from a purely utilitarian perspective, were more often found in alliances of
the highest commitment level, that alliances of stable regimes were more
likely to be renewed, and that they were less likely to be broken prior to
the termination date. We would also expect that wartime alliances would
endure for only short periods of time—usually no longer than the end of
the conflict. The data indicate substantial support only for the last of these
propositions. Although the evidence is clearly insufficient for a full-scale
test of power theories, the results suggest that the motives underlying the
nature and performance of alliances are more complex and varied than en-
visaged in many balance of power formulations.[1]

Finally, we can use these data for a very preliminary and crude assessment of one facet of coalition theories—the theorem that alliances will increase in size only to the point that they are sufficient to win. A corollary
is that those exceeding this optimal size will tend to experience defections,
expulsions, or disintegration. Our data do not provide a clear and direct
test of the size principle, but for the period 1815–1939 we may assume
that alliances of only two nations would not violate the size principle,
whereas those of three or more members might do so. Thus, coalition
theories would lead to the prediction that the larger alliances (three or
more members) were more likely to be broken by the defection or expulsion of one or more members prior to the termination date. Moreover, the
larger alliances should have been renewed less frequently and should have
been less likely to survive over an extended period of time. In short, although alliances that violate the size principle may be formed—owing to
inadequate information, miscalculation, and the like—according to the
theory they should endure in their original form less frequently than the
smaller alliances.

The evidence for these propositions is mixed. More small alliances survived until the formal termination date, but only by a small margin, and
they did last for longer periods of time than alliances comprised of many
nations. They were also renewed less often. Although such an indirect test
is clearly an insufficient basis for rejection of the size principle, the find-

ings perhaps sustain some of the doubts expressed in Chapter One about the applicability of this aspect of coalition theories to international alliances. At least they suggest the need for more systematic research before the size principal can be accepted as a regular feature of alliance behavior.

We can also summarize our findings from a different perspective. The results of the preceding chapters may be used for a very preliminary assessment of the potency of various levels of explanation.

The effects of *national attributes* of alliance behavior are the most difficult to assess. The survey of alliances formed during 1815–1939 examined two variables frequently associated with alliances—ideological homogeneity and regime stability. The results suggest that neither of these attributes was strongly related to the nature or performance of alliances. In Chapter Five we developed a line of reasoning to indicate that political stability might be a necessary, but not sufficient, condition for deviation from alliance commitments. It was further suggested that nations with authoritarian and pluralistic political systems are likely to cope with intra-alliance conflicts in quite different ways. The data on France and China presented in Chapter Six were consistent with these speculations, but the results cannot be viewed as more than a very preliminary assessment of the impact of political systems on alliance politics.[2]

The findings on the effects of *alliance attributes* are similarly mixed. Although size, geographical dispersion, and the nature of goals are often linked with aspects of alliance performance, they appear to have had only limited effect on alliances formed during the period 1815–1939. But we also tested the proposition that centralized and authoritarian alliances would be less capable than pluralistic ones of containing serious intra-bloc conflicts. These were well supported with data on French and Chinese relations with their erstwhile allies, but only modest claims can be made for the generality of findings based on two alliances. No doubt further investigations along these lines would point to the need for additional qualifications. For instance, we might find that the incidence of "across the board" rupture in alliance relations is very rare among weak nations, even in highly centralized and authoritarian alliances. The Dubcek regime in Czechoslovakia tried very hard to make a distinction between domestic and external policy. Although internal reforms were acknowledged to vary from the Soviet brand of Marxist-Leninist practice, the Dubcek government was highly circumspect in repeatedly pledging allegiance to the Warsaw Pact. A relatively weak nation might be expected to have difficulties in wholesale repudiation of alliance links, as the Hungarian government of Imre Nagy discovered in 1956. In the Czech case, it could not succeed even in modest efforts to maintain a distinction between internal and foreign policy.

As might be expected, the preceding chapters provide considerable evidence that alliance behavior is affected by the state of relations within the *international system,* especially by the level of conflict between contending nations and alliances. The impact of international conflict is evident in the survey of pre-World War II alliances. Wartime pacts, for instance, differed from those contracted in peacetime with respect to level of commitment, renewal rate, and duration. Although the correlations were not uniformly high, they were generally consistent with the view that wartime alliances are often short-term compacts of expediency. As Winston Churchill stated in justifying British assistance to Russia after the Nazi invasion of June, 1941, "I have only one purpose, the destruction of Hitler, and my life is much simplified thereby. If Hitler invaded Hell I would make at least a favourable reference to the Devil in the House of Commons." [3]

The widely articulated proposition that alliance cohesion is a direct function of inter-bloc conflict was tested in Chapter Four. Data from NATO and the Communist system indicated that external threat facilitates cohesion, but it is neither a necessary nor a sufficient condition. Some exceptions to the general proposition were discovered, especially in the case of the Atlantic alliance. Specifically, an external threat directed at only part of the alliance may not be conducive to unity; conversely, efforts toward a détente with adversaries may have sufficient support from the entire alliance membership to produce at least a short-term unity of outlook and strategy.

French and Chinese experiences within their alliances also appear to indicate that international crises and conflict, even those that had a decidedly "cold war" flavor, may loosen as well as strengthen alliance bonds. Conflict over Indo-China (1954), Suez (1956), Quemoy-Matsu (1958), the Sino-Indian border (1962), Soviet missiles in Cuba (1965), and Vietnam (since 1964) may have had precisely this effect. From the perspective of Peking and Paris, it must have seemed that inter-alliance conflicts that involved the interests of the junior partners—Indo-China, Suez, the offshore islands, and the Himalayan frontier—were always deemed either too trivial or too dangerous to receive much support from the alliance leaders. Their chagrin could scarcely have been assuaged, moreover, by the willingness of Washington and Moscow to run considerable risks on behalf of minor "Johnny-come-lately" allies in South Vietnam and Cuba. Thus, international conflict is usually the occasion for allies to conceal or defer their differences in order to present a united front to the adversary, but this would appear to depend on at least a minimal degree of consensus about the existence and the nature of the threat. In the instances cited above this condition appears to have been missing, with the consequence that each of these episodes seems to have contributed to friction between

France and the United States, China and the Soviet Union, or both.

Finally, we shall speculate about some possibly promising questions for future research. In doing so we shall emphasize the development and testing of middle-range theories, with special attention directed to the conditions under which alternative explanations are likely to apply. Several examples based on the findings of the previous chapters may illustrate this point.

In Chapter Two we considered the effects of the international system on alliance behavior. Our findings suggested that even a crude distinction between the pre-World War I balance of power system and the post-1919 system seemed to result in somewhat different forms of alliance behavior. Several further questions are suggested by this very tentative finding. A reasonable next step is determining more precisely which structural features of the international system make a significant difference. Which ones intervene to limit the generality of central propositions about alliance formation, performance, and disintegration? We need not, of course, confine our inquiry to the more familiar balance of power or bipolar international configurations.[4] Indeed, we might wish to consider the implications for alliance behavior of international structures that have not existed for any length of time in modern history such as, for example, a truly multipolar system. Simulations offer one possible research strategy when historical data are not available. For example, Brody and Benham used manned simulations to analyze alliance behavior before and after nuclear proliferation.[5] Alternatively, the logical consequences of some hypotheses can be explored through computer simulations, such as Levitt's analysis of different effects of bipolar and multipolar international systems on the behavior of alliances.[6] In carrying out this type of research it is important, of course, to avoid circular reasoning. System structures must be defined in terms that are independent of alliance configurations. It would not do, for example, to define bipolarity as a system dominated by two tightly-knit alliances, and then use that definition to predict attributes of alliance structures in a bipolar world.

The structure of the international system also emerged as a significant variable in Chapters Three and Four. External conflict had less impact on alliance cohesion in a loose bipolar system than in a tight one. Further comparisons might usefully be made with other international system structures. For example, the effects of external threat might be tested in the various balance of power systems which existed during the two centuries prior to World War I.

In summary, we might proceed on the premise that the structure of the international system is one important scope variable. Should this prove a valid assumption, the result would be a series of middle-range theories that explain alliance behavior within specified systemic structures.

The impact of alliance structure also merits further consideration. Although external conflict and perceived threat seemed to result in increased cohesion within both the centralized Communist system and the pluralistic NATO alliance, there were also important differences. External conflict appeared to exert greater impact on attitudinal consensus within the Communist bloc, whereas in NATO the degree of intra-alliance cooperation was more markedly affected. It remains to be determined whether this is a regular feature of centralized and pluralistic alliances, whether we could explain the results by reference to the level of coercion employed to maintain alliance unity, or whether NATO and the Communist bloc are unique in this respect.

The study of French and Chinese alliance policies reported in Chapters Five and Six also considered the structure of alliances, as well as that of national regimes. We found that France, a pluralistic nation within a pluralistic alliance, was able to maintain normal relations with its allies in most issue-areas, despite sharp disagreements on security and military problems. China, a highly authoritarian polity within a monolithic alliance, found itself in conflict with virtually all its erstwhile allies. Moreover, the conflict spread rapidly to all issue-areas. But with only two cases it was impossible to determine whether the differences in French and Chinese alliance behavior arose from alliance structure, polity attributes, or a combination of the two. Future studies that include pluralistic nations within centralized and authoritarian alliances as well as authoritarian regimes within pluralistic alliances would provide at least a partial answer to this question.

In addition to these structural variables, further investigation on the effects of external threat seems warranted. The general proposition that alliance cohesion is related to external threat may often be valid. But is the relationship a linear one, as many seem to imply? Or, are there conditions under which the relationship could be described as an inverted V? That is, is there a point beyond which increasing external threat leads not to greater cohesion and collaboration, but rather to disintegrative behavior —for example, seeking a separate deal with the adversary? Moreover, is the threat-cohesion relationship an invariant one, or might it be affected by one or more intervening variables? Candidates that come to mind include: the level of consensus on basic values and alliance norms, the degree of regime stability among alliance members, and the extent to which the alliance is based on coercion. Answers to such questions should help us identify with greater precision the circumstances under which external threat is a necessary or sufficient condition for central aspects of alliance performance.

In attempting to answer these and related questions there are, of course, many research strategies that might be followed. It would be highly presumptuous to suggest that there is a single royal road to knowledge about such complex institutions as alliances. By stating a preference we do not mean to imply that alternative approaches—ranging from insightful speculation to detailed case studies of specific alliances—should be accorded second-class citizenship by students of alliances. With that qualification clearly stated,[we would place our bets on a research strategy which emphasizes comparative studies that include several levels of analysis, hypothesis testing as well as hypothesis formulation, multiple indicators of key concepts, and special attention on identifying the conditions that limit the generality of prominent theories and propositions.]

This interpretation of the alliance literature and of our findings is *not* an argument against efforts to develop valid generalizations and theories. Nor does it require us to stress the unique aspects of every alliance, in effect forming a separate category for each one. It does suggest, however, that we look critically at efforts to impose grand, overarching theories on alliance behavior.[7] These theories may provide a useful starting point, but we need also to examine the effects of intervening variables in order to define the scope and limits of alternative explanations of the causes and effects [8] of alliances. For example, there are probably limited rewards to be reaped from continuing to argue whether or not alliances are formed in response to the dictates of balance of power politics. Clearly many are, but others are not. What are the shared properties of the former that distinguish them from the latter? How do alliances formed from diverse motives differ with respect to structure, intra-alliance politics, longevity, and national or international effects? It is our guess that the answers to these and many other central questions will lead us to increasingly complex conceptions of alliance, not back to global theories that attempt to explain the cause and effects of all alliances with references to broad principles such as ideological affinity, balance of power, the size principle, and the like.

The preceding pages have raised many more such questions than they have answered. Hopefully this will be of assistance to others, however, who seek to extend our understanding of this central aspect of international politics.

Notes

1. A recent study of 137 alliances formed during the period 1920–1957 revealed a number of continuities between the pre- and post-World War II in-

ternational systems. It also found support for both the power and affiliation theories. Bruce M. Russett, "An Empirical Typology of International Military Alliances," *Midwest Journal of Political Science,* 15, 1971.

2. The thesis that the nature of political and bureaucratic systems has a deep impact on the processes and outcomes of intra-alliance politics receives support from Richard Neustadt, *Alliance Politics,* Columbia University Press, New York, 1970.

3. Winston S. Churchill, *The Grand Alliance,* Houghton Mifflin Co., Boston, 1951, p. 370.

4. Some alternative candidates are described in Richard N. Rosecrance, "Bipolarity, Multipolarity, and the Future," *Journal of Conflict Resolution,* 10, 1966; and Wolfram Hanrieder, "The International System: Bipolar or Multibloc," *Journal of Conflict Resolution,* 9, 1965.

5. Richard A. Brody and Alexandra H. Benham, "Nuclear Weapons and Alliance Cohesion," in Dean G. Pruitt and Richard C. Snyder, eds., *Theory and Research on the Causes of War,* Prentice-Hall, Englewood Cliffs, N.J., 1969.

6. Michael R. Leavitt, "A Computer Simulation of International Alliance Behavior," Ph. D. Dissertation, Northwestern University, 1971.

7. For a more general discussion of the retreat from efforts to develop "grand theories" of international relations, see K. J. Holsti, "Retreat from Utopia: International Relations Theory, 1945–1970," *Canadian Journal of Political Science,* 4, 1970.

8. Although we have not considered the effects of alliances, the Singer-Small studies would also seem to support this argument. For a further discussion of their findings, see Chapter One, pp. 35–38, and the sources cited there.

APPENDIX A:
CODING DATA ON ALLIANCES,
1815–1939

This appendix discusses the coding procedures employed to generate the data reported in Chapter Two.

Alliance Variable Coding Sheet. In order to generate data on the independent and dependent variables, each treaty was read and coded as indicated below. This provided the basic information for all of the variables except ideological similarity and regime stability.

Columns	Coding Instructions
1	Blank
2–4	Alliance ID
5–7	Year—last three digits
8–10	Year in which treaty signed—last three digits
11–12	Size—number of members at time the treaty signed (If enlarged during this year, give *new* size)
13	Was the alliance enlarged during this year? Yes—1; No—2.
14	If the answer to 12 is yes, number of new members added (If no new members code 0)
15–19	Alliance dispersion index—average distance, in miles, between capitals of alliance members (If only two members, give actual distance)
20	Number of times alliance renewed
21	Is a specific nation or nations or area mentioned as the object of the treaty? Yes—1; No—2.
22	If the answer to question 21 is yes, how many specific references are made? (If the answer is no, code 0)
23	Is a specific type of military problem mentioned? Yes—1; No—2.
24	If question 23 is yes, how many specific types are mentioned (references are made)? (If no, code 0)
25	If the answer to question 23 is yes, code the problem(s) into one

and only one of the following categories: (If no, code 0)
(1)   aggression without specific referent
(2)   aggression with specific referent
(3)   revolutionary aggression
(4)   legitimacy plus aggression
(5)   both 3 and 4
(6)   general concern for peace and for past agreements
(7)   commitment [limited to promise] not to commit aggression against each other or permit such actions from own soil
(8)   concern for peace between third parties or with restoring peace between third parties
(9)   other
(Use cols. 26–28 if answer to 23 more than 1)
(If 23 is 0 or 1, code these columns 0)

29   In addition to military commitments, does the treaty mention additional future types of activities resulting from war to which the contracting parties commit themselves? Yes—1; No—2.

30   If the answer to 29 is yes, how many distinct types of activities are listed? (If no, code 0)

31   If the answer to 29 is yes, code the commitments into the following categories:
(1)   offer of mediation or consultation in the event of war or to solve existing war or conflict between selves or others
(2)   offer to assist or confer in territorial settlements after war
(3)   offer to aid in putting down internal insurrection should such occur in the domain of one of the contracting parties
(4)   maintain occupation troops
(5)   specific peace proposals to solve threat of war or promise to conclude peace together
(6)   diplomatic aid to cope with existing threat
(7)
(8)
(9)
(Use cols. 32–34 if answer to 29 more than 1. If answer to 29 is 1 or 0, code these columns 0)

35   Does the treaty have provisions requiring that the contracting parties consult before making commitments with third parties? Yes—1; No—2.

36   Does the treaty contain provisions for adjusting or altering non-military relations of the contracting parties? Yes—1; No—2.

37   If the answer to question 36 is yes, how many specific references are made? (If answer to 36 is no, code this 0)

38   If the answer to 36 is yes, code the provision into one of the following categories:
(1)   territorial adjustments of one or more of the contracting parties; guaranteed territorial integrity

(2) territorial adjustments of third parties; guaranteed territorial integrity

(3) political status (e.g., sovereignty) of one or more of the contracting parties or their citizens

(4) political status of third parties or their citizens

(5) provisions for the establishment, extension or protection of trade relations between contracting parties

(6) provisions for trading and economic rights in territory of third parties

(Use cols. 39–41 if answer to 36 more than 1. If 1 or zero, code 39–41 0)

(9) other

42 Does the treaty contain provisions specifying one of the following:

(1) amount of troops or material to be supplied in the event of war; including "whole" military force

(2) special meetings to be held in the event of war to determine contribution each member will make

.
.
.
.
.

(9) no arrangements specified beyond general commitment to give aid or to consult

51 Type of alliance

1) defense pact

2) neutrality pact

3) entente

52 Alliance effectiveness

(1) alliance is invoked and honored

(2) alliance is invoked and *not* honored

(3) alliance is never invoked or no information available

(4) more than one of 1, 2, 3; see cols. 72, 73

53 Was the alliance renewed during this year? Yes—1; No—2.

54 If the answer to 53 is yes, indicate change in treaty, if any: (If 53 is no, code this 0)

(1) stayed the same—includes tacit renewal

(2) commitment increased

(3) commitment decreased

(4) added or changed articles of military nature not affecting commitment (e.g., new target nations; change in proposed length)

(5) added articles of nonmilitary nature

(6) both 4 and 5

55 Was the alliance terminated in this year? Yes—1; No—2.

56 Mode of termination of alliance

(1)   lapsed without renewal
(2)   lapsed after renewal
(3)   broken before termination date (or just broken)
(4)   broken after renewal but before new termination date
(5)   not renewed at termination date (including second termination date)
(6)   merged into larger alliance or larger political entity (e.g., Italy); or replaced by another treaty

57–61   Actual length of alliance in months
62   Proposed length of treaty was
(1)   specified
(2)   indefinite
63–68   Proposed length, if specified, in months (If indefinite, code 0; if renewed in this year, give *new* proposed length if available)
69–71   Year in which treaty terminated
72   Number of times alliance invoked and honored
73   Number of times alliance invoked and *not* honored
74–75   Mean alliance score computed from the score of each pair in the alliance to the following question:
Is the pair
(1)   contiguous and regional
(2)   regional but not contiguous
(3)   contiguous but not regional
(4)   not regional or contiguous
79–80   Card number

Distance. The geographical distance between each pair of nations in the data was recorded and a mean score of each alliance was computed. In alliances with two nations, the distance between the two was employed as the dispersion score. Two sources were consulted in compiling these data. The *World Almanac* for the years 1899, 1935, and 1939, provided distances, either in miles or kilometers, between all of the European capitals and many major cities outside of Europe.[1] In cases where actual distances were not available the dispersion index was estimated from historical atlases.[2]

Ideological Similarity. The sets of issues described in Chapter Two formed the basis for making judgments about the ideological similarity or dissimilarity of members of alliances. The coding procedure employed was the following: In order to develop such a score, each dyad in an alliance was rated for similarity or dissimilarity. Similar dyads were assigned a code of "1." Dissimilar dyads were assigned a code of "2." For each alliance a total ideology score and a mean ideology score were computed. The mean score was the mean dyadic score for each alliance.

The number of dyads to be coded was quite large and the judge could not claim detailed knowledge of the nations in many of the dyads. In order to introduce some degree of reliability into the coding, an attempt was made to derive codings from historical accounts of the alliances or descriptions of the members of each dyad. The Franco-Russian alliance of 1894 provides a good example. Albrecht-Carrié's judgment that these two nations were poles apart on the ideological issues of republicanism, popular sovereignty, and the like, formed the basis for the judgment that these two nations were ideologically dissimilar. Whenever possible, such judgments were employed in the rating of dyads in each alliance. When it was not possible to obtain such comparisons, an attempt was made to derive from historical descriptions some indication of the ideological orientation or the nature of the regime in question. For instance, the *Statesman's Year Book* indicates that Rumania in 1921 had a popularly elected assembly but that the king had suspensive veto over all laws passed. Czechoslovakia, on the other hand, had a democratic republic with a president.[3] This information formed the basis for a judgment that this dyad was ideologically dissimilar. Thus, in a few cases, it was necessary to make inferences about the ideological orientation of nations on the basis of information about the nature of the regime since more explicit data were not available.

Leadership Stability. In recent years there have been numerous attempts to define and to operationalize the concept of stability. Lipset employed a simple coding system which made a distinction between stable and unstable democracies and between popular and elite-based dictatorships.[4] Cutright suggested a more precise system in which points are given for the existence of political parties and for popularly elected chief executives.[5] Russett *et al.*, following Rummel, employed as one of their measures the number of deaths which resulted from domestic group violence.[6] A second measure these writers employed was "the rate of turnover in office of legally designated chief executives." [7] Finally, Eckstein employed a count of violent events such as rioting, civil war, and guerrilla war.[8]

Implicit in our concern for stability is the assumption that nations seeking to ally themselves with other nations will be concerned with the ability of other nations to live up to their commitments. A change in chief executive might result in a nation's pursuing an altogether different alliance policy. The kind of stability assumed in these hypotheses would therefore best be investigated by a measure of change of chief executive. The measures proposed by Russett *et al.*, therefore, would seem most appropriate. In gathering the relevant data, however, we have departed from the measure proposed by these writers. The following measure was employed: In parliamentary systems or in systems in which a prime minister appeared to play an important policy role, we listed both the sovereign, whether he was a figurehead president as in France during the Third Republic or an autocrat as in Russia under the Tsars, and the prime minister. In purely presidential systems, on the other hand, a list of presidents was developed.

In coding these data, sovereigns were given one code while presidents and prime ministers were given another. This procedure permitted an examination of rate of change of chief executive and the rate of change of sovereign in nations with such a position.[9] The data were coded in the following manner: for each member of an alliance, a count was made of the number of changes of

Alliance	Type	Inception	Termination	Source
201 England France	1	4/1854	1863	Martens, 15, pp. 569–573 Taylor, p. 72
202 Austria Prussia	1	4/1854	1855	BFS, 44, p. 85 Taylor, pp. 62–63
203 England France Austria	1	12/1854	1856	Martens, 15, pp. 600–602 Taylor, pp. 69–70 Albrecht-Carrié, p. 91
204 Austria Turkey	1	6/1854	1856	Martens, 15, p. 594
205 England France Turkey	1	3/1854	1856	Martens, 15, p. 565
206 France Russia	2	3/1859	1863	Taylor, pp. 105–106, 137
207 England France Russia Italy	1	4/1915	1918	BFS, 112, p. 973 Taylor, p. 566
208 Russia Japan	2	6/1916	1918	BFS, 110, p. 922–923 Black and Helmreich, p. 59
209 England Poland	1	3/1939	1939	Albrecht-Carrié, p. 539
210 France Austria	1	12/1854	1855	Taylor, pp. 70 and 77

chief executive and sovereign for five time periods: the first, second, third, and fourth decades prior to the signing of the treaty and the years during which the alliance was in force. For each of these five time periods, the sovereign stability score and the chief executive stability score were summed, thus producing five scores for each member of an alliance. The scores for each member of an alliance were summed producing five alliance scores. It was discovered that the number of nations for which data were available for four decades prior to the formation of the alliance was quite small, which necessitated limiting the analysis to two decades prior to the formation of the alliance. For each alliance, then, there are three stability scores: a score for the period during which the alliance was in force, a score for the members of the alliance-to-be for the first decade prior to the formation of the alliance, and a score for the first *and* second decades prior to the formation of the alliance.

These alliance stability scores were employed in the following manner: the first decade and the sum of the first and second decade scores were compared to the type of alliance and its proposed length. This was done to ascertain if relatively long-term instability had more of an impact on these two attributes than short-term instability. The stability score for the period during which the alliance existed was also compared to alliance effectiveness, mode of termina-

Alliance	Type	Inception	Termination	Source
211 Prussia Italy	1	4/1866	1866	Taylor, pp. 160–161
212 England France Russia	1	4/1915	1918	Taylor, pp. 541 ff.
213 Germany Russia	2	8/1939	1941	Sontag and Beddie, pp. 76–78
214 Germany Austria Bulgaria	1	9/1915	1918	Albrecht-Carrié, p. 356
215 Germany Turkey	1	8/1914	1918	Taylor, p. 533 Albrecht-Carrié, p. 335 Black & Helmreich, p. 58
216 England Japan	1	2/1917	1918	Black & Helmreich, p. 70
217 England France Turkey	1	10/1939	1940	Black & Helmreich, p. 411 Albrecht-Carrié, pp. 532–533
218 England France Russia Rumania	1	8/1916	1916	Albrecht-Carrié, p. 341

tion, alliance renewal, and length of alliance. These analyses would assess the impact of instability on patterns of alliance maintenance.

War Years. As noted in Chapter Two, war years were identified from the list developed by Singer and Small. Two criteria guided this selection. An examination of their data suggested that wars of a magnitude of greater than 4000 battle deaths were sufficiently important to be included in the study. It was decided not to include wars in which all participants were "peripheral nations," as defined by Singer and Small. The list of war years is as follows:

1828–29—Russo-Turkish War
1848　　 —Austria-Italy
1854–56—Crimean War
1859　　 —Italian War
1864　　 —Schleswig-Holstein (Prussia-Austria against Denmark)
1866　　 —Austria and Prussia
1870–71—Franco-Prussia War
1877–78—Russo-Turkish War
1904–05—Russo-Japanese War
1912–13—First Balkan War
1914–18—World War I

1931–33—Sino-Japanese War
1935–36—Italian-Ethiopia War
1939   —World War II

Alliances Concluded During War Years. The main source of alliances
for this study was Singer and Small.[10] In their research, these writers did not
wish to analyze alliances which were concluded during a war or within three
months of the outbreak of war and hence excluded such alliances from their
list. A list of such alliances was compiled for this study and is presented in this
appendix. The first citation listed after each alliance is the source for the
treaty. BFS refers to the *British Foreign and State Papers.* The number preceding each alliance is the identification number assigned for this study.

Notes

  1. *World Almanac, 1899–1900,* The Press Publishing Company, New York
     World Telegram, New York, pp. 58–59; *World Almanac,* 1935, New York
     World Telegram, New York, pp. 784–785; *Ibid.,* 1939, pp. 694–695.
  2. William R. Shepard, *Historical Atlas,* 9th Ed., Barnes and Noble, Inc.,
     New York, 1964; R. R. Palmer, *Atlas of World History,* Rand McNally,
     Chicago, 1957.
  3. *The Stateman's Year Book,* Macmillan & Co., London, 1921, pp. 789 and
     1213.
  4. Seymour Martin Lipset, "Some Social Requisites of Democracy: Economic
     Development and Political Legitimacy," in Nelson W. Polsby, Robert A.
     Dentler, and Paul A. Smith, eds., *Politics and Social Life,* Houghton Mifflin
     Co., Boston, 1963, pp. 541–568.
  5. Phillips Cutright, "National Political Development: Social and Economic
     Correlates," *Ibid.,* pp. 569–581.
  6. Bruce M. Russett *et al., World Handbook of Political and Social Indica-
     tors,* Yale University Press, New Haven, 1964, pp. 97–104.
  7. *Ibid.,* p. 101.
  8. Cited in *Ibid.,* p. 98.
  9. In addition to these two lists, it would have been desirable to develop a list
     of each country's minister of foreign affairs or secretary of state. While it
     was possible to do this for some countries, the number of lists was incom-
     plete and hence could not be utilized.
 10. J. David Singer and Melvin Small, "Formal Alliances, 1815–1939." *Jour-
     nal of Peace Research,* No. 1, 1966, pp. 1–32.

APPENDIX B:
THE MEASUREMENT OF ALLIANCE
COHESION

In Chapters Three and Four we employed an analysis of alliance cohesion using attitudinal and behavioral measures. In this appendix we will discuss both the theoretical foundations of the measurement models and the measurement techniques employed in those chapters.

The A–B–X Model

The model upon which our measures of attitudinal cohesion were based was the $A–B–X$ system. In this system the degree of co-orientation between two actors, A and B, toward an external object, X, is assumed to be an indicator of the relationship between A and B. In other words, this model assumes that more similar orientations by A and B toward X enhance the cohesion in the relationship between A and B, whereas dissimilar evaluations of X lead to increased conflict between A and B. These assumptions are based on theoretical and empirical work on cognitive balance and consistency theory. The common strain running through this work is "the notion that thoughts, beliefs, attitudes, and behavior tend to organize themselves in meaningful and sensible ways." [1]

The forerunner of the $A–B–X$ model is Heider's work on the $P–O–X$ unit, in which a person (P), another person (O), and an impersonal object (X) are interdependent and linked by attitudes such as liking (L) and unit relations (U).[2] He suggests that relations among P, O, and X may have positive or negative bonds; the more P perceives that O's beliefs, sentiments, and goals are similar to his own, the more positive will his own attitude toward O be. Heider further contends that P's cognitive structure may either be balanced or unbalanced. A balanced state exists if one or three relations are positive. Balanced configurations indicate an absence of cognitive stress for P, so that there is no pressure to change. Unbalanced states create a cognitive stress for P and pressures to reduce stress by cognitive reorganization. This led Heider to the conclusion upon which all subsequent theory building in this area has been based, that "a good deal of interpersonal behavior and social perception is determined—or at least codetermined—by simple cognitive configurations." [3]

The $A-B-X$ model developed out of this configuration. Newcomb transformed Heider's theory into a model of communications between two people (A and B) about something or someone (X).[4] The result is that the model may be based on attitudes of each person toward X rather than on P's perceptions of these attitudes, as was the case in Heider's model. Because A and B are interdependent, they may have simultaneous affective and cognitive orientations toward X. Thus, there are four possible joint orientations by A and B toward X, depicted in Figure 1, Chapter Three. Co-orientation is defined as a situation in which A and B have similar orientations toward X. Therefore, co-orientation is predicted to be associated with positive relations between A and B. This conclusion is based on the assumption that the $A-B-X$ system is characterized by a balance of forces in which changes in any part of the system lead to changes in other parts. Thus, there are always present within any system " 'strains' toward preferred states of equilibrium." [5] As a result, if both A and B have symmetrical orientations (either positive or negative) toward X, then, for the system to be in balance, the relationship between A and B tends to be positive; if their orientations differ, then the relationship between them tends to be negative. Therefore, if we assume that an $A-B-X$ system is balanced, we may be able to infer the relationship between A and B from the degree of their co-orientation toward X.

Balance within an $A-B-X$ system depends upon a number of scope conditions which must be met in order for valid inferences to be drawn. First, the strength of attraction between the persons (A and B) affects the amount of strain that nonconsensus about the object of reference (X) will produce. Second, the importance or salience of the object of reference affects the degree to which nonconsensus about the object will produce strain. Nonconsensus over an object of virtual indifference would thus produce little strain toward balance. Third, the joint relevance for both of the objects of reference affects the amount of strain that assymetrical orientations will produce. Discrepancies in perceptions of an item which has no common impact on both parties will produce little or no strain.[6] In spite of these limitations, some experimental evidence supports the position of both Heider and Newcomb that there is a strain toward balance in $A-B-X$ situations.[7] When this model is applied to international alliances, however, several additional limitations must be made explicit.

First, similar orientations at the time of an event can only be expected to facilitate cohesion with respect to *that* event. This model says nothing about the relationship among A, B, etc., toward other objects (eg., Y and Z) at the same time or toward the same object (X) at the time of other events. For example, Sino-Soviet consensus about the role of the United States in the escalation of the Vietnam War in February 1965 does not imply consensus about other actors, such as North Vietnam, nor does it imply consensus about the role of the United States in other events, such as arms control negotiations going on simultaneously in Geneva. However, there may be a "spill-over" effect from one event or object to another. A series of events during which positive relations are established might carry over to other events in which orientations are more dissimilar. The same principle would probably apply equally to the establishment of negative relations. The amount of spill-over should be a function of the salience of any particular object or event or of the length of the series of events during which a particular relationship was established. The following hypotheses might be suggested:

The greater the salience of an object (X), *the greater the spill-over in the relationship* (+ *or* −) *established among* A, B, *etc., from their position with respect to the object* (X) *to their relationship vis-à-vis other objects* (Y, Z, *etc.*).

The longer the series of events during which a particular relation (+ *or* −) *among* A, B, *etc., is established, the greater the spill-over to later events.*

Second, there may be circumstances in which similar orientations do not indicate cohesion. Two nations may have similar orientations toward object *X* for entirely different reasons. For example, the consensus between the Soviets and Chinese over the United States' role in Vietnam may have been a function of their competition to secure influence in North Vietnam rather than an indication of a cohesive relationship between them. Furthermore, the balance model does not apply to possession relations.[8] Two nations may be positively oriented toward a given object, such as territory which both hope to possess. In this case, clearly, similar orientations would lead to conflict rather than to cooperation. Thus, similar orientations are neither a necessary nor a sufficient condition but merely a facilitative condition for cohesion.

Third, quantitative measures of attitudinal interactions must be supplemented by an analysis of the processes of decision making and their effect on the transformation of perceptions into overt behavior. Social psychologists working with theories of cognitive balance have also reached the conclusion that these models must be supplemented by decision-makers' calculations of costs and gains in making policy decisions. For example, Rosenberg and Abelson found that, in resolving cognitive discrepancies, "subjects seek out not only the attainment of cognitive balance but they seek also to alter their beliefs and evaluations in ways that will maximize expected gain and minimize expected loss." When both forces were congruent, then a balanced outcome resulted, but when they diverged, the outcome often did not meet the requirements of a formal definition of cognitive balance.[9]

Procedures for Computer Content Analysis

Joint orientations within the *A–B–X* model were measured through computer content analysis. Relations among members of each alliance were then inferred from the degree of symmetry in their perceptions of their enemies. These perceptions were measured by use of a computer program based on three dimensions: evaluation, potency, and activity. This program was first developed by Ole R. Holsti and Robert C. North as an outgrowth of the work of Philip Stone on the General Inquirer Program.[10] A modified version of this Stanford General Inquirer program was used in this research. It is written in PL/1 programming language for use on any model IBM 360 system with core storage of at least 236K.[11] The program consists of a dictionary, a set of dimension names, coded documents, a list of retrieval categories or format names, and a cross-referencing list of proper names.[12]

Dictionary. The original political dictionary for the Stanford version of the General Inquirer contained 3628 words, each defined on three dimensions ranging along a seven point scale:

Evaluative: (Positive) $+3, +2, +1, 0, -1, -2, -3$ (Negative)
Potency: (Strong) $+3, +2, +1, 0, -1, -2, -3$ (Weak)
Activity: (Active) $+3, +2, +1, 0, -1, -2, -3$ (Passive)

Words appearing frequently in documents from nine Communist countries analyzed for a previous study [13] which were not contained in the dictionary were added for purposes of the analysis in Chapters Three and Four. A total of 434 new words brought the total dictionary size up to 4062 words.

Inter-coder reliability for coding the dictionary has generally been high; for the set of 434 words added to the dictionary reliability scores across three judges were:

Dimension	Between Judges			Composite
	1 and 2	1 and 3	2 and 3	
Evaluative	.74	.71	.85	.91
Potency	.50	.56	.70	.80
Activity	.45	.39	.70	.76

A score for a pair of judges of .70 or better or a composite of .85 is generally considered to be very good. Because the evaluative dimension was most reliable and because the positive-negative continuum is also most relevant for the $A-B-X$ model, virtually all analysis in Chapter Four was based on that dimension alone.

This dictionary then provides a precoded set of modifying words and action words according to which one actor's perceptions of another actor can be evaluated. This dictionary serves as an unchanging instrument to be applied over time, enabling us to make reliable comparative studies. The values attached to any single word are arbitrary and not absolute, but the dictionary does provide a common relative standard against which differences and changes can be measured. In this respect it is roughly analagous to other measuring instruments, like a thermometer, which measure relative changes rather than absolute values.

Document Sampling and Coding. Documents to be content analyzed for the research in Chapters Three and Four were selected for each of eleven members of the Communist system and eight members of NATO for each of the four time periods covered. The sources of the documents were somewhat different for the Communist system and NATO.

For the Communist system we sampled forty-four documents consisting of the first commentary over government-controlled radio stations following each event in which the object of perception, the United States or the western bloc, was highly salient. Although the authorship of some statements cannot be determined, it was assumed that the documents fairly accurately reflected the attitudes of key decision-makers because the stations were state controlled. In many cases, however, the radio stations broadcast official government statements or statements by national leaders. In most cases the broadcasts concerning the events were made within a few days after the event, although in a few cases there were time lapses up to three weeks before any response was made over government controlled stations.

Three countries ruled by the Communist party had to be excluded from this analysis for different reasons. Yugoslavia was not considered to be a member of the Communist system even though it was a Communist party state throughout this entire period. Since Yugoslavia was expelled from the Cominform in 1949, it was not really an integrated part of the system; in particular, it has not been a member of either of the major multilateral organizations of the Communist system in Eastern Europe, the Warsaw Treaty Organization or the Council of Mutual Economic Assistance. Outer Mongolia was excluded from the analysis due to the failure to obtain the necessary documents from three of the four relevant periods. We were unable to determine whether no official statements were made or whether they were just not reported in the sources available to us. Cuba was also excluded from this list inasmuch as it was not a part of the Communist system prior to January 1, 1959; the inclusion of Cuba in the later two periods would have hindered us in making comparisons among all four periods.

Problems of document availability were far more serious for NATO than for the Communist system. Seven NATO countries were excluded from the content analysis because of our inability to locate documents responding to all four events. In addition, the sources of documents for the NATO countries were much more varied, inasmuch as the mass media could not generally be considered to reflect accurately the attitudes of key decision-makers. Therefore, in virtually all cases, the documents were texts either of speeches by top decision-makers or were official government statements by an anonymous author. The sources also varied widely and included United Nations documents, *The New York Times,* and government documents and bulletins published by the various NATO countries. The document sampling reflected in large part the availability of documents in these sources. No systematic bias could be determined, and the major problem was often the unavailability in any of these sources of any relevant documents from several countries for all four time periods.

An additional problem in the analysis of both sets of documents is that our computer content analysis program at present requires that all documents be processed in English. Some distortion can enter as a result of translation. Since we selected all Communist system documents from one source, the translations were assumed to be fairly consistent, presumably minimizing the extent to which differences among documents could have been caused by different translations. This problem was much more serious for NATO because documents were translated by many different sources, including the home government of the documents' authors, official translations at international meetings and conferences, newspapers and journals in which the documents were printed, and one of the authors and others hired by him. We assume that this source of error is fairly random and that, over the entire set of documents, individual errors will tend to cancel one another out.

The coding procedures involve breaking each document down into themes consisting of an agent, an action, and a target. Thus, the theme simply describes who does what to whom. Words modifying the agent and the target are also coded as being associated with the appropriate actor. This enables one to obtain information about the document author's perception of an actor as agent, based on the modifying words, as target, based also on modifying words, and of the action connecting the agent and target. Therefore, the dictionary provides the source for both modifying words and action words, scaled on the semantic differential dimensions. This syntactical coding procedure makes it possible to obtain measures of two types of perceptions: *evaluative* perceptions of actors in their roles as both agent and target and *action* perceptions of the actions of one agent toward another target.

The document coding, therefore, requires coders to identify the agent and its modifiers, the action, and the target along with its modifiers. This coding procedure is purely syntactical and is thus unrelated to the content or "meaning" of the documents. The meaning attributed to the various actors is assigned by the computer program on the basis of constant scores prepared independently for the dictionary. Therefore, the opportunities for the coders' bias to enter at this stage are strictly limited.

The major problem with document coding involves coder reliability, that is, the consistency and stability of coding procedures from one document to the next. Problems of intercoder reliability were eliminated altogether by only using one coder for all documents. Problems of intracoder reliability were minimized by the use of an experienced coder, under the assumption that a coder is more likely to have established a set pattern of coding if he has had substantial previous experience in coding, in contrast to an individual who is coding for the first time and thus adjusts his technique as he gains experience. As a further check, after all documents had been coded, one of the first documents was recoded, and the results were almost identical. All documents were then read through carefully before processing, and other minor inconsistencies in coding procedures were corrected.

Bias which might have been introduced by using only one coder was minimized by the fact that the coding procedure is largely syntactical and has little relation to the final scores assigned to actors in terms of their location in "semantic space." In addition, what bias might have still been introduced would, so long as intracoder reliability was high, be fairly consistent throughout all documents, and it could not account for any significant differences found from one document to the next. Since all the theoretical questions raised in this project involved comparisons of differences among documents (among different countries and different time periods), it appears unlikely that coding procedures account for any substantial distortion of results.

After documents were coded in this manner, they were then analyzed by computer. The results enabled us to determine each alliance member's perceptions of its enemy in its roles as agent and as target and in all its actions towards all other actors with whom it was perceived as interacting. These perceptions on the evaluative dimension provided the basis for the measurement of co-orientation as an attitudinal indicator of alliance cohesion.

Limitations. Several limitations to these content analysis procedures must be made explicit.

First, the content analysis dictionary assumes that the same word has approximately the same meaning (in terms of the three "semantic" dimensions) in a number of different countries. To the extent that this assumption is not true, some important differences between countries may be overlooked.

Second, the content analysis dictionary is not fully equipped to deal with words having mutliple meanings in different contexts, so that the word codings often reflect some "average" or most common meaning. But the meaning attributed to most words is assumed to be relatively constant regardless of context.

Third, the content analysis procedures assume that explicit statements of decision-makers in some way reflect their attitudes. It is often argued that national leaders may attempt to distort their statements for purposes of suppressing information⸱ or to deceive their audiences and that computer content analysis may not be sensitive to this fact. Jervis has charged that "a country's statements of perception cannot be taken at face value by other states or scholars." This tendency of states to attempt to create false impressions "makes especially questionable the attempts to apply the Stanford techniques and model to recent history where the scholar can only use public documents." [14] While this statement may often be true, this problem is hardly confined to computer content analysis as any kind of textual analysis such as that undertaken by the diplomatic historian may be subject to the same kind of distortion. Furthermore, we assume that when a nation's leader makes a statement that does not accurately reflect his private attitudes, then he does so for a reason, and this reason may be directly relevant to our investigation. For example, if the leader of an Eastern European country issues a statement almost identical to that of the Soviet leaders, it makes little difference if his private attitudes are different; this is still representative of his desire, whether voluntarily or as a result of coercion, to exhibit some degree of unity with the Soviet Union. Thus, in this case, it is the overt verbal behavior rather than the private attitude which is most relevant to the testing of our hypotheses. In interpreting the results of this research it must clearly be understood that our content analysis instrument primarily measures the manifest and not the latent content of messages. But the fact that it does not measure what decision-makers are "really" thinking does not invalidate it for testing many international relations hypotheses. Therefore, in spite of some significant limitations of the content analysis methodology, we were relatively confident that it produced fairly reliable and valid data for testing our hypotheses about the attitudinal component of alliance cohesion.

Procedures for Events Data Analysis

Scaling Procedures. Events interaction data were used in Chapter Four to measure the degree of conflict or cooperation in interactions among nations in the same alliances and between alliances, thus serving as a behavioral indicator of alliance cohesion and inter-alliance conflict. Approximately 9000 bilateral and multilateral events were collected for the 19½-year period between July 1, 1948, and December 31, 1967. These 9000 events were drawn from all issues of *Keesing's Contemporary Archives.* While this was not the most comprehensive chronology of events available, it did appear to provide a fairly comprehensive summary of major events in Europe and North America. Since it concentrates on major events, its use also enabled us to keep the sample down to a manageable size.

The 9000 original events were then reduced to 496 *different* interaction items for scaling. In other words, all events which were essentially the same were reduced to one item. For example, approximately 100 instances of the extension of diplomatic recognition could be reduced to one item. For these 496 items the identity of actors and targets were masked. Relations between allies were identified as a relationship between *A* and *B,* whereas those between traditional enemies were masked as the relationship between *A* and *X*. This provided a minimal amount of context to assist the coders in distinguishing among ambiguous events. Hence, an item might read: "*A* holds maneuvers near the frontier of *X*" if *X* is an enemy or "*A* holds maneuvers near the frontier of *B*" if *B* is an ally. A major limitation of this procedure was that this was all the contextual information which could normally be supplied easily without giving away the actual events being scaled. It was assumed that knowledge of the actors might bias the codings of at least some judges; the cost of avoiding this bias was the loss of substantial contextual information.

These 496 items were then scaled by four judges on a thirty-point continuum from conflict to cooperation.[15] Each judge was instructed to place each event into one of the thirty categories which he felt represented as closely as possible the same degree of conflict or cooperation. Despite some difficulties in distinguishing between the concrete events representing the thirty categories on the scale and the abstract level of conflict or cooperation found in these items, inter-coder reliability ratings among the four judges were quite high, as follows:

		Judge	
Judge	4	3	2
1:	.66	.59	.71
2:	.82	.74	
3:	.70		

Composite: .90

The final score for any action was then determined as the average of the scores assigned by the four judges. The scores for the 496 items were then transferred back to the 9000 events from which they were drawn, so that scores could be associated with the specific dates and actors involved. These data then provided the basis for our analysis of conflict and cooperation among members of the Communist system and of NATO and between the two alliances during the period from 1948 through 1967. Data were aggregated in six-month periods and twelve-month periods. For each period an average score was computed for the interactions within every possible dyad, and summary statistics indicated the average scores for all interactions within each bloc and between the two blocs. These data thus served as behavioral indicators of inter-alliance conflict and of intra-alliance cohesion (cooperation).

There follows a summary of the thirty-point conflict/cooperation scale employed in the research reported in Chapter Four. For every point on the scale the category definition item is presented. After this is an example of an actual event scaled at that intensity on the scale. In some cases events and scale items may not appear to match well. This is generally because the event score is the average of the scores given by the four judges, and it may thus fall between two points frequently identified by the different judges. In addition, the four most cooperative items (1–4) and the most conflictual item (30) had no events corresponding to them in the data analyzed in this research, so no examples are provided:

The Conflict/Cooperation Scale.

1. Member nations $A, B, \ldots n$ of an international organization agree to allow the executive of the organization to tax them in order to raise funds.

2. Member nations $A, B, \ldots n$ create an international executive organization which can make decisions with the approval of a majority of the legislatures of the member nations.

3. Nation A engages in joint military maneuvers with nation B, but identity of each national unit is preserved.

4. International organization of member nations $A, B, \ldots n$ controls production of some nonmilitary materials in nations $A, B, \ldots n$.

5. Nation A's legislature votes funds to support an international military organization. June 11–18, 1955: The Soviet Union, Poland, Czechoslovakia, East Germany, Hungary, Rumania, Bulgaria, and Albania meet to form a military alliance, the Warsaw Treaty Organization.

6. Nations $A, B, \ldots n$ create and join a mutual defense organization in which aid is not automatic in case of an attack. August 2, 1954: Yugoslavia and Greece sign an agreement for joint defense works on borders with Albania and Bulgaria.

7. Nations $A, B, \ldots n$ form new governmental agencies concerned with international and internal security. February 23, 1953: Yugoslavia, Greece, and Turkey sign a Treaty of Friendship and Cooperation.

8. Nation *A* extends military aid to Nation *B*. November 14, 1951: United States agrees to supply military aid to Yugoslavia.

9. Nations *A* and *B* conclude a cultural exchange treaty. September 13, 1951: The Soviet Union and the United Kingdom sign a grain trade agreement.

10. Nation *A* agrees to attend an international meeting with nation *B*. August 23–24, 1951: British Undersecretary of Foreign Affairs has discussions with Tito in Yugoslavia.

11. Nation *A* invites nation *B* to an international meeting. August 12, 1951: Soviet Union accepts invitation to attend international conference in United States.

12. Nation *A* initiates universal military training. May 25, 1950: The United Kingdom sends France a note expressing reservations about attending a conference to discuss the Schuman Plan.

13. Nation *A* increases the size of its armed forces: June 9, 1950. West Germany issues a statement denouncing agreement between East Germany and Poland on the Oder-Niesse line.

14. Nation *A* extends military aid to an enemy of Nation *B*. March 25, 1952: Polish government note to Canada demands return of Polish art treasures given to Canada during World War II.

15. Nation *A* imposes selective tariff increases which are aimed at nation *B*. August 17, 1951: Chinese note to United States denounces draft of U.S.–Japanese security treaty.

16. Nation *A* halts the flow of refugees from nation *A* into lands under the control of nation *B*. September 11, 1951: Soviet note to France denounces Schuman Plan and Pleven Plan.

17. Nation *A* makes an oral protest to the ambassador of nation *B* concerning a specific action of nation *B*. November 27, 1951: Soviet UN resolution condemns U.S. Mutual Security Act as an act of aggression.

18. Nation *A* holds maneuvers near its frontier with nation *B*. November 15, 1951: Yugoslavia denounces Soviet Union in UN for building troop strength in Eastern Europe in excess of treaty limits.

19. Nation *A* threatens nation *B* that it (nation *A*) will take a particular issue it has with nation *B* to an international body. October 15, 1951: Soviet note to Norway warns Norway against adherence to the NATO treaty.

20. Nation *A* calls military staff conference on short notice. August 8, 1951: Poland demands closing of U.S. Information Service office in Warsaw.

21. Nation *A* initiates subversion in nation *B*. March 13, 1953: United Kingdom announces that Soviet jet fighter flew alongside British aircraft in Berlin air corridor.

22. Nation *A* places a partial censorship on all outgoing communications. November 23, 1954: China announces sentencing of thirteen Americans to four-year imprisonment for espionage.

23. Nation *A* moves its troops toward its frontier with nation *B* in transportation units. July 19, 1949: Greek government accuses Albania of assisting guerrillas fighting in Greece.

24. Nation *A* confines its military units to their barrack areas until further notice. December 23, 1951: Hungarians try and sentence American airman forced down over Hungary.

25. Nation *A* militarizes its transportation system. May 8, 1952: Soviet Union interferes with American military vehicles on Berlin autobahn for over a week.

26. Nation *A* moves a large number of its troops from one post to another, both posts being within nation *A*. May 1, 1960: Soviet Union shoots down United States spy plane over Soviet territory.

27. Nation *A* stops nation *B*'s ships at sea. December 3, 1951: Hungary forces down United States aircraft over Hungary.

28. Nation *A* makes frontier incursions which are not clearly attacks on Nation *B*. August 15, 1952: Bulgaria occupies disputed island on its border with Greece, but retreats under fire.

29. Nation *A* begins a general offensive against Nation *B*. June 25, 1950: North Korean troops cross border and invade South Korea.

30. Nation *A* executes prisoners of war of nation *B*.

Notes

1. Robert B. Zajonc, "The Concept of Balance, Congruity, and Dissonance," *Public Opinion Quarterly,* 1960, p. 280.
2. Fritz Heider, "Attitudes and Cognitive Organization," *The Journal of Psychology,* 21, 1946, pp. 107–112. Fritz Heider, *The Psychology of Interpersonal Relations,* John Wiley and Sons, Inc., New York, 1958.
3. Heider, "Attitudes and Cognitive Organization," *op. cit.,* p. 111.
4. Theodore M. Newcomb, "An Approach to the Study of Communicative Acts," in A. F. Hare, E. F. Borgatta, and R. F. Bales, eds., *Small Groups,* Alfred Knopf, New York, 1955, p. 149.
5. *Ibid.,* p. 152.

6. Theodore Newcomb, "The Study of Consensus," in Robert K. Merton, Leonard Broom, and Leonard S. Cottrell, eds., *Sociology Today: Problems and Prospects*, Vol. II, Harper and Row, New York, 1965, p. 283.

7. Kendall O. Price, Ernest Harburg, and Jack M. McLeod, "Positive and Negative Affect as a Function of Perceived Discrepancies in ABX Situations," *Human Relations*, 18, 1965, p. 99.

8. Davis B. Bobrow, "The Transition From International Communication to International Relations as Communications," in Richard L. Merritt, ed., *Communication in International Politics*, University of Illinois Press, Urbana, 1972.

9. Milton J. Rosenberg and Robert F. Abelson, "An Analysis of Cognitive Balancing," in Carl C. Hovland and Milton J. Rosenberg, eds., *Attitude Organization and Change*, Yale University Press, New Haven, 1960, p. 145.

10. Philip J. Stone, Dexter C. Dunphy, Marshall S. Smith, and Daniel M. Ogilvie, eds., *The General Inquirer: A Computer Approach to Content Analysis*, The M.I.T. Press, Cambridge, Mass., 1966, *passim*, especially Ch. 3 and Ch. 5, pp. 170–191.

11. An original version of this program was prepared by Horace and Anne Enea in Balgol, and it was subsequently rewritten in PL/1 by Kuan Lee.

12. Details about these procedures may be found in Ole R. Holsti, *Content Analysis for the Social Sciences and Humanities*, Addison-Wesley, Reading, Mass., 1969, Ch. 7.

13. See P. Terry Hopmann, "International Conflict and Cohesion in the Communist System," *International Studies Quarterly*, 11, 1967.

14. Robert Jervis, "The Costs of the Scientific Study of Politics: An Examination of the Stanford Content Analysis Studies," *International Studies Quarterly*, 11, 1967, p. 380.

15. For a description of the scale and its development see Lincoln E. Moses, *et al.*, "Scaling Data on Inter-Nation Actions," *Science*, 156, 1967, pp. 1054–1059.

APPENDIX C:
PROPOSITIONS ON ALLIANCES

A survey of articles and books on international alliances was undertaken with a view to uncovering some of the major explanations of alliances. Most of the vast literature on coalition formation in experimental settings, supra-national community-building, and electoral or legislative coalitions is not reflected in the present list of propositions. The exceptions are identified by an asterisk (*).

The propositions listed below are concerned with both causes and effects. The 347 items that deal with the causes of alliances—that is, those in which some aspect of alliances is the dependent variable—are classified into twenty groups, depending upon the aspect of alliance behavior being considered and the level of explanation. Table 1 summarizes the classification scheme and indicates the number of propositions in each category. The letters in parentheses indicate the category code. There are, in addition, 70 propositions that consider the international (51) and national (19) effects of alliances.

TABLE 1. Distribution of Propositions in Which Alliance is the Dependent Variable

	Alliance Formation and Participation	Alliance Structure, Formal and Informal	Alliance Purposes and Policies	Alliance Efficacy	Alliance Duration and Termination
Attributes of the International System	20 (A)	7 (B)	4 (C)	2 (D)	13 (E)
Situational Factors	11 (F)	31 (G)	7 (H)	13 (I)	8 (J)
Attributes of Alliances	3 (K)	35 (L)	6 (M)	25 (N)	19 (O)
National Attributes and Comparisons	60 (P)	39 (Q)	10 (R)	24 (S)	10 (T)

Although several propositions are relevant for more than a single category, none appears more than once.

Attributes of the International System

A. Alliance Formation and Participation

1. "Wherever in recorded history a system of multiple sovereignty has existed, some of the sovereign units when involved in conflicts with others have entered into alliances." Wolfers, 1968, p. 269.

2. Nations join alliances of a given size at a rate proportional to the total number of nations in alliances of that size. Horvath and Foster, 1963, p. 116.

3. Geographic conditions do not appear to play a significant role in alliance making. K. Holsti, 1967, p. 111.

4. The greater the number of actors in a balance of power system, the greater the uncertainty as to the combinations opposing each other. Morgenthau, 1959b, p. 325.

5. Larger than minimum winning coalitions will occur when the system is composed of many states. Russett, 1968, p. 291.

6. As great power conflict becomes limited, small powers are sought as allies *in place of,* not *because of* an imminent great power war. Rothstein, 1966, p. 407.

7. A policy of nonalignment can only be successful in a particular type of [bipolar] power configuration. Rothstein, 1966, p. 398.

8. Alliances are "a natural and unexceptionable product of the working logic of the international political system." Friedman *et al.,* 1970, p. 15.

9. As the world becomes relatively war-free, it will also become relatively alliance-free. Modelski, 1963, p. 776.

10. In a bipolar world alliance leaders will strive to win as many allies as possible, even if they are not of military significance. Lall, 1966, p. 179.

11. Perceived imbalances in the distribution of international power will give rise to alliance formation. Gulick, 1955, pp. 61–62.

12. In a balance of power system, only nations with no territorial ambitions, or against whom others did not have territorial claims, can remain unaligned. Dinerstein, 1965, pp. 592–593.

13. In a system with reduced likelihood of war, it is easier for some states to remain unaligned. Dinerstein, 1965, p. 594.

14. The greater the number of essential actors in an international system, the greater the opportunity to remain outside alliances. Kaplan, 1957, p. 130.

15. Alliances are formed when the balance of power is threatened. Organski, 1968, p. 277.

16. As a bipolar system changes, the gap between alliance and nonalignment is likely to be reduced. Liska, 1968, p. 19.

17. "The historically most important manifestation of the balance of power . . . is to be found not in the equilibrium of two isolated nations but in the relations between one nation or alliance of nations and another alliance." Morgenthau, 1967, p. 175.

18. "Alliances are a necessary function of the balance of power operating within a multiple-state system." Morgenthau, 1967, p. 175.

19. If balance of power politics are pursued earnestly, the eventual result will be two nations or two alliances. Waltz, 1967b, p. 217.

20. A high level of status inconsistency in the international system will result in an increased level of alliance activity, with the aim of altering the status quo. Wallace, 1970, p. 7.

B. Alliance Structure, Formal and Informal

1. The tighter the bipolar system, the greater the intra-bloc communication and the less the inter-bloc communication. Kaplan, 1957, p. 120.

2. The availability of alternative alliance partners enhances the ability of one alliance member to restrain others. Liska, 1962, p. 140.

3. The greater the number of actors in a balance of power system, the greater the uncertainty as to the role of individual actors in opposing combinations. Morgenthau, 1959b, p. 325.

4. In a bipolar system competing alliances will tend to resemble one another. Triska and Finley, 1965, pp. 37–53.

5. In diffuse-bloc systems, alliances tend to be closely-knit structures from which smaller alliance partners do not easily remove themselves. K. Holsti, 1967, p. 110.

6. In polar systems alliances tend to be closely-knit structures from which smaller alliance partners do not easily remove themselves. K. Holsti, 1967, p. 110.

7. Geographical distance between allies can be detrimental to alliance unity. Wolfers, 1959, p. 7.

C. Alliance Purposes and Policies

1. Diffusion of military technology will change alliances, making them less military in nature. Morgenthau, 1957, p. 24.

2. In an international system dominated by superpowers, the disparity between their power and that of allies gives rise to interests common to the superpowers, and not shared by their allies. Dinerstein, 1965, pp. 593–594.

3. The specific character of alliances differs in various historical periods, depending on the nature and number of actors in the system. Rothstein, 1968, pp. 46, 116.

4. When international factors determine alignment, the commitment is likely to rest on broader and less homogeneous foundations [than alliances based on domestic needs]. Liska, 1962, p. 23.

D. Alliance Efficacy

1. Alliances not buttressed by geography are difficult to maintain. Strausz-Hupé and Possony, 1950, p. 240.

2. Nuclear diffusion in the long run may stabilize alliances [by decreasing the freedom of governments to determine alliance functions and commitments]. Liska, 1962, pp. 276–277.

E. Alliance Duration and Termination

1. In an international system dominated by nuclear deterrence, alliances will tend to disintegrate. Burton, 1965, p. 209.

2. In a balance of power system there is a high rate of alliance disintegration. Kaplan, 1957, p. 129.

3. The diffusion of military technology is disruptive of alliances. Steel, 1964, pp. 34–37.

4. In diffuse international systems, alliances tend to be temporary because objectives derive from interests rather than ideology. K. Holsti, 1967, p. 110.

5. In an international system characterized by great power stalemate, alliance switching is unlikely because the opposing alliance cannot offer territorial compensation. Dinerstein, 1970, p. 23.

6. In a balance of power system nations frequently and rapidly shifted alliance commitments. Dinerstein, 1965, p. 592.

7. In polar and diffuse-bloc systems, alliances tend to persist because they reflect ideological cleavages rather than just dynastic or commercial rivalries. K. Holsti, 1967, p. 110.

8. Alliances cannot be shifted in a bipolar system with great differences in power between alliance leaders and followers in each bloc. Dinerstein, 1965, p. 596.

9. In a disarming world, alliances would tend to dissolve. Hammond, 1966, p. 87.

10. The greater the number of essential actors in an international system, the greater the opportunities to shift among competing alliances. Kaplan, 1957, p. 130.

11. Steps taken toward inter-alliance détente have a disintegrative effect on alliances. Marshall, 1964, pp. 18–19.

12. Increases in alternatives available contribute to realignment and alliance dissolution. Liska, 1962, pp. 193–194.

13. Alliances cannot be reshuffled in a system in which both bloc leaders are status quo powers. Dinerstein, 1965, p. 596.

Situational Factors

F. Alliance Formation and Participation

1. Nuclear weapons make alliances less likely to occur or persist, because allies are not necessary to gain preponderant power. Kissinger, 1964, p. 3.

2. "It is only when the common interests are inchoate in terms of policy and action that a treaty of alliance is required to make them explicit and operative." Morgenthau, 1967, p. 177.

3. When alliance benefits can be shared noncompetitively, alliances will be larger than minimum winning coalitions. Friedman *et al.,* 1970, p. 235.

4. Alliances are the result of disappointed hopes for collective security. Haas, 1969, pp. 97, 115.

5. The more international conflict takes on the character of a war between ideological camps, the stronger public resistance against alliances with governments of the opposing ideology. Wolfers, 1968, p. 270.

6. In an age of mass politics, alliances will tend to become larger than suggested by calculations of "interest," because it is hard to define any nation or area as of peripheral value. Deutsch and Kaplan, 1964, p. 178.

7. Fear of an external threat may produce either alignment or nonalignment. Liska, 1962, p. 213.

8. Great powers ally because of threats to the balance of the entire international system; small powers do so because of threats to the local balance. Rothstein, 1968, p. 62.

9. Political alliances result from perceptions of a situation that can be exploited by an alliance. Rothstein, 1968, p. 52.

10. Military alliances result from the perception of external threat that cannot be met by one's own resources. Rothstein, 1968, p. 52.

11. "Despite popular assumptions, the existence of an alliance does not indicate substantive common interests between the members, except insofar as the immediate adversary is concerned." Fedder, 1968, p. 86.

G. Alliance Structure, Formal and Informal

1. Diminution of external threat, or of the will to meet it, will tend to undermine alliance cohesion. Wolfers, 1962, p. 29.

2. External danger causes allies to rally around alliance leaders. Wolfers, 1959, p. 3.

3. Discrepancy in variety of external conflicts faced by alliance members reduces alliance unity. Wolfers, 1959, p. 11.

4. Need is a more stable basis for group cohesion than is similarity.* Gross, 1956, pp. 174–179.

5. Group cohesiveness can be increased by external threat.* Sherif and Sherif, 1953.

6. Social support is greater when members are strongly threatened by external sources.* Festinger, Riecken and Schachter, 1956.

7. Commonly perceived threat is likely to overcome other incompatibilities among alliance members. K. Holsti, 1967, p. 116.

8. Development of nuclear weapons may have a divisive effect on alliances. K. Holsti, 1967, p. 119.

9. Wartime alliances operate under continual internal tensions, because "military operations seldom pose burdens of similar magnitude upon all allies." Haas and Whiting, 1956, p. 164.

10. Lack of a strong threat weakens alliance cohesion. Stevens, 1961, p. 45.

11. Decreased external threat will lead to decreased alliance cohesion. Calvocoressi, 1966, p. 358.

12. Alliances based on the confrontation of two superpowers may result in

tensions within the alliances because the interests of minor members are neglected. Calvocoressi, 1966, p. 359.

13. Existence of an external enemy serves to unify alliances. Boulding, 1962, p. 162.

14. As stress due to time constraints increases, group cohesion tends to increase.* Lanzetta, 1955.

15. Group integration increases during a crisis if a likely cooperative solution to the crisis problem is present.* Hamblin, 1958.

16. Group integration decreases during a crisis if a likely solution to the crisis problem is unavailable.* Hamblin, 1958.

17. The greater the between-group competition, the greater the in-group solidarity and cooperativeness.* Sherif, 1961, pp. 428–429.

18. Increases in external threat or pressure tends to consolidate alliances. Liska, 1962, pp. 97–100.

19. Conditions of peace permit more flexibility in alliance activity than do conditions of war. Haas and Whiting, 1956, p. 167.

20. When pressured by military demands outside of the alliance, the alliance leader may demand greater assumption of burdens by other members. Calvocoressi, 1966, p. 357.

21. The greater the external threat, the greater the organizational rigidities of all blocs, whereas easing international tensions tends to make blocs less hierarchical. Kaplan, 1957, p. 45.

22. The greater the extent to which alliance members perceive the enemy as threatening, the greater their reliance on the bloc leader. Gorden and Lerner, 1965, pp. 419–433.

23. Alliance decison making becomes more difficult when an external threat is directed at only a few members rather than the alliance as a whole. Liska, 1962, p. 129.

24. A common external danger does not necessarily produce an equitable division of labor among alliance members. Waltz, 1967c, p. 11.

25. Conflict may be functional for the cohesion of a group only if it does not strike at the consensual basis of the group. * Coser, 1956, p. 80.

26. Inter-alliance negotiations tend to be disruptive of intra-alliance cohesion. Liska, 1962, p. 147.

27. "It is virtually impossible to predict the effect of a spread of individual nuclear capabilities on alliance cohesion." Liska, 1962, p. 93.

28. "Nuclear diffusion may therefore be expected to have a disruptive ef-

fect on the cohesiveness and unity of the major alliance system—particularly the western alliance system." Tucker, 1962, p. 13.

29. Groups engaged in outside conflict tend to be intolerant of dissent within.* Coser, pp. 103–104.

30. "Considerable strains within the alliance must be expected, particularly if the alliance . . . goes into effect in time of peace." Wolfers, 1968, p. 270.

31. After the spread of nuclear weapons within an alliance, cohesion will decline.* Brody, 1963, pp. 735–736.

H. Alliance Purposes and Policies

1. Common perceptions of threat are probably the most frequent source of alliance strategies. K. Holsti, 1967, p. 111.

2. Wartime alliances tend to be general, comprising the total interests of the partners both with respect to conduct of the war and the peace settlement. Morgenthau, 1967, p. 179.

3. Alliances undertaken in war differ from those contracted in peacetime; the former often evolve into alliances of self-extension, whereas the latter are usually for self-preservation. Haas and Whiting, 1956, p. 163.

4. "Peacetime alliances tend to be limited to a fraction of the total interests and objectives of the signatories." Morgenthau, 1967, p. 179.

5. With an increase in external threat, an alliance with multiple conflicting goals will be transformed into one with a single goal. Steel, 1964, pp. 27–28.

6. An aim common to all alliances is to augment power by securing help from other nations. Haas and Whiting, 1956, p. 160.

7. Sheer necessity is the common core of all alliances. Haas and Whiting, 1956, p. 160.

I. Alliance Efficacy

1. "When there is not a single unifying conflict, the concern of allies over each other's capabilities will be even greater." Liska, 1962, p. 89.

2. The assumption of alliance responsibilities varies with the perception of threat to immediate interests. Stevens, 1961, p. 45.

3. Actors in a competitive situation will tend to overrate the strength of allies and underrate that of opponents. * Bass and Dunteman, 1963, pp. 16–20.

4. The greater the danger to the security of an alliance member's terri-

tory, the less the credibility of his guarantee to defend other alliance members. Liska, 1962, pp. 8–9.

5. The greater the conflict between systems [alliances], the greater the need for cooperation within each system [alliance]. Kaplan, 1957, p. 139.

6. Suspicions concerning the reliability of allied pledges of future assistance are the most disruptive element of peacetime alliances. Wolfers, 1962, p. 29.

7. Fear of separate peace is the most disruptive element in wartime alliances. Wolfers, 1962, p. 29.

8. As military power becomes less usable, because of either its more restricted legitimacy or the risk of escalation, alliances should be somewhat less valuable. Knorr, 1966, p. 153.

9. Nuclear weapons introduce inconsistencies into traditional alliances, because no country will die for another. Kissinger, 1964, p. 3.

10. Nuclear weapons do not reduce the value or number of alliances. Organski, 1968, pp. 331–332.

11. Nuclear weapons have made alliances obsolete. Gallois, 1963, pp. 226–249.

12. In crisis, alliance members tend to exhibit "bandwagon behavior," either toward new structures and tasks, or toward disintegration. Beer, 1969, p. 268.

13. The less extensive the external threat, the more likely are the allies to risk intra-alliance friction. Rothstein, 1968, p. 59.

J. Alliance Duration and Termination

1. Groups disintegrate during a crisis if a likely competitive solution to the crisis is available.* Hamblin, 1958.

2. Disappearance of an external threat will produce alliance disintegration. Scott, 1967, p. 112.

3. Withdrawal of external threat may cause alliances to break up. Hardy, 1919, p. 260–265.

4. Alliance strains are less likely to deepen into disintegration when there is an ideological conflict with the enemy. Liska, 1962, p. 90.

5. "The emergence of new issues might eventually contribute to a sharp shift in alignments." Russett, 1965, p. 236.

6. "As the possession of the technology of nuclear warfare spreads, such defections [from alliances] may well become more frequent." Riker, 1962, p. 183.

7. "The invention of a very cheap make-it-yourself, all-purpose deterrent would invite every nation to be isolationists in military affairs, fragmenting such alliances as NATO and the Warsaw Pact. . . ." Burns, 1961, p. 188.

8. "Alliances may extend to forms of cooperation other than military ones, but they are unlikely to survive if the military reasons disappear." Wolfers, 1968, p. 269.

Attributes of Alliances

K. Alliance Formation and Participation

1. Coalitions will increase in size only to the minimum point of subjective certainty of winning. Riker, 1962, pp. 32–33.

2. The larger the number of nations desiring to form an alliance, the more difficult it will be to do so. Gulick, 1955, p. 78.

3. Status quo alliances will be larger than the minimum winning coalition because the gain [maintaining status quo] satisfies all members. Friedman *et al.*, 1970, p. 261.

L. Alliance Structure: Formal and Informal

1. Alliance decisions are usually made more by national actors rather than by international organizations. Kaplan, 1957, p. 115.

2. In the absence of external threat, alliance cohesion cannot be saved by inward-directed "diversions." Wolfers, 1962, p. 29.

3. Centralized alliances tend to create intra-alliance frictions because of constant intervention in domestic affairs. Rothstein, 1968, p. 178.

4. "A hegemonic alliance would repress strains underneath the supremacy of the leading ally." Liska, 1962, p. 73.

5. The best thing for cohesion is an even and moderate rise in capability rather than extreme failure or excessive success in increasing capabilities. Liska, 1962, p. 89.

6. Alliances that supplement collective benefits with private benefits are more cohesive than alliances that provide only collective benefits.* Burgess and Robinson, 1969, pp. 194–218.

7. "Offensive alliances of autocratic states will be held together [in time of war] by the prospect of gain." Liska, 1962, p. 62.

8. "Considerable strains within the alliance must be expected, particularly if the alliance is of long duration." Wolfers, 1968, p. 270.

9. "The chief motivation for the acquisition of nuclear capabilities within a coalition, and for neutrals who might join a colition, is the payoff as-

sociated with greater control over future decision." Snyder, 1961, p. 71.

10. The greater the differentiation of functions, the greater the unity of the group.* French, 1941, pp. 365–366.

11. Status inconsistency is detrimental to alliance cohesion. Liska, 1962, p. 107.

12. Disparity in the degree of protection against external threat reduces alliance cohesion. Liska, 1962, p. 93.

13. The greater the capacity of alliances to absorb *faits accomplis* [by alliance members], the greater their cohesion. Liska, 1962, pp. 85–86.

14. Consultation enhances alliance cohesion as it affirms the equality and solidarity among allies. Liska, 1962, p. 69.

15. In nonhierarchical alliances, the greater the perceived joint interest, the greater the cohesion. Kaplan, 1957, p. 80.

16. The longer an alliance exists, the greater its solidarity and legitimacy. Kaplan, 1957, pp. 108–109.

17. The greater the status inconsistency within a group, the greater the conflict within the group.* Exline and Ziller, 1959, p. 160.

18. An alliance not characterized by doctrinal unity will more easily resolve internal conflicts without disrupting the alliance. Iklé, 1967, p. 236.

19. Inefficient intra-alliance machinery for policy coordination reduces alliance cohesion. Bowie, 1963, pp. 63–64.

20. A loose system of states in alliance may be more cohesive than a tight one. Kissinger, 1964, p. 6.

21. "The more highly structured the alliance, the greater the likelihood of conflict among members." Fedder, 1968, p. 83.

22. Lack of a division of labor within alliances leads to dissension because minor partners have no distinct, useful role. Calvocoressi, 1966, p. 360.

23. Cohesion of an alliance for deterrence varies with the credibility of the deterrent. Calvocoressi, 1966, p. 359.

24. Centralization of alliance decision making leads to greater alliance cohesion. Haas and Whiting, 1956, p. 183.

25. The larger the group, the less likely it is to be cohesive.* Hare, 1952,

26. Democratic styles of leadership produce greater group cohesion.* Cartwright and Zander, 1960, p. 87.

27. Group cohesiveness is greater for groups that perform better.* Seashore, 1959, p. 81.

28. In alliances based on ideology, bargaining and compromise are far more difficult. Lowenthal, 1963, p. 113.

29. The more successful the group, the more likely it is to restructure its hierarchies to reduce status inconsistencies.* Burnstein and Zajonc, 1965, p. 360.

30. There is a direct relationship between the source of power in an influence situation and the type of conformity: means control leads to compliance; attractiveness leads to identification; credibility leads to internalization.* Kelman, 1958, pp. 234–235.

31. Decision making in groups with well-defined power structures will be a function of power.* Torrance, 1955, pp. 491–492.

32. The distribution of benefits is likely to reflect the distribution of power within an alliance. Morgenthau, 1959a, p. 190.

33. Groups with strong ideological orientations are more likely to break up into splinter groups.* Cartwright and Zander, 1960, pp. 86–87.

34. "The group whose members are not able to leave will develop more overt or noninternalized conformity than the group whose members remain because they are attracted to it." * Cartwright and Zander, 1960, p. 180.

35. Inconsistencies between achievements and status within an alliance give rise to intra-alliance conflict. Bowie, 1963, p. 51.

M. Alliance Purposes and Policies

1. "Alliances are against, and only derivatively for, someone or something." Liska, 1962, p. 12.

2. Alliances of democratic states, when under stress, use ideology to transform the alliance into "communities of friendship among peoples." Liska, 1962, p. 62.

3. Highly cohesive groups will be less restrained when under attack than relatively less cohesive groups.* Pepitone and Reichling, 1955, p. 142.

4. The determination of policies in an alliance is likely to reflect the distribution of power. Morgenthau, 1959a, p. 190.

5. Multilateral alliances seem less aggressive than bilateral ones. Rothstein, 1968, p. 124.

6. Two features of alliance remain constant: The goals states seek to achieve by alliance, and the factors that determine the success or failure of alliances. Rothstein, 1968, p. 46.

N. Alliance Efficacy

1. Alliances are "not particularly viable" components of the international system. Fedder, 1968, pp. 82–83.

2. Alliances require coordinated foreign and economic policies before the military goals can be achieved. Haas and Whiting, 1956, p. 183.

3. "Only when a leading ally cannot count on support or sympathy in a multilateral conclave, will he incline to unilateral or bilateral action." Liska, 1962, p. 172.

4. "The more structurally centralized ('system dominant') as well as the more autocratic ('directive') the organizational structure of a bloc, the greater the potential energy with which the bloc could act. . . ." Masters, 1961, p. 795.

5. A very autocratic bloc, "because of its control over resources, can readily respond to external threats or opportunities." Masters, 1961, p. 795.

6. "A structurally decentralized bloc . . . is likely to hold together only in opposition to some external 'enemy.' " Masters, 1961, p. 795.

7. Small power alliances usually fail because the sum of their power is too unsubstantial. Fox, 1959, p. 185.

8. "Failure to clarify the scope and conditions of commitment will impede the cohesion of the alliance and its chances for evolving effective strategy." Liska, 1962, p. 111.

9. The greater the ratio of bilateral to multilateral implementing agreements, the greater the real integration of an alliance. Liska, 1962, p. 123.

10. The requirements of alliance cohesion may, but do not necessarily, coincide with those of alliance efficacy. Liska, 1962, p. 116.

11. Alliances formed for purposes of deterrence will only be successful if they can assemble overwhelming force. Strausz-Hupé and Possony, 1950, pp. 231–232.

12. Alliance cohesion based on the oppressive rule of a single power, or a single principle, will give rise to reduced efficacy. Liska, 1962, p. 116.

13. Alliances will continue to maintain themselves as long as a favorable balance between gains and liabilities is maintained. Liska, 1962, p. 108.

14. Too great a concern with consultation may impede the military efficacy of the alliance. Liska, 1962, p. 69.

15. "The smaller the alliance, the more viable." Fedder, 1968, p. 83.

16. The greater the level of communication, the greater the perceived trust and, therefore, the greater the cooperative behavior.* Loomis, 1959, p. 305.

17. "The level and frequency of contact associated with structured alliances is so great that it acts as an impediment to efficient concentration upon decreasingly salient threat." Fedder, 1968, p. 84.

18. "The larger the group, the less it will further its common interests." * Olson, 1965, p. 36.

19. The keys to alliance maintenance are continuous consultation and adjustment of policies. Haas and Whiting, 1956, p. 178.

20. Pluralistic alliances have greater vitality. Ball and Killough, 1956, p. 478.

21. Total alliances [those which practice solidarity in conduct and are global in concern] are fragile owing to an imbalance between commitments and the scope of consultation. Liska, 1962, p. 78.

22. Only voluntary groups can develop lasting changes of attitude and motivation.* Cartwright and Zander, 1960, p. 180.

23. The less rational an alliance commitment appears, the more difficult it will be to convince the adversary that the commitment even exists. O. Holsti, 1972, p. 220.

24. The fewer historical precedents for a particular alliance, the less credible the alliance commitments will appear to adversaries. O. Holsti, 1972, p. 220.

25. Ideology is a relatively minor factor in alliance cohesion, incapable of making or breaking the system, but ideological affinity is an asset. Haas and Whiting, 1956, p. 168.

O.   Alliance Duration and Termination

1. The greater the maximization beyond a minimum winning coalition and overpayment to allies, the greater the decline of international coalitions. Riker, 1962, pp. 213–214; 238.

2. A rigid alliance system is likely to suffer much greater disintegration than a loose one. Dinerstein, 1965, p. 601.

3. The more extensive the formation of sub-coalitions within an international alliance, the greater the likelihood of alliance disintegration. Halpern, 1963, p. 117.

4. Alliances led by a "superpower" are especially prone to erosion. Duchacek, 1966, pp. 342–343.

5. Offensive alliances tend to disintegrate easily. Liska, 1962, pp. 39–40.

6. Alliances break up at a constant rate independent of size. Horvath and Foster, 1963, p. 116.

7. Nonaggression and mutual defense alliances have a short existence. Lerche, 1956, p. 50.

8. The more general the alliance, the shorter its duration. Morgenthau, 1959a, p. 191.

9. Failure to solve major problems will lead to alliance disintegration. Scott, 1967, p. 111.

10. The greater the need to maintain ideological homogeneity in an alliance, the greater will be the tendencies toward disintegration. Dinerstein, 1965, p. 601.

11. Political structures that are authoritarian tend in time to disintegrate as a result of pent-up frustrations exploding in violence.* Jacob and Teune, 1964, p. 35.

12. Alliances led by rich nations are more stable than those led by poor nations, because the former can offer economic incentives to allies without disrupting domestic programs. Dinerstein, 1965, p. 601.

13. "Other things being equal, a coalition will be more stable to the extent that decision making is centralized, i.e., the coalition is hierarchically organized." Snyder, 1961, p. 70.

14. The greater the ability of an alliance to respond to external disturbances, the greater its stability. Kaplan, 1957, p. 99.

15. The larger the number of nations in an alliance, the more difficult it will be to maintain. Gulick, 1955, p. 78.

16. Coalitions that have established institutional means of settling intra-alliance disputes are most likely to persist even when external threat is reduced.* Kelley, 1970, p. 486.

17. Alliances of limited purpose are most stable and durable. Dinerstein, 1965, p. 599.

18. The duration of alliances is dependent on how they are maintained more than upon how they are drafted. Haas and Whiting, 1956, p. 173.

19. "Once an alliance has been created, there is positive value placed on continuing it, even if it seems to perform very few functions." Rothstein, 1968, p. 119.

National Attributes and Comparisons

P. Alliance Formation and Participation

1. The decision to align or not to align, in what form, and with whom is made with reference to the national interest. [In theory: to supplement

each others' capabilities and to reduce impact of antagonistic power].
Liska, 1962, p. 26.

2. External threat, rather than national strength or weakness, is the primary source of alliances. Liska, 1962, p. 13.

3. Alliances are formed primarily for security rather than out of a sense of community. Liska, 1962, pp. 12–13.

4. Accurate knowledge of the true power relationships will produce "rational" strategies of coalition formation.* Vinacke *et al.,* 1966, pp. 180–189.

5. The less complete the decision-makers' information, the larger the size of coalitions and the greater the excess beyond the maximum winning size. Riker, 1962, pp. 88–89.

6. Larger than minimum winning coalitions will occur when intelligence-gathering is poor. Russett, 1968, p. 291.

7. Community of interest is a necessary but not sufficient condition for alliance. Morgenthau, 1959a, p. 186.

8. Alliance policy is a matter of expediency, not principle. Morgenthau, 1959a, p. 185.

9. States make alliances because alliances are the most binding obligations that states can make to stabilize the configurations of power that affect their vital interests. Osgood, 1968, pp. 19–20.

10. "Nations join alliances only if they are unable or unwilling to develop sufficient military power of their own to accomplish objectives for which they judge military means to be necessary." Schleicher, 1962, p. 305.

11. For most states alliances represent the only method by which they can significantly increase their international power. Claude, 1962, p. 89.

12. The choice of alliance partners depends upon power *and* interest. Haas and Whiting, 1956, pp. 167–168.

13. Alliances depend on identical interests. Liska, 1962, pp. 27–28.

14. "Religious or ideological homogeneity has not been a traditional prerequisite of alignment among states." Wolfers, 1968, p. 270.

15. Alliances can be concluded between dissimilar states, but their duration depends on the existence of a common enemy. Frankel, 1964, p. 133.

16. The nature of a state's political structure may influence the choice of alliance partners. Teune and Synnestvedt, 1965, p. 188.

17. The greater the extent to which isolation satisfies internal or group leadership needs, the greater the tendency to avoid alliances. Guetzkow, 1957, p. 157.

18. Politically and economically stable nations are more likely to join alliances than are unstable ones. Teune and Synnestvedt, 1965, p. 189.

19. The desire to subsume potential rivals or aggressors while utilizing their present military capabilities tends to encourage alliance formation. Beloff, 1955, p. 71.

20. Faced with a perceived threat, weak nations will seek strong alliance partners. Morgenthau, 1957, p. 22.

21. The attraction of strong states for the weak is based primarily on economic need. Liska, 1962, p. 14.

22. Nations undertake alliance commitments with nations which face similar external problems. K. Holsti, 1967, p. 110.

23. Nations may be unable or unwilling to align rationally for reasons of ideology or historic biases. Liska, 1962, p. 27.

24. Alliances generally presuppose national or ideological affinities that go beyond expediency. Osgood, 1968, p. 20.

25. The more successful a nation's past experience with self-reliant policies, the lesser the tendency to join alliances. Guetzkow, 1957, p. 154.

26. Unpleasant historical experience may prevent alignment with countries associated with that experience. Teune and Synnestvedt, 1965, p. 189.

27. Ideology provides the rationalization for alliances. Liska, 1962, pp. 61–62.

28. The greater ideological emphasis on independence, the greater the tendency to shun alliances. Guetzkow, 1957, p. 154.

29. "A weaker power will be commonly anxious to seek alignment with geographically remoter powers." Liska, 1962, p. 13.

30. "Where they exist, ideological affinities among regimes are merely the immediate impetus to such alignments or their consequences." Liska, 1962, p. 14.

31. The greater the cultural similarity among nations, the greater the likelihood of collaboration [alliance]. Guetzkow, 1957, p. 158.

32. A nation's alliance strategies are closely linked to domestic needs. K. Holsti, 1967, p. 110.

33. The three main grounds for alignment are: security, status, and internal stability. Liska, 1962, p. 30.

34. When needs of security are compelling, internal stability and status are subordinated as goals of alignment policy. Liska, 1962, p. 39.

35. Alliances are more often undertaken for the purpose of self-preservation than that of self-extension. Haas and Whiting, 1956, p. 161.

36. The motives of lesser powers to ally with great powers are: security, stability, and status. Liska, 1968, p. 27.

37. A nation may seek alliances with irresponsible partners in order to increase the credibility of its commitments [a form of the "rationality of the irrational" strategy]. Maxwell, 1968, p. 8.

38. If states have no interests that they need to support by military power against other states, they lack sufficient incentives to form alliances. Osgood, 1968, p. 23.

39. Weakness is an impetus to follow a policy of nonalignment. Schleicher, 1962, p. 306.

40. As a nation's economic position relative to other nations declines, it will be motivated to seek alliances. Waltz, 1967a, pp. 67–68.

41. If a nation is economically developed relative to other nations, it will not be motivated to seek alliances. Waltz, 1967a, pp. 67–68.

42. Leaders of newly independent nations will use a policy of nonalignment to maintain power at home. Good, 1962, p. 9.

43. Underdeveloped nations will seek to pursue a policy of nonalignments with existing blocs. Good, 1962, p. 8.

44. Newly independent nations will seek to establish a unique identity by pursuing a policy of nonalignment with existing blocs. Good, 1962, p. 8.

45. New states tend to pursue a policy of avoiding alliances. Rothstein, 1966.

46. Militant neutralism is usually associated with "one-party domestic systems and remote geographical location." Liska, 1962, p. 248.

47. "Too great a facility in separate-peace making lowers one's value as an ally in the future despite a temporary rise in status." Liska, 1962, pp. 47–48.

48. "If you can 'stand off' every other nation in the world [with own nuclear weapons], there is not a pressing necessity to be connected [in alliance] with someone else who can do so, too." Burns, 1958, p. 38.

49. "When community feeling is sufficiently strong, it commonly seeks other institutional forms of expression" [than alliances]. Liska, 1962, p. 12.

50. The greater the internal difficulties within a nonaligned state, the greater the temptation to go beyond nonalignment to militant neutralism. Liska, 1962, p. 214.

51. Policies of small and poor states are too inchoate and unreliable to attract great powers to alliances. Osgood, 1968, p. 163.

52. "The optimal alliance strategies for Great Powers and Small Powers tend to differ." Rothstein, 1968, p. 177.

53. "Countries that have been allied tend to remain allied or to return to an alliance after periods of interruption." Padelford and Lincoln, 1967, pp. 204–205.

54. "The role of ideology, political system, and other nonutilitarian preferences are more likely to be important" in peacetime alliances. Russett, 1968, p. 298.

55. "A nation will never ally with a stronger power (or alliance) against a power (or alliance) that is weaker than itself." Russett, 1968, p. 295.

56. "Ideology is at best inadequate in explaining why or how an alliance comes into existence." Fedder, 1968, p. 86.

57. Nonalignment and neutralism are policies that arise from domestic concerns, especially economic needs and interests. Liska, 1962, p. 217.

58. "The basic motive, that of the additional power of lesser allies, is no longer necessarily the primary one." Liska, 1968, p. 30.

59. A convergence of economic interests helps to establish a favorable atmosphere for alliance. Renouvin and Duroselle, 1967, p. 85.

60. Alliances do not preclude conflicting interests and ideologies. Haas and Whiting, 1956, p. 160.

Q. Alliance Structure, Formal and Informal

1. "A measure of independent [nuclear] strength for each of the NATO allies is likely to contribute to the cohesiveness of the alliance." Hilsman, 1959, p. 168.

2. "In an alliance of states very unequal in size and strength, differences are almost certain to arise." Kissinger, 1965, p. 226.

3. "The internal workings of modern government are so complex that they create a variety of obstacles to meaningful consultation [among allies]. Nations sometimes find it so difficult to achieve a domestic consensus that they are reluctant to jeopardize it afterwards in international forums." Kissinger, 1965, pp. 225–226.

4. "Unless allies have an ideal basis for identifying with one another, unequal increase in their present and likely future capabilities will not favor cohesion." Liska, 1962, p. 89.

5. "The pattern of roles and claims within an alliance will change with the rise and decline of national capabilities." Liska, 1962, p. 88.

6. "Equality among allies would convert strains into stimuli for accomodation." Liska, 1962, p. 73.

7. "Another likely effect of heterogeneity among allies, inimical to cohesion, is a derangement of the relationships underlying status." Liska, 1962, p. 70.

8. Common ideology may provide a source of alliance unity in the absence of common interests. Lowenthal, 1963, p. 107.

9. The greater the divergence in tactical and strategic priorities, the less the cohesion among allies. Brzezinski, 1963, pp. 516–517.

10. In alliances of equally mature powers, cohesion will grow as allies spontaneously compensate unequal expenditure by unequal risks, or other kinds of efforts. Liska, 1962, p. 102.

11. In alliances which are built around a core power, the capability of the major ally counts most in determining the degree of cohesion. Liska, 1962, p. 87.

12. Progress in integration among some alliance members may detract from cohesion of the alliance as a whole. Calvocoressi, 1966, pp. 360–361.

13. Growing strength of minor alliance members will lead to alliance strains. Calvocoressi, 1966, p. 358.

14. Great disparity in the relative strengths of alliance members may cause alliance dissension. Calvocoressi, 1966, p. 361.

15. Changing international role of an alliance partner tends to damage alliance cohesion. Hardy, 1919, p. 260.

16. Incompatibility of major social and political values is a major source of strains in alliances. K. Holsti, 1967, pp. 117–118.

17. Discrepancy in capabilities of allies reduces alliance cohesion. Wolfers, 1959, p. 8.

18. In alliances, different "styles" of organizational behavior disrupt alliance cohesion. Craig, 1965, p. 336.

19. Ideological differences will not disrupt alliance relations if none of the nations is intent on political revolution in the others. Dinerstein, 1965, p. 592.

20. One-sided dependence of one ally on another is simultaneously a source of alliance unity and conflict. Lowenthal, 1963, p. 111.

21. Alliances with both status quo and revisionist powers will tend to lack cohesion. Dinerstein, 1965, p. 601.

22. Alliance policy is produced by the interaction of intra-governmental bargaining. Neustadt, 1970, p. 140.

23. Alliances led by nations which have not established regime legitimacy will not tolerate political diversity among alliance members. Dinerstein, 1970, p. 13.

24. The degree of economic dependence of one country on another influences their degree of alignment. Teune and Synnestvedt, 1965, p. 188.

25. The degree of cultural or psychological penetration of one country by another determines the degree of alignment of the two states. Teune and Synnestvedt, 1965, p. 188.

26. The greater the perceived competence of one's partner, the greater the conformity of one's own behavior.* Willis, 1965, p. 378.

27. Nuclear diffusion may render nations which receive nuclear weapons more cooperative. Liska, 1962, pp. 93–94.

28. The more complementary the interests of alliance members, the more easily intra-alliance compromises are achieved. Liska, 1962, p. 82.

29. The greater the extent to which conflict results from clashing interests rather than values or beliefs, the greater the likelihood of resolution through bargaining or compromise. Aubert, 1963, p. 27.

30. Coalition members will expect that payoffs are proportional to contributions to the coalition.* Gamson, 1961, p. 592.

31. Small states may increase their influence in an alliance by withholding resources from the alliance. Liska, 1962, p. 180.

32. Small nations usually have disproportionate power in intra-alliance bargaining, because (1) it is hard for a large nation to threaten credibly to reduce its contribution and (2) a large nation has less to gain by bargaining hard than does a small nation. Olson and Zeckhauser, 1966, p. 274.

33. A small power has disproportionate influence in an alliance because it has the ability to commit its larger ally, who cannot accept the losses attendant upon the weaker partner's defeat. Rothstein, 1966.

34. States strongly requiring allies are in a weaker position within the alliance than nations which are requested to join. Lerche, 1956, p. 90.

35. The stronger alliance partner is in a weaker bargaining position within the alliance, because it is usually the keener of the two to maintain the alliance. Lall, 1966, p. 182.

36. The greater the anxiety of individual group members, the greater the rejection of deviants from group norms.* Weller, 1963, p. 190.

37. In small groups with common interests the great tend to be exploited by the small. Olson, 1965, p. 35.

38. Small powers normally have a more effective voice in large than in small alliances. Rothstein, 1968, p. 125.

39. The distribution of payoffs within an alliance will be a function of relative size. Russett, 1968, p. 296.

R. Alliance Purposes and Policies

1. "States neither should, therefore—nor do they any more as a rule—embark on an aggressive career unless they can do without allies or can fully control them." Liska, 1962, pp. 39–40.

2. "A power with less capability than concern will, as a rule, seek to expand alliance functions in both scope and depth." Liska, 1962, p. 76.

3. Faced with alliance setbacks, a regime depending on popular support is likely to press for expanding alliance functions. Liska, 1962, p. 115.

4. "Any weakening of the leading bloc actor, nevertheless, may permit non-leading bloc members to assert greater independence in policy." Kaplan, 1957, pp. 79–80.

5. "Two contradictory aims of allies sometimes tend to cancel each other out: Each wants to avoid being forced into nuclear war against its will, and it wants to be certain of nuclear support when its existence is at stake." Kissinger, 1965, p. 139.

6. Ideological affinity has an important influence on alliance policies. Greene, 1964, p. 34.

7. Ambiguities arise in alliances of unequal partners because each ally operates on the basis of different perspectives. Rothstein, 1968, p. 57.

8. Most parties to an alliance are motivated by conflicting desires: They want to give strong warning to potential adversaries, but they want to assume only weak obligations, Van Dyke, 1966, p. 234.

9. "When domestic factors determine alignment, the groups committed to an alliance are likely to be more homogeneous and the commitments of individuals more personal." Liska, 1962, p. 23.

10. The addition of allies is governed by the same factors as the original alliance, but the problems are more complex because the original purpose of the alliance may be reinterpreted or violated. Haas and Whiting, 1956, p. 171.

S. Alliance Efficacy

1. Alliances among democratic governments are less stable, because elite stability is not assured. Haas and Whiting, 1956, p. 182.

2. Alliance effectiveness depends in good measure upon the relations of

trust and respect among its principal statesmen. Morgenthau, 1959a, p. 201.

3. Alliances tend to be only as strong as their weakest link. Rothstein, 1968, p. 175.

4. Feelings of inner-community ["we feelings"] are an important element in any international coalition. Nitze, 1959, p. 23.

5. States join a struggle as allies only when they are directly assaulted in their territory or interests. Liska, 1962, p. 64.

6. The more similarly the members of an alliance perceive an external change, the greater the success of the alliance in responding to that change. Scott, 1967, p. 222–223.

7. States can never be certain of the assistance of allies. Lerche, 1956, p. 90.

8. When a new member joins an alliance, both the assets and liabilities of the alliance increase. Scott, 1967, p. 116.

9. Domestic instability of an alliance member may be a source of weakness in an alliance. Liska, 1962, p. 44.

10. Differences in purpose may improve alliance effectiveness, because they increase private, noncollective benefits from the national contributions to the alliance. Olson and Zeckhauser, 1966.

11. Relatively few states have the resources, internal cohesion, or coherence of national interest to become effective allies. Osgood, 1968, p. 21.

12. The greater an alliance member's national income, the greater the percentage of its income spent on defense. Olson and Zeckhauser, 1966, pp. 274–275.

13. The power of an alliance is not equal to the sum of the power of its individual members. Russett, 1968, p. 294.

14. A combination of small powers in alliance is not equivalent to a great power. Rothstein, 1968, p. 171.

15. Small powers are less likely to use their power on behalf of the alliance. Rothstein, 1968, pp. 60–61.

16. "Viable alliances are grounded in mutuality of strategic interests." Padelford and Lincoln, 1967, p. 401.

17. "The ideological factor, when it is superimposed upon an actual community of interest, can lend strength to the alliance by marshalling moral conviction and emotional preferences to its support." Morgenthau, 1967, p. 178.

18. The ideological factor may weaken alliances by obscuring interests and by raising false expectations as to the extent of concerted policies and actions. Morgenthau, 1967, p. 178.

19. A democratic nation is less likely to make a separate peace with an actual or potential adversary. Liska, 1962, p. 50.

20. A democratic nation is more likely to make grave compromises in order to avert a separate peace by its allies. Liska, 1962, p. 50.

21. "Alliances between greater and lesser powers are likely to be most useful in implementing an international order that is maintained by interstate restraint, surveillance, intervention, legitimation, and other forms of 'control.' " Liska, 1968, p. 42.

22. Changes in relative power are a major source of difficulty within alliances. Haas and Whiting, 1956, p. 175.

23. Ideological and institutional dissimilarities do not have unduly negative consequences for the operation of alliances. Haas and Whiting, 1956, p. 168.

24. "Authoritarian regimes seem inherently hostile to the necessary consultations and compromise which make alliances viable." Haas and Whiting, 1956, pp. 182–183.

T. Alliance Duration and Termination

1. Alliance strains are less likely to deepen into disintegration when there are ideological ties between allies. Liska, 1962, p. 90.

2. "A marked decline in the capability of a crucial ally is even more likely to set off dissolution." Liska, 1962, p. 89.

3. The more alliances a nation enters, the more it usually breaks. Strausz-Hupé and Possony, 1950, p. 154.

4. The most straightforward cause of alliance disintegration is domestic instability producing radical change in the governing elite. Liska, 1962, p. 103.

5. A purely ideological alliance cannot but be stillborn. Morgenthau, 1959a, p. 189.

6. Despite their absence of shifting elites and representative government, dictatorships are no more likely than democratic states to honor alliance commitments. Haas and Whiting, 1956, p. 182.

7. Desire for independence from a limited alliance may encourage membership in a universal alliance. Claude, 1962, p. 144.

8. Between friendly countries, alliances will endure irrespective of the dic-

tates of the balance of power. Dawson and Rosecrance, 1966, pp. 50–51.

9. "Expediency overrides communality" in alliance policies. "Hence, alliance tends to be unstable and of temporary duration." Friedman *et al.,* 1970, p. 10.

10. Reinterpretation of interest accompanying a change in elites is a major source of tensions within alliances. Haas and Whiting, 1956, p. 175.

The Effects of Alliances

U. International

1. Nonalignment can reduce inter-bloc tensions and stabilize inter-bloc relations. Liska, 1962, pp. 225–231.

2. Groups may search for outside enemies where none exist in order to preserve internal cohesion.* Coser, 1956, p. 110.

3. Alliances are incompatible with any system of collective security. Burton, 1965, p. 79.

4. Alliances increase tensions rather than promote security. Burton, 1965, p. 79.

5. The more the international system is polarized into competing alliances, the fewer the summit conferences. Galtung, 1964, pp. 36–54.

6. The greater the emphasis on strengthening alliance, the less the emphasis on achieving international détente. Rosecrance, 1966, p. 325.

7. Alliance processes are more likely to undercut than underpin collective security, because the aggressor, too, can acquire allies. Friedman *et al.,* 1970, p. 25.

8. To establish a system of "effective law between states" nations must shun alliances. Wright, 1965, p. 1494.

9. Alliances tend to be incompatible with collective security because a collective security system requires flexible national policies. Claude, 1962, p. 129.

10. Alliances tend to be incompatible with collective security, because a collective security system requires widespread diffusion of international power. Claude, 1962, p. 129.

11. The search for allies increases international tensions. Liska, 1962, p. 19.

12. Alliances intensify the atmosphere of distrust in the international system. Buell, 1925, p. 483.

13. The alliance is one of the most prominent means of putting the balance of power theory to work. Gulick, 1955, p. 61.

14. "Whenever an aggressor arises, alliances are indispensable to avoid war." Strausz-Hupé and Possony, 1950, p. 236.

15. Alliances uphold the balance of power by facilitating alert responses to developing imbalances. Friedman *et al.*, 1970, p. 20.

16. Alliances among great powers are conducive to instability in a balance of power system. Wright, 1965, p. 1494.

17. The stability of balance of power systems is more threatened by counter-alliances than by efforts to break up dangerous alliances. Wright, 1965, p. 774.

18. *Ad hoc* alliances are most favorable to the perpetuation of a balance of power system. Wright, 1965, p. 773.

19. The formation of alliances is necessary for the operation of a balance of power system. Claude, 1962, p. 89.

20. Alliances frequently have the function of preserving the status quo. Morgenthau, 1959b, p. 38.

21. Alliances serve as power balancing devices. Hill, 1963, pp. 254–255.

22. The less the difference in capability between two conflicting parties, the greater the influence of a weaker third party. Liska, 1962, p. 204.

23. "Alliances which are not implemented by adequate political, economic, and military means, or are not backed up by adequate offensive striking power, are indeed 'dangerous' [i.e. war-causing] alliances." Strausz-Hupé and Possony, 1950, p. 236.

24. "Power predominance within the alliance may stimulate its accumulation outside the alliance." Haas and Whiting, 1956, p. 180.

25. Alliances may spread conflict to a region previously free of it. Scott, 1967, p. 117.

26. Rigid alliances lead to war. Frankel, 1964, p. 162.

27. Alliances make it more probable that a localized war will spread. Ball and Killough, 1956, p. 178.

28. Among the causes of war most frequently considered are alliances. Ball and Killough, 1956, pp. 176–177.

29. The greater the number of alliance commitments in the international system, the more war the system will experience. Singer and Small, 1968, p. 251.

30. Alliances "may submerge only temporarily the conflicts among allies." Liska, 1962, p. 13.

31. "In themselves, alliances neither limit nor expand conflicts any more than they cause or prevent them." Liska, 1962, p. 138.

32. Only a very few alliances succeed in transforming themselves into federal unions. Duchacek, 1966, p. 341.

33. Where there is an alliance, there tends not to be a community. Fedder, 1968, p. 84.

34. Alliances can be transformed into regional supranational organizations. Haas and Whiting, 1956, p. 183.

35. Alliances entail political costs vis à vis the external enemy: counterattack, counteralignment, or other adverse responses. Liska, 1962, p. 27.

36. The greater the extent to which coalitions become threatening to others, the greater the likelihood that opposing coalitions will be formed. Kaplan, 1957, p. 24.

37. The opposition of two alliances is the most frequent configuration of the international system. Morgenthau, 1959b, p. 171.

38. In the loose bipolar system, the more hierarchical the blocs the greater the likelihood of transformation to a tight bipolar or hierarchical system. Kaplan, 1957, pp. 37–41.

39. The greater the cohesion of alliances on matters of substance and strategy, the more polarized the international system. Liska, 1962, p. 149.

40. Alliances prevent or retard the spread of nuclear weapons. Beaton, 1966, ch. 6.

41. The more multipolar the international system, the less the significance of shifts in alliances. Rosecrance, 1966, p. 320.

42. The more multipolar the international system, the greater the uncertainty resulting from shifting alliances. Rosecrance, 1966, p. 320.

43. "Alliances may be regarded as essential methods in the regulatory process of international politics. . . . They help fill the gap between the ideals of organization and the realities of quasi-anarchy in the international system. Lerche and Said, 1963, p. 117.

44. Military alliances are a relatively poor instrument for integration. Deutsch *et al.*, 1957, p. 190.

45. Alliances may serve to restrain the more aggressive member nations. Liska, 1962, p. 40.

46. Alliances among small states are unlikely to become self-sufficient bases of regional order. Liska, 1968, p. 57.

47. Alliances fulfill a vital role as institutional stabilizers of political behavior, fostering the growth of conventions and reducing the impact of outright coercion. Liska, 1968, p. 61.

48. Alliance is a poor base for integration because activities that might provide a technical impetus for growth will be dominated by politics, and undermined by conflicts of interest. Beer, 1969, p. 7.

49. Alliances are usually met by counteralliances. Rothstein, 1968, p. 48.

50. Alliances serve admirably the purpose for which they were intended: To preserve the state system. Haugse, 1955, p. 159.

51. "Alliances, counter-alliances, and treaties of guarantee and neutralization are held to produce in favourable conditions a certain amount of stability in international relations. This equilibrium is described as the balance of power." Schwarzenberger, 1951, p. 178.

V. National

1. When nations are allied, their leaders often overestimate the degree to which interests are shared. Jervis, 1968, p. 463.

2. Alliances limit and may even weaken the power position of a state. Lerche, 1956, p. 89.

3. Membership in an alliance detracts from members' decision-making independence. Claude, 1962, p. 128.

4. Underdeveloped nations will develop more rapidly to the extent that they align themselves with other underdeveloped nations. Casanova, 1966, p. 144.

5. Alliances increase rather than decrease defense costs for members [because they provoke counter-alliances and arms races]. Burton, 1965, p. 78.

6. In a rigid alliance, disruptive tendencies will produce feedback into the internal politics of member nations. Dinerstein, 1965, p. 601.

7. The political significance of alliances is greater in an era of popular (including undemocratic) governments [because alliances presuppose ideological affinities]. Osgood, 1968, p. 20.

8. "If ideological erosion does take place, it will probably begin with doubts about the general desirability of a cohesive [communist] bloc. . . ." Brzezinski, 1960, p. 408.

9. As a loose alliance system becomes even looser, there is little feedback to internal politics. Dinerstein, 1965, p. 601.

10. As a rigid alliance system becomes looser, the feedback to internal politics is significant and of dimensions difficult to forsee and assess. Dinerstein, 1965, p. 601.

11. "Under conditions of ideological conflict alliances may also be used to bolster regimes that share the ideology of the ally." Wolfers, 1968, p. 270.

12. "A country may gain prestige from having powerful allies or from denying them to its opponents." Wolfers, 1968, p. 269.

13. An alliance may be more of a drain on a nation's strength than a supplement. Wolfers, 1968, p. 269.

14. "Alliance does not transform national political systems but national values undergo transformation in alliances." Fedder, 1968, p. 86.

15. In the present "anti-colonialist age, alliance with a major power has come to cost status rather than confer it." Liska, 1962, p. 39.

16. "In the past, alliance with a respected power was especially valuable for unstable regimes." Liska, 1962, p. 37.

17. Nations that acquire allies incur costs in the form of added political commitments, risks, and reduced flexibility of policy, without necessarily gaining greater security. Snyder, 1971, pp. 69–70.

18. Alliances reduce the freedom of action of allies by changing their status in the eyes of all others. Haas and Whiting, 1956, p. 161.

19. "A coalition approach to security is a greater political problem for each nation involved than a unilateral approach." Padelford and Lincoln, 1967, p. 401.

References

Aubert, Vilhelm. "Competition and Dissensus: Two Types of Conflict and of Conflict Resolution," *Journal of Conflict Resolution,* 7, 1963.

Ball, M. M. and H. B. Killough, *International Relations.* New York: The Ronald Press Co., 1956.

Bass, Bernard M., and Dunteman, George. "Biases in the Evaluation of One's Own Groups, Its Allies and Opponents," *Journal of Conflict Resolution,* 7, 1963.

Beaton, Leonard. *Must the Bomb Spread?* Harmonsworth: Penguin Books Ltd., 1966.

Beer, Francis A. *Integration and Disintegration in NATO: Processes of Alliance Cohesion and Prospects for Atlantic Community.* Columbus: The Ohio State University Press, 1969.

Beloff, Max. *Foreign Policy and the Democratic Process.* Baltimore: Johns Hopkins Press, 1955.

Boulding, Kenneth E. *Conflict and Defense: A General Theory.* New York: Harper and Row, 1962.

Bowie, Robert R. "Tensions Within the Alliance," *Foreign Affairs,* 42, 1963.

Brody, Richard A. "Some Systemic Effects of the Spread of Nuclear Weapons Technology: A Study Through Simulation of a Multi-Nuclear Future," *Journal of Conflict Resolution,* 7, 1963.

Brzezinski, Zbigniew K. *The Soviet Bloc: Unity and Conflict.* Cambridge, Mass.: Harvard University Press, 1960.

―――. "Threat and Opportunity in the Communist Schism," *Foreign Affairs,* 41, 1963.

Buell, Raymond L. *International Relations.* New York: Henry Holt & Co., 1925.

Burgess, Philip M., and Robinson, James A. "Alliances and the Theory of Collective Action: A Simulation of Coalition Processes," *Midwest Journal of Political Science,* 13, 1969.

Burns, Arthur Lee. "Military Technology and International Politics," *Yearbook of World Affairs.* London: Stevens and Sons Ltd., 1961.

Burnstein, E., and Zajonc, R. B. "The Effect of Group Success on the Reduction of Status Incongruence in Task-Oriented Groups," *Sociometry,* 28, 1965.

Burton, John W. *International Relations: A General Theory.* Cambridge: Cambridge University Press, 1965.

Calvocoressi, Peter. "Europe's Alliance Blues," *Political Quarterly,* 37, 1966.

Cartwright, Dorwin, and Zander, Alvin. *Group Dynamics: Research and Theory.* New York: Harper and Row, 1960.

Casanova, Pablo Gonzolez. "Internal and External Politics of Underdeveloped Countries," in R. Barry Farrell, ed., *Approaches to Comparative and International Politics.* Evanston, Illinois: Northwestern University Press, 1966.

Claude, Inis L. Jr. *Power and International Relations.* New York: Random House, 1962.

Coser, Lewis. *The Functions of Social Conflict.* Glencoe, Illinois: The Free Press, 1956.

Craig, Gordon A. "The World War I Alliance of the Central Powers in Retrospect: The Military Cohesion of the Alliance," *The Journal of Modern History,* 37, 1965.

Dawson, Raymond and Rosecrance, Richard N. "Theory and Reality in the Anglo-American Alliance," *World Politics,* 19, 1966.

Deutsch, Karl W., and Kaplan, Morton A. "The Limits of International Coalitions," in James N. Rosenau, ed., *International Aspects of Civil Strife.* Princeton, New Jersey: Princeton University Press, 1964.

Deutsch, Karl W., *et al. Political Community and the North Atlantic Area.* Princeton: Princeton University Press, 1957.

Dinerstein, Herbert S. "The Future of Ideology in Alliance Systems," Paper read at the annual meeting of the American Political Science Association, 1970.

―――. "The Transformation of Alliance Systems," *American Political Science Review,* 59, 1965.

Duchacek, Ivo D. *Nations and Men: International Politics Today.* New York: Holt, Rinehart and Winston, Inc., 1966.

Etzioni, Amitai. "The Dialectics of Supranational Unification," *American Political Science Review,* 56, 1962.

Exline, Ralph V., and Ziller, R. C. "Status Congruency and Interpersonal Conflict in Decision-Making," *Human Relations,* 12, 1959.

Fedder, Edwin H. "The Concept of Alliance," *International Studies Quarterly,* 12, 1968.

Festinger, Leon, Riecken, H. W., and Schachter, Stanley. *Whén Prophecy Fails.* Minneapolis: University of Minnesota Press, 1956.

Fox, Annette Baker. *The Power of Small States.* Chicago: University of Chicago Press, 1959.

Frankel, Joseph. *International Relations.* London: Oxford University Press, 1964.

French, J. R. P. "The Disruption and Cohesion of Groups," *Journal of Abnormal and Social Psychology,* 36, 1941.

Friedman, Julian R., Bladen, Christopher, and Rosen, Steven, eds., *Alliance in International Politics.* Boston: Allyn and Bacon, 1970.

Gallois, Pierre. "U.S. Strategy and the Defense of Europe," *Orbis,* 7, 1963.

Galtung, Johan. "Summit Meetings and International Relations," *Journal of Peace Research,* 1, 1964.

Gamson, William A. "A Theory of Coalition Formation," *American Sociological Review,* 26, 1961.

Good, Robert C. "State-Building as a Determinant of Foreign Policy in the New States," in Lawrence W. Martin, ed., *Neutralism and Nonalignment: The New States in World Affairs.* New York: Frederick A. Praeger, 1962.

Gorden, Morton, and Lerner, Daniel. "The Setting for European Arms Control: Political and Strategic Choices of European Elites," *Journal of Conflict Resolution,* 9, 1965.

Greene, Fred. *Dynamics of International Relations: Power, Security, and Order.* New York: Holt, Rinehart and Winston, 1964.

Gross, Edward. "Symbiosis and Consensus in Small Groups," *American Sociological Review,* 21, 1956.

Guetzkow, Harold. "Isolation and Collaboration: A Partial Theory of Inter-Nation Relations," *Journal of Conflict Resolution,* 1, 1957.

Gulick, Edward Vose. *Europe's Classical Balance of Power.* Ithaca, New York: Cornell University Press, 1955.

Haas, Ernst B. *Tangle of Hopes: American Commitments and World Order.* Englewood Cliffs, N.J.: Prentice-Hall, 1969.

————, and Whiting, Allen S. *Dynamics of International Politics.* New York: McGraw-Hill, 1956.

Halpern, A. M. "The Emergence of an Asian Communist Coalition," *Annals,* 349, 1963.

Hamblin, Robert L. "Group Integration During A Crisis," *Human Relations,* 11, 1958.

Hammond, Paul Y. "Nonmilitary Instruments of Policy in a Disarming World," in Arnold Wolfers *et al.,* eds., *The United States in a Disarmed World.* Baltimore: Johns Hopkins Press, 1966.

Hardy, Osgood. "South American Alliances: Some Political and Geographic Considerations," *Geographical Review*, 8, 1919.

Hare, A. Paul. "A Study of Interaction and Consensus in Different Sized Groups," *American Sociological Review*, 17, 1952.

Haugse, Eugene S. "Alliances in International Relations Since 1920." Ph. D. dissertation, University of Nebraska, 1955.

Hill, N. L. *International Politics*. New York: Harper and Row, 1963.

Holsti, K. J. *International Politics: A Framework for Analysis*. Englewood Cliffs, N.J.: Prentice-Hall, 1967.

Holsti, Ole R. *Crisis, Escalation, War*. Montreal and London: McGill-Queen's University Press, 1972.

Horvath, William J., and Foster, Caxton C. "Stochastic Models of War Alliances," *Journal of Conflict Resolution*, 7, 1963.

Iklé, Fred C. *How Nations Negotiate*. New York: Harper and Row, 1964.

Jacob, Philip E., and Teune, Henry. "The Integrative Process: Guidelines for Analysis of the Bases of Political Community," in Philip E. Jacob and James V. Toscano, eds., *The Integration of Political Communities*. Philadelphia: J. B. Lippincott, 1964.

Jervis, Robert. "Hypotheses on Misperception," *World Politics*, 20, 1968.

Kaplan, Morton A. *System and Process in International Politics*. New York: John Wiley and Sons, 1957.

Kelley, E. W. "Utility Theory and Political Coalitions: Problems of Operationalization," in Sven Groennings, E. W. Kelley, and Michael Leiserson, eds., *The Study of Coalition Behavior: Theoretical Perspectives and Cases From Four Continents*, New York: Holt, Rinehart and Winston, 1970.

Kelman, Herbert C. "Compliance, Identification, and Internalization: Three Processes of Attitude Change," *Journal of Conflict Resolution*, 2, 1958.

Kissinger, Henry A. "The Changing Nature of Alliances." Paper read at a meeting of the U.C.L.A. National Security Studies Program (May 15, 1964).

―――. *The Troubled Partnership*. New York: McGraw-Hill, 1965.

Knorr, Klaus. *On the Uses of Military Power in the Nuclear Age*. Princeton: Princeton University Press, 1966.

Lall, Arthur. *Modern International Negotiation*. New York: Columbia University Press, 1966.

Lanzetta, John T. "Group Behavior Under Stress," *Human Relations*, 8, 1955.

Lerche, Charles O. *Principles of International Politics*. New York: Oxford University Press, 1956.

―――, and Said, Abdul A. *Concepts of International Politics*. Englewood Cliffs, N.J.: Prentice-Hall, 1963.

Liska, George. *Alliances and the Third World*. Baltimore: Johns Hopkins Press, 1968.

―――. *Nations in Alliance: The Limits of Interdependence*. Baltimore: Johns Hopkins Press, 1962.

Loomis, James L. "Communication, The Development of Trust, and Cooperative Behavior," *Human Relations*, 12, 1959.

Lowenthal, Richard. "Factors of Unity and Factors of Conflict," *Annals*, 349, 1963.

Marshall, Charles Burton. "Détente: Effects on the Alliance," in Arnold Wolfers, ed., *Changing East-West Relations and the Unity of the West.* Baltimore: Johns Hopkins Press, 1964.

Masters, Roger D. "A Multi-Bloc Model of the International System." *American Political Science Review,* 55, 1961.

Maxwell, Stephen. *Rationality in Deterrence.* London: Institute for Strategic Studies, Adelphi Paper No. 50, 1968.

Modelski, George. "The Study of Alliances: A Review," *Journal of Conflict Resolution,* 7, 1963.

Morgenthau, Hans J. "Alliances in Theory and Practice," in Arnold Wolfers, ed., *Alliance Policy in the Cold War.* Baltimore: Johns Hopkins Press, 1959a.

———. *Politics Among Nations,* 2d edition, revised. New York: Alfred A. Knopf, 1959b.

———. *Politics Among Nations.* 4th edition. New York: Alfred A. Knopf, 1967.

———. "Sources of Tension Between Western Europe and the United States," *Annals,* 312, 1957.

Olson, Mancur, Jr. *The Logic of Collective Action: Public Goods and the Theory of Groups.* Cambridge: Harvard University Press, 1965.

———, and Zeckhauser, Richard. "An Economic Theory of Alliances," *The Review of Economics and Statistics,* 48, 1966.

Organski, A.F.K. *World Politics.* 2d edition. New York: Alfred A. Knopf, 1968.

Osgood, Robert E. *Alliances and American Foreign Policy.* Baltimore: Johns Hopkins Press, 1968.

Neustadt, Richard E. *Alliance Politics.* New York: Columbia University Press, 1970.

Nitze, Paul, "Coalition Policy and the Concept of World Order," in Arnold Wolfers, ed., *Alliance Policy in the Cold War.* Baltimore: Johns Hopkins Press, 1959.

Padelford, Norman J., and Lincoln, George A. *The Dynamics of International Politics.* 2d edition. New York: The Macmillan Co., 1967.

Pepitone, Albert, and Reichling, George. "Group Cohesiveness and the Expression of Hostility," *Human Relations,* 8, 1955.

Renouvin, Pierre, and Duroselle, Jean-Baptiste. *Introduction to the History of International Relations.* New York: Frederick A. Praeger, 1967.

Riker, William H. *The Theory of Political Coalitions.* New Haven: Yale University Press, 1962.

Rosecrance, Richard N. "Bipolarity, Multipolarity, and the Future," *Journal of Conflict Resolution,* 10, 1966.

Rothstein, Robert L. "Alignment, Nonalignment, and Small Powers: 1945–1965," *International Organization,* 20, 1966.

———. *Alliances and Small Powers.* New York: Columbia University Press, 1968.

Russett, Bruce M. "Components of an Operational Theory of International Alliance Formation," *Journal of Conflict Resolution,* 12, 1968.

Russett, Bruce M. "An Empirical Typology of International Military Alliances," *Midwest Journal of Political Science,* 15, 1971.

—————. *Trends in World Politics.* New York: The Macmillan Co., 1965.

Schleicher, Charles P. *International Relations: Cooperation and Conflict.* Englewood Cliffs, N.J.: Prentice-Hall, 1962.

Schwarzenberger, Georg. *Power Politics.* New York: Frederick A. Praeger, 1951.

Scott, Andrew M. *The Functioning of the International System.* New York: The Macmillan Co., 1967.

Seashore, Stanley. *Group Cohesiveness in the Industrial Work Group.* Ann Arbor, Michigan: Institute for Social Research, 1954.

Sherif, Muzafer, *et al. Intergroup Conflict and Cooperation: The Robbers' Cave Experiment.* Norman: University of Oklahoma Press, 1961.

Sherif, Muzafer, and Sherif, Carolyn. *Groups in Harmony and Tension.* New York: Harper, 1953.

Singer, J. David and Small, Melvin. "Alliance Aggregation and the Onset of War: 1815–1945," in J. David Singer, ed., *Quantitative International Politics: Insights and Evidence.* New York: The Free Press, 1968.

Snyder, Glenn H. " 'Prisoner's Dilemma' and 'Chicken' Models in International Politics," *International Studies Quarterly,* 15, 1971.

Snyder, Richard C. *Deterrence, Weapons Systems and Decision-Making.* China Lake, Calif.: U.S. Naval Ordnance Test Station, 1961.

Steel, Ronald. *The End of Alliance: America and the Future of Europe.* New York: The Viking Press, 1964.

Stevens, F. B. "Why Alliances Fall Apart," *U.S. News and World Report,* 50, 1961.

Strausz-Hupé, Robert, and Possony, Stefan. *International Relations in the Age of Conflict between Democracy and Dictatorship.* New York: McGraw-Hill, 1950.

Teune, Henry, and Synnestvedt, Sig. "Measuring International Alignment," *Orbis,* 9, 1965.

Torrance, E. Paul. "Some Consequences of Power Differences on Decision Making in Permanent and Temporary Three-Man Groups," in A. P. Hare, E. F. Borgatta, and R. F. Bales, eds., *Small Groups: Studies in Social Interaction.* New York: Alfred A. Knopf, 1955.

Triska, Jan F., and Finley, David. "Soviet-American Relations: A Multiple-Symmetry Model," *Journal of Conflict Resolution,* 9, 1965.

Tucker, Robert W. *Stability and the Nth Country Problem.* Washington: Institute for Defense Analyses, 1962.

Van Dyke, Vernon. *International Politics.* 2d edition. New York: Appleton-Century-Crofts, 1966.

Vinacke, W. Edgar, *et al.* "The Effects of Information About Strategy on a Three Person Game," *Behavioral Science,* 11, 1966.

Vincent, Jack E. "Generating Some Empirically Based Indices for International Alliance and Regional Systems Operating in the Early 1960's," *International Studies Quarterly,* 15, 1971.

Wallace, Michael D. "Status, Formal Organization, and Arms Levels as Factors Leading to the Onset of War, 1820–1964," Paper read at the annual meeting of the American Political Science Association (September, 1970).

Waltz, Kenneth N. *Foreign Policy and Democratic Politics: The American and British Experience*. Boston: Little, Brown and Co., 1967a.

———. "International Structure, National Force, and the Balance of Power," *Journal of International Affairs*, 21, 1967b.

———. "The Relation of States to the World," Paper read at the annual meeting of the American Political Science Association, (September 7, 1967c).

Weller, Leonard. "The Effects of Anxiety on Cohesiveness and Rejection," *Human Relations*, 16, 1963.

Willis, Richard H. "Conformity, Independence, and Anticonformity," *Human Relations*, 18, 1965.

Wolfers, Arnold. "Alliances," in David L. Sills, ed., *International Encyclopedia of the Social Sciences*. Vol. I. New York: Macmillan and The Free Press, 1968.

———. *Discord and Collaboration*. Baltimore: Johns Hopkins Press, 1962.

———. "Stresses and Strains in 'Going it with Others,' " in Arnold Wolfers, ed., *Alliance Policy in the Cold War*. Baltimore: Johns Hopkins Press, 1959.

Wright, Quincy. *A Study of War*. 2d edition. Chicago: University of Chicago Press, 1965.

Author Index

Subject Index

289